Wounded Eagle

Chain of Deceit, Book 5

By

D.A. McIntosh

Wounded Eagle

Chain of Deceit Book 5

Copyright© 2015 by D.A.McIntosh

All rights reserved. No part of this book may be reproduced in any form by any means, electronic or mechanical, including photocopying, recording, or by an information storage system, without the written permission of D.A. McIntosh.
For information contact David McIntosh
591 E Plaza Circle #1006
Litchfield Park, AZ 85340

Cover, photography and internal design by D.A.McIntosh©

All rights reserved

The characters and events portrayed in this book are fictitious. Any similarity to real persons, living or dead is purely coincidental and not intended by the author.
Manufactured and published in the United States of America

ISBN: 13-978-0-9856276-2-1

Special thanks to the following for assistance and encouragement in completion of this book and my previous books. There are more to come and they support me by adding quality comments and suggestions.
Carol, my wife, Tony and Cynthia, John and Mona, and
Jack and Marie.

This novel is dedicated to all the men and women who have served or are serving in our Armed Forces defending our nation from enemies both foreign and domestic. To those who have given some and especially to those who gave it all. Without those we would not be a free country. Thank you for your dedication.

Other Novels by D.A. McIntosh
The Chain of Deceit series
Chain of Deceit, Book 1
Retribution, Book 2
T-Minus 36, Book 3
Final Report, Book 4

Table of Contents

Wounded Eagle 1
Main Characters 8
Secondary Characters 9
It all began with a Revolution 10
Chapter 1 Checkmate... 12
Chapter 2 Defining the Future 19
Chapter 3 Key West Nightmare 24
Chapter 4 Fort Bragg, North Carolina 30
Chapter 5 Electronic Warfare 35
Chapter 6 Key West Naval Air Station... 43
Chapter 7 Cyber Warriors 50
Chapter 8 Orders from the Desert 55
Chapter 9 New Appointments, Later That Day 59
Chapter 10 Death under the Bridge.. 66
Chapter 11 History Revisited 71
Chapter 12 Don't Shoot the Messenger 76
Chapter 13 San Francisco.. 81
Chapter 14 Dead Ends.. 87
Chapter 15 Dark Night in California 94
Chapter 16 South of the Border.. 99
Chapter 17 Dinner at Six, Sex at Eleven 103
Chapter 18 Back to the Stone Age 106
Chapter 19 Do You Really Want to Do That?... 111
Chapter 20 Missing in Mexico... 116
Chapter 21 Executive Dilemma 121
Chapter 22 Mexican Jail, Well, Sort Of 126
Chapter 23 You Can't Do That 130
Chapter 24 The Basement 135
Chapter 25 Just Kidding, Really... 140

Chapter 26 Out of the Frying Pan, Into the Fire 145
Chapter 27 Hospital Blues 151
Chapter 28 Down in the Bayou 158
Chapter 29 White House Blues 164
Chapter 30 Is There a Doctor in the House? 168
Chapter 31 Out in the Cold 172
Chapter 32 Cyber War Turns Hot 175
Chapter 33 Retaliation 179
Chapter 34 Aerial Cat Fight 182
Chapter 35 Shoot the Messenger 187
Chapter 36 Made in Korea 191
Chapter 37 Touch and Go 195
Chapter 38 KaBoom? 198
Chapter 39 GITMO 203
Chapter 40 Recovery 207
Chapter 41 Cyber Warriors Strike Back 210
Chapter 42 Discovery 213
Chapter 43 Bait and Switch 216
Chapter 44 Betrayal 222
Chapter 45 If Penguins Could Fly 224
Chapter 46 Berlin Germany 228
Chapter 47 Mount Weather 232
Chapter 48 Cyber Meltdown and Nuclear Waste 236
Chapter 49 Who's in Charge Here 239
Chapter 50 South of the Border 243
Chapter 51 Healing 247
Brief History of American Military Deployments 250
Excerpt from Schutzstaffel Rising, Chain of Deceit, Book 6 255
Chapter 1: New Life 255

Main Characters

Davin Pierce - retired Military Intelligence NCOIC, CIA Field agent
Connie Pierce - female FBI agent, wife of Davin
Josh Randal - CIA Field Agent
Stephanie Randal - wife of Josh Randal, ex-secretary to Davin
Darrell Mitchell – President of the United States
Tara Mitchell – President Mitchell's daughter
Tony Sanford - National Security Advisor, former FBI agent, retired USAF
Douglas Williams – Director Secret Service, White House detail
Ashley Marie Peterson – Director of Covert Operations, CIA
John Ramsay – Director of Homeland Security
Eric Fredericks - Director of National Security Agency
John Polson – Section head, White House Secret Service
Gregory Dietrich - grandson of SS General Josef "Sepp" Dietrich
Hans Bormann – Gregory Dietrich assistant
Jessica Angela Moore – aka Dusty, 2nd Lt. USAF Cyber Command
William James Savage – Ensign JG, US Navy, USAF Cyber Command
Master Sergeant Todd Wiggins – NCOIC USAF Cyber Command
Major Amanda 'Spooky' Sorenson – OIC USAF Cyber Command
John Polson – Secret Service Agent
Amber Miller – Secret Service Agent

Secondary Characters
Alfred - the President's residence butler
Harvey Stewart – Assistant Director of Homeland Security
Lt. Commander Frost – executive officer of U.S. Coast Guard Cutter
Sergeant First Class Eric Clark – NCOIC In-processing Ft. Bragg, NC
Lieutenant Goodman – Executive Officer, Ft. Bragg, NC
Sergeant Bettes – Fort Bragg In-processing specialist
Calib Abdul Mohamed – Leader of the Terrorist group
Savon Hussain Laden – Lieutenant to Calib
Matthew Harmon – NSA Section Head
Hamilton Bradley Jones - Nuclear Defense Employee
Valerie Marie Sikes – Nuclear Defense Employee
Harry Snow – San Francisco police officer
Sergeant Lascell – San Francisco police officer
Agent Monica Blair – Colonel, Senior ARMY CID Chief Investigator
Agent Ricky Donald – Lieutenant, ARMY CID Investigator
Agent Todd Sandlewood – Lieutenant, ARMY CID Investigator
Agent Angela 'Angel' Parks – Sergeant First Class, ARMY CID Investigator
Dr. Rachel 'Mac' Mackey – Major, ARMY CID Medical Examiner
Jonathan 'Spock' Nimoy – Captain, ARMY CID Forensic Scientist
SS Colonel General Josef "Sepp" Dietrich – a legend that never died
Michelle Dietrich – aspiring model and actress
Weasel – nickname for criminal in San Francisco, aka Eric Schubert
Tamako 'Tam' Takahashi - Detective with the San Francisco Police Homicide Division
Eric Fredericks - Director of NSA
Miguel – Mexican Drug Enforcement Agent, Nogales, Mexico
Murphy – U.S. Border Patrol supervisor
Gomez – U.S. Border Patrol officer
Mark Harrington - Chief of Police in Los Angeles
Seaman Murphy – Naval Security Group communications expert
Master Chief Damon – Naval Security Group Section Chief
Commander Phelps – Naval Security Group Section Officer
Marvin Gibson – Washington Navy Yard Contractor
Henry James – Washington Navy Yard Contractor
General Margaret Hunt – Commander of Mount Weather
Admiral Scott Hamner – Commander Atlantic Fleet
Natalie Mitchell – President Mitchell's wife, First Lady
Plus many more

It all began with a Revolution

In July 1776, the United States of America was formed. At that time, it was thought to be the perfect union. With the Declaration of Independence and Bill of Rights, the United States started to become the most powerful country on planet earth. However, this was not accomplished without conflict. Over the years that followed, the United States saw depressions, recessions, World Wars, multiple conflicts in Korea, Viet Nam, the Middle East, Panama as well as several on home soil. The Civil War pitted the northern states against the south over a dispute concerning slavery, the right to own humans. But was that the only reason? Wars were fought to claim our independence; wars were fought to maintain that and to also help other countries maintain their own independence.

Wars tended to bring people together for the greater good; and along with this, technology increased at a rapid pace to help in the war effort. The Enigma machine, an encryption device used by the Germans to transmit classified messages to their U-Boat fleet, was one of those inventions. The machine was deemed unbreakable. Even with the capture of several of the Enigma machines it was impossible to crack the code without the code book that controlled it. The code was finally broken by Alan Turing when he and his team developed a computer to crack the code during World War II. This was just the beginning of the rapid development of computers.

Not too many years after the end of World War II, a young engineer by the name of Gordon Moore made a prediction that the future would bring home computers, mobile phones and automatic control systems for cars. His prediction stated that technology would double year after year and has become known as 'Moore's Law'. This has proven to be true and technology as we know it today keeps on advancing. Computers that once filled entire rooms, have even more capabilities, can be carried in our pockets, and connect to the world in an instant. However, issues have arisen along with these technological advances. One of those issues, network security, has become a big concern with the nations of the world, with the single question being asked, "How do we secure a network that was never designed to be secure?"

There are skeptics that say technological advancements are driven by competition, the greater good, or just plan smarts. But, whether it is competition or something else, technology has been doubling each year. The use of a single external hard drive with the capacity to hold over two terabytes of information is not uncommon today. A single compact hard drive has been developed to hold up to six terabytes of information. To put that into perspective, two terabytes is the equivalent of all the contents of an academic library such as the United States' Library of Congress, on one hard drive. Theoretically, this allows an individual to load an entire library and carry it in their pocket.

Because technology has become readily available to every country on our planet and there are individuals and governments that wish to do harm to our country, the United States has taken precautions to protect our nation. The United States government formed a group known as the United States Cyber Command (USCYBERCOM) to provide protection. They are an armed forces sub-unified command subordinate to the United States Strategic Command located at Fort Mead, Maryland. They plan, coordinate, integrate, synchronize and conduct activities to direct operations and defense of specified Department of Defense information networks. And when directed, conduct full spectrum military cyberspace operations to enable actions in all domains to ensure United States/Allied freedom of action in cyberspace and deny the same to our adversaries.

The following story is fiction, but based on possibilities that could happen. The United States infrastructure is attacked by multiple sources and Cyber Command has its hands full stopping an attack of this magnitude. Along with the attack, terrorist forces are mounting continuous physical attacks which are taxing government and military resources. President Mitchell was recently rescued from being held captive by a terrorist group and now with the loss of his wife and his only daughter off to college, he is being stressed to the max.

Davin Pierce and Josh Randal are CIA Field Operatives tasked to locate a computer's stolen two terabyte hard drive, which could, if the encryption is broken, change the face of the free world. The adventures continue and the life and death of the United States is on a very slippery slope.

Chapter 1 Checkmate

Four months had passed since President Darrell Mitchell had been rescued from a group of terrorists in the Iranian desert. Mitchell was six foot three inches tall with grey hair cut short just like he had it cut while in the army. He kept in shape by running daily and using the White House gym; his doctor had given him a clean bill of health after his ordeal in the desert at the hands of a group of Islamic terrorists. Physically he was in great shape for a man of sixty years of age; mentally his doctor was not so sure. He had suffered a great deal of stress and mental trauma while he was held captive by terrorists in Iran.

Add that to the loss of his wife, Natalie, and her parents who died when the nuclear bomb detonated in Boston. It was only luck that his daughter, Tara, was not with his wife but at school in California working on her undergraduate degree; she had been accepted to Harvard for her Law degree but that would not happen for awhile. Harvard was almost completely destroyed when the bomb detonated. It was only a bit of luck that many of the students were on break and away from the campus when it happened; many of the professors were not as lucky.

President Darrell Mitchell sat in his private residence contemplating his next move. Politics was like playing chess, looking into the future and planning your moves to put your opponent in checkmate. Right now he was playing chess with his friend and new National Security Advisor, Tony Sanford.

Looking over the chess board in front of him and then up to his competition, he knew that his next move could mean a sure win or defeat. This wasn't life or death, but very similar to the decisions he made on a daily basis. Life was like a game of chess, wasn't it?

"Darrell, are you going to move or wait till I die of old age?" Tony Sanford, his new National Security Advisor (NSA), asked and then picked up his cup of coffee and took a sip. Tony was a slim almost bald man standing five foot ten inches. He was intelligent, and kind of a smart mouth at times, but good at what he did for the President. He had retired as an Air Force Colonel after working as a Weapons Control Officer on AWAC aircraft and then posted as liaison to the NATO Forces command which allowed him to continue to work with AWAC aircraft, but this time as an interface with the powers of the countries they were tasked to defend. Tony became the NSA by accident; the accident was when the nuclear warhead detonated outside of Denver and caused the crash and destruction of Air Force Two. The crash killed fifteen senators, twelve Congressmen, several news media representatives, several aides and other members of the government, the entire flight crew and the National Security Advisor.

"Just a second, Tony. The wrong move now could mean a loss. Don't rush perfection," Darrell commented without looking up, and to himself he continued, *'I've got you by the short hairs and you don't even know it yet.'*

"What did you say, sir?" Tony asked thinking he may have heard a comment.

It was business as usual, political back stabbing, positioning for a better vote, nothing changed except for the recovery from the destruction of Boston and death of members of Congress outside of Denver. The North Koreans had settled down, the Chinese were happy selling America its cheap imitations of technology, which worked better than the original most of the time. There were a few incidents of terrorist influence, but nothing major had happened in several weeks, at least not since the fires in several of our national parks, which were suspected of being set by terrorist groups, but unproven as yet.

"Saved by the knock," Darrell said after hearing a knock on his door. He looked up at the door then over to Tony and smiled, "Enter, its open."

"That's... saved by the bell" Tony commented. "Don't change the rules;" after pausing for a second he continued, "I don't make the rules."

"Good morning, Mr. President, Mr. Sanford. How is your morning going?" Doug Williams, Director Secret Service, White House Division, the tall African American asked as he crossed the room. It was eight a.m. on a snowy Tuesday morning. The weather outside was wet and cold; it was early in November, Thanksgiving was just around the corner, and Christmas was not far behind. There was an early snow this year that covered the ground with about two inches of fresh powder. Out west, the rim fire around Yosemite National Park was out, but not until after it had destroyed over sixty homes and tens of thousands of acres of pristine forest. It would recover but would take years to do so. The individual hunter that started it would spend many years in jail for his crime of stupidity; he was not a terrorist, just stupid.

"So far, pretty quiet. What brings you to my office on this fine Tuesday morning? I see we finally arrested the hunter that started the fire in Yosemite," Darrell asked and then sipped his cup of coffee and eyed the donut on his plate, but did not touch it.

"Oh, not much, yeah he actually turned himself in, feeling guilty about what he did. I just wanted to check in and let you know that we have had two more suspected terrorist attacks, minor but they did get our attention. No one hurt. Now we have twenty-four wildfires burning out of control in the northwest and a couple in West Virginia. And the weather is not helping, even with the heavy snowfall, the fires are still burning; however, they have been contained and the firefighters feel they are winning."

"What are we doing about those terrorists?" Darrell asked his friend. "All indications are terrorists are setting these fires to drain our resources, and damn it, they are doing a good job of it. Except of course the Yosemite fire, and he is awaiting trial now."

"Not sure; FBI, CIA, and Homeland Security have been working hard to discover who and where they are but have not had much luck. We did get lucky and caught one cell just two days ago, but they are not talking and will not be talking anytime soon," Doug replied. "Our firefighters are doing the best they can, but water, weather and the terrain is causing us problems. We may need to do something drastic to stop this."

"They are draining our resources; the previous administration gave away the farm with lots of stupid, money sucking programs. Now with the Syria problem blowing up in our faces, some of the remaining Congressmen, within the House of Representatives and the Senate, want us to bomb them to hell. But the rest of Congress does not want to get into another war; and I agree. The fighting needs to stop. We can't be everywhere. Sometimes I wonder what the hell we are fighting for! We still have troops in Iraq and Afghanistan neither of which look like they will end soon. I did order another downsizing of troops, but the Generals want more men and equipment. It is looking like the war is being run by this office and it should be run by the Generals in the field. Maybe I should just give them what they want and need and let them finish it, as they were trained to do."

"Darrell you have just returned from a horrible situation and lucky to be alive. Your wife was killed when the bomb went off in Boston and your recovery has been something books will be written about. You are one lucky man to be alive. You have a wonderful daughter that is going to be a lawyer in a couple of years. You are the most powerful man in the world," Doug commented and then continued with a thought, "Maybe you should let the Generals have what they need and let them finish the job, not have another Viet Nam. And then you can concentrate on other matters of importance."

"I know, I know, and as soon as I got back I started to get more requests," he continued, "And I don't need to get into all the ones I had to cancel when I got in, but the money I saved our country is now being sucked up by all those fires and the war. I don't know when it is going to end and I don't know who has declared war on us. We need to find out who is behind the attacks and stop them, permanently. Tony would you get in contact with the command in Iraq and Afghanistan and get a list of what they need to finish the job, ASAP."

"Yes, sir, I will advise you when I have the list and if we need to get approval and the money allocated," Tony answered.

"No, just do it and I will take the hit; consider it an executive decision and order. Don't worry about the money, we are at war and we need to end this," Darrell stated. "The longer we are there, the more it costs in lives and money."

"If this job was easy, Darrell, then anyone could do it. But it isn't easy and only a few select men and women can do it. You know, a few years ago, Harrison Ford played in a movie called 'Clear and Present Danger', where the President gave authority to a team to go down to South America on a kill and destroy mission. You know the movie?" Doug commented.

"Wait!" Tony finally spoke up, "As your National Security Advisor I am here to advise you not to go there."

"Yeah, goes in and saves the day but not before the team is killed or captured. What does that have to do with our current situation?" Darrell asked, wondering where Doug was going with his comment.

"I know what I'm doing Tony and we can discuss the ramifications later. But for now I think we need to do something out of the box," Doug replied.

"You know it is kind of funny that Hollywood can come up with solutions to world crisis, get it done within the time frame of a movie and have one man or woman doing the saving; where it takes us years to do the same," Tony commented.

"Darrell let's think about this a bit. We already have troops in the Middle East; why not assign some of them to go on a search and destroy mission. We have the intel that tells us where the heads of each terrorist group is located. Chop off the heads and the snakes will die; at least that is what they say," Doug said calmly, looking seriously at Darrell and Tony.

"Well, what you are suggesting is murder, Doug. I can't do an order like that, but the thought is way too intriguing that I don't know what to say," Darrell agreed and then looked at his friend and Director of the Secret Service, then out the window and the snow that just started to fall again. He then turned to his new National Security Advisor and said, "Tony, you are new to this, but I picked you because of your past experience and expertise in world matters. Would this work or are we just day dreaming?"

"Darrell, I know what you are saying. It is an interesting idea and we can keep it classified. Nobody but the players needs to know; and if it works, we will be rid of those damn terrorists. We need to make the world a safer place and you have the power and resources to do it. You just have to make a decision. Save the country with brute force by allowing our guys to do their job," Doug jokingly suggested before Tony had a chance to open his mouth.

"Actually Darrell, it may work but it is very risky. Remember when Seal Team Six went in to get Bin Laden and the flack we got from your own rescue. Very risky; could cause some repercussions with Iran. But we were successful twice; they would never suspect we would be bold enough to send in another team. It may just work," Doug stated and then picked up his coffee and tasted it; finding it had turned cold, he put it back on the table.

"Are you joking guys? We can't do that," Darrell questioned his friends. "Not a third time, we know who is behind the attacks. Intelligence has confirmed that the responsible group is run by Calib Adul Mohammed, head of an Islamic group. We do know where they are, at least generally, and we know they use the Internet. Why not just flood the servers in their area and create a little denial of service. Maybe that will slow them down. And when they get agitated and do something stupid, we can just go in and blow the hell out of them."

"Yes, we know who they are and where they are, but that is only one group. I know we can't just go in and start killing people without justification," Doug started to say but was interrupted by Tony.

"We know who they are, and they are guilty of killing Americans and anyone that will not conform to their ways. It is justified; they started by killing and bombing. I know we should go and capture them; but hell, while being judge, jury and executioner would be wrong, it would save lives and millions of dollars." Tony had changed his mind after listening to Doug and Darrell.

"It is against our principals. But, just like Bin Laden, once we get confirmation as to who and exactly where, we could mount a strike or send in a team again," Doug agreed smiling and then looked over at Tony and back to Darrell and said, "It is ultimately your call, sir. The denial of service will work in stopping them from using the Internet to give orders; they will have to revert to cell phones or other forms of communication. You know it may just work and we can track and jam the cell phones too. That will take time and money, but we will be able to capture their teams and get them off the streets. But this will only slow them down until they can regroup."

"Yeah, you know we can do that, would be nice to be rid of those damn terrorists and their support groups and countries. But any decision will be mine in the end, Doug. I just don't believe we can defeat our enemies by going in and killing everyone that looks like a threat. First things first, identify exactly who and then I can make a firm decision as to what to do next. In the mean time, Tony contact NSA and have them work up a plan of attack for a little cyber war and as soon as it is ready execute it. Call it *Operation Blindfold.*"

"We are already working on it, sir," Tony commented. He then looked at the chess board and said, "We can finish this game later. By the way, how is your daughter doing at Berkeley?"

"She is doing fine, third year and holding a 4.0 average. It is a shame she will not be able to go to Harvard for her law degree. But they may be able to get it back together before she graduates with her BS degree. Well now gentlemen, it's about time for our guests to show up; we need to go downstairs. I asked Homeland Security to get me an update on our disaster areas. Doug, have you heard anything about Denver, Boston and our other disaster areas? The country is in bad shape and we need to repair it before it gets worse. Are they getting the help they need to recover and rebuild?" President Mitchell asked and started for the door.

"I haven't heard, but John should be able to give us a good update," Doug replied, referring to John Ramsay the Director of Homeland Security. He started for the door when he heard a soft knock and said, "That must be our guests."

As the door opened, a head peaked around the edge, "Sir, your guests are gathering downstairs," Alfred, the President's residence butler quietly said to the men in the room.

"Tell them we will be right down, Alfred, thank you," Darrell stated. He then stood, picked up his suit jacket, and slipped it on as all three headed for the door.

Chapter 2 Defining the Future

Minutes later Darrell, Tony and Doug entered the Oval Office via the residential private stairway. They paused and waited until the door opened and six of Darrell's top advisors walked in. "Come in ladies and gentlemen. Please help yourselves to some coffee and take a seat; we have a lot to discuss. Ashley, I am really glad you decided to take the job, welcome to the big league." Darrell paused for a second, and then to the group, he continued, "Ladies and gentlemen, please let me introduce the new Director of the Central Intelligence Agency, Ms. Ashley Peterson."

"Thank you for your confidence, Mr. President. I will not let you down," Ashley Peterson replied, as the new Director of CIA. Her predecessor was killed when he was a passenger on Air Force Two when it crashed outside of Denver. She had the experience, with twenty years as a field agent working her way up to Director of Covert Operations and now the newly appointed Director of CIA. Her ability to plan, execute and complete missions was almost second nature to her. She was the perfect choice to head up the Central Intelligence Agency.

"Ladies and Gentlemen, I need an update and hope you have good news for me; presently, I see the country is severely wounded and to coin a new acronym I have to say we are a '*Wounded Eagle*'."

"Good choice, sir," Ashley Peterson started, "Thank you."

"Home Land Security, please begin with the status of the country," President Mitchell ordered.

"Good morning, sir. Well as you just stated, the country is a '*Wounded Eagle*'. First, there was the bomb that exploded outside of the Denver International Airport. The count is in and we have reported three thousand five hundred twenty-six confirmed dead, including members of Congress, twenty-nine from the Senate and twenty-two from the House of Representatives, the Director of CIA, and several aides, who were in Air Force two on approach into Denver. We have reports of an additional one hundred seventy-five missing and presumed dead. Ground zero is still hot and has been designated off limits for at least the next one hundred plus years. At least they were not dirty bombs. The blast area caused major damage to the airport. However, it should be back up and running in about six months, but there will be a No Fly zone on the eastern approach. The FAA says there is enough room to fly around it and make a safe approach," John Ramsey, Director of Homeland Security stated and then paused to take a sip of water.

"Damn, they really did a number on us," President Mitchell commented, "Go on, John."

"Yes, sir, more details are in the report I submitted this morning. But you need to know about Boston. Well, Boston did lose a lot more. Ground Zero was a block east of the Commons. We have an estimated 1.2 million dead, over six hundred thousand suffering from radiation sickness, one hundred thirty-five thousand missing and presumed dead. Ground Zero is designated off limits, along with a five mile circumference around ground zero. We were lucky with the fallout; the winds were blowing from the west and pushed most of it out to sea. Most of the six hundred thousand with radiation sickness are on Cape Cod. We have medical teams on site and they are doing what they can, but it is not looking good for a lot of them. We also received reports from four ships at sea that are experiencing some illness, possibly radiation poisoning. We will know more when the medical teams we dispatched to each of them report in. That should be later today. And of course you know that Harvard was severely damaged and will not be operating for at least a year, possibly two. We lost a lot with that bomb. That's about it for now, sir," John finished and then took another long sip of water.

"Damn, I am really glad my rescue team took out that ..." Darrell Mitchell said showing his anger and almost said some things he would regret; he then started again, "As I was about to say, if my rescue team had not taken out the terrorist group that took me, I would order something I cannot order, and that would be a strike on all the terrorist camps in all the countries that house them. I would start World War III and finish it in one day. But as you know I can't do that, can I?"

"No, sir, you can't do that; but it would really make us feel good to rid the earth of those people," Tony Sanford stated, attempting to keep the President honest.

"Okay, let's move on; we have a lot to cover. Ms. Peterson, your turn," Mitchell said.

"Sir, the Embassy in Kiev has just reported more troop movements in the area, looks like a possible build up for a preemptive strike. We will know more shortly. And….." she continued to brief the room on everything she had in a condensed form ending with, "all of this is in my intel report on your desk."

Forty minutes later the meeting was over and all were dismissed except for Ashley Peterson and Tony Sanford.

"I have asked you two to remain because we have a problem. Ms. Peterson we need you to help us with using resources of the agency that you now control. Mr. Sanford knows and is here to fill in the blanks when I miss them. What I am about to tell you is meant for my eyes only and the National Security Advisor, Tony Sanford. I must ask you not to repeat any of this to anyone. Do you understand?" Darrell started and continued pausing to catch his breath. "We have had a major robbery."

"Yes I do, I hold almost as high a clearance as you do, don't I?"

"Of course you do, but not for *'Presidents Eyes Only'* information that is presented from sources other than yours," he continued and without stopping except to take a breath, "Let me tell you a little story, or rather some history; back a few administrations ago, there were several high level scientists and senators working on a project that would, at least on paper, would promise permanent peace to our country. Well, the project did not turn out as planned and was scrapped a few years later. The project I am referring to is known as *'Raven Claw'*. The overall plan was to build and deploy small six kilo ton nuclear weapons. They were built and deployed in various locations; it has been nearly twenty years since they were built and deployed. The movie *'RED'* starring Bruce Willis is loosely based on our *'Raven Claw'*, due to the Freedom of Information Act. They had one bomb to recover and a nut job scientist that wanted to use it. Our problem is not the recovery of the bombs because we have already recovered them and they are safely stored. The problem is that several of the scientists that worked on and helped recover them have gone missing. That alone is a problem, but they also took several highly classified documents, actually a portable hard drive, which holds all the names, code names, current assignments of all your field agents and location of our legal and illegal nuclear and chemical arsenal. What is listed on that hard drive could cause World War III, get your agents killed, and we will not have any allies to help because they would become our enemies."

"Holy crap, sir. Who's bright idea was it to put that kind of information on a single hard drive?" Ashley Peterson questioned.

"It wasn't on one hard drive; it was down loaded from multiple sources by one of the scientists and then removed from the facility. How? We don't know how yet, but will shortly. The bottom line is we know it was downloaded, and we know it was missing along with two scientists. We are not sure if they stole it or are innocent victims or if there is possibly a third party involved."

"Where was this information taken from?" Ashley questioned.

"Mount Weather research lab," Darrell stated and then continued, "You know where it is; have you been there, yet?"

"Yes, got my first tour yesterday. Awesome facility, a lot of security and impenetrable; if the public knew about what is going on there, they, well, I am not sure what they would do."

"Well, that is why it is classified and it along with the other six facilities similar to it needs to stay that way. They were built during the Cold War with a purpose to protect our country and its many secrets. Mount Weather is the main facility, kind of like the headquarters for a very large complex system of secrets," Darrell stated.

"Am I to be read on to all those or is it in the Presidents' Book of Secrets and only for your eyes and only the Presidents?" Ashley asked Tony Sanford, questioning her purpose.

"In time you will learn more but you will not know everything that goes on within those facilities. Only the Presidents can know everything and trust me I don't know everything. This is a burden for me and those that preceded me and those that will follow. As for a Presidents' Book of Secrets, well, it does not exist, except in the movies," Darrell stated and turned and walked across his office to his desk stopping to pick up a folder.

"I noticed when I was there that they had multi-level security systems; how the hell did they get a disk drive in much less get it back out without being detected?"

"The security system had a glitch; normally anything going out would be wiped clean when it goes past the door, which has a very strong classified system within its walls that will wipe any electronic device clean as it passes through it. We don't know for sure if the drive was wiped or not, but we do know it got out. We had a system failure for twenty minutes when the entire security system was down, all the cameras, tracking and well, the entire system was down, so we have no video, sound, or any kind of sensor working during that time. A coincidence, probably not; they may have caused the system to go down so they could get the disk out of the facility. We know they got it out because a low life in San Francisco contacted a cryptologist from the Presidio and asked him if he could crack an encryption system on a hard disk. A coincidence? Not likely! That crypto specialist was found dead a few hours ago. We also have two dead scientists in the lab. They were working on the system that held the information that was stolen. Two scientists are missing; they were assigned to work on the system that we believe was compromised. We are not sure if they were part of the theft or victims…"

"If the information is encrypted and possibly wiped when it left the facility, why are you worried?" Ashley asked looking closely at Darrell and Tony Sanford, who were sitting quietly on the sofa across from her.

"The system they were working on holds information that is Top Secret. But I will tell you that if the information becomes knowledge, well, I will not have to start World War III because our allies will and we will be the target. Remember what I said earlier about nuclear warheads and our Star Wars program; well, that alone will get us in deep," Darrell stated and then sat quietly watching Ashley, "And our illegal stash of nuclear weapons which is only known by a few select people."

"Damn!" Ashley commented with a scared look on her face.

Chapter 3 Key West Nightmare

Key West, the most southern point in the Continental United States attracts all kinds of people, from all over the world. Many come for the sun, others to enjoy the night life at places like Sloppy Joe's, the world famous hangout of Ernest Hemingway and the infamous rum runner Habana Joe. As with most days, when it wasn't raining, the morning broke with a sunrise that many visitors saw through blood shot eyes as they walked home or back to their hotel after a night of partying at one or all of the many adult drinking establishments located on and around Duval Street.

Key West also has a darker side. At night, when the bars were open and visitors were celebrating a cause that was forgotten after the third or fourth drink, all along the coast small boats ranging from eighteen foot to large cruisers and fishing boats cruised up and down delivering everything from illegal aliens to drugs.

Stationed in Key West is a contingency of the United States Coast Guard, operating various high speed ocean going craft, helicopters and aircraft. The most formidable ocean craft were the three Hydrofoils. They patrolled the waters surrounding Key West in an attempt to capture those illegal activities. The station was manned by one hundred and fifteen men and women dedicated to the protection of the United States and to the apprehension of all those that participated in illegal activities in and around the Florida Keys.

Anchored a mile south of Key West was a beautiful fifty foot Cigarette boat rolling slowly over the calm warm waters. The weather was perfect and the sunrise broke just as it was supposed to. It was a perfect morning during a nearly perfect vacation.

"Davin, we have been down here for two months already. Isn't it time we went home?" Connie asked as she and Davin laid on the lounge in the back of their custom built fifty foot AMG Cigarette Black Series boat, drifting comfortably on the rolling waves off the coast of Key West.

Connie was wearing her favorite tiny white bikini bottom and small white top to match and Davin wore a Hawaiian print baggy bathing suit. Connie was in her early forties, but to look at her you would think she was in her early to middle twenties. She kept herself in near perfect shape; exercising, running and watching what she ate. But she did like a cold beer on a hot summer day; too bad this was the middle of November. The temperature was in the mid-eighties and there was not a cloud in the sky. Connie picked up her beer and took a sip.

Davin was a bit older, but it was hard to tell since he only had a little bit of gray showing around his temples. He was in pretty good shape for his fifty-eight years. Davin stood five foot eleven inches tall and had an average build for a man of his age. After spending over twenty years in the army, he retired as a Master Sergeant and then was convinced to work with his Army buddy, Josh Randal with the Central Intelligence Agency. Davin had lived in Palm Beach and was enjoying his retirement and being a part time insurance investigator. He had been doing a bit of scuba diving and treasure hunting before Josh convinced him to join.

Prior to joining the CIA, with Josh's help, they were able recover a fortune in gold with the discovery of the war time ship wreck, the *MaryJean*. Connie, an FBI agent, and Davin began working with his old friend Josh with the CIA soon after the discovery. They had worked several cases together; but after the last operation, they decided they needed a long vacation. So here they were with Josh and Stephanie in Key West doing what they loved to do, drink beer and relax. He and Connie had time to keep in shape, and enough money to not worry about the bills.

"Honey, Josh and I still haven't discovered the mother lode yet. We are going out in the morning, one more time and if we don't find it then I promise we go home. Deal?" Davin promised and then took a sip of his beer. "Where did Josh and Stephanie say they were going?"

"They went down to get some groceries and more beer," Connie responded, "didn't we make enough money off the *MaryJean*?"

"Good, we need more beer for the trip home," Davin agreed. "And yes we did, pretty much set for a long time, but it isn't about the money this time. It's the mystery and the why; why did they disappear and where are they now?"

"Sure more beer, I know you love the stuff, and well, I do too, but shouldn't we be thinking about our future a little more?" Connie asked as she leaned on her elbow and looked sternly at Davin.

"Our future is set; we have enough money in the bank and invested to live comfortably for a long time. What's the problem?"

"I know we have the money, but I have been thinking of retiring from the bureau and have been thinking I would like to, well, have a family."

"Whoa, families that means, oh, wait are you, now?" Davin fumbled through his question.

"Maybe, but it doesn't matter if I am or not right now. I am up for a desk job or retirement in the next six months, and you are past time to get out of the field and get behind a nice desk job. Look at Ms. Peterson; she is much younger than you and now the head of the company. A job you or Josh should have and could have if you wanted it; but no, you wanted the freedom of being in the field and not stuck behind a desk."

"You know damn well that a desk job is just not me. Josh has seniority on me so he should get at least the Assistant Director's position. I will retire at the end of the year if that works for you. And you my beautiful sexy wife can either retire and travel with me or take a desk job and stay at work while I travel and..."

"Wow. Do you see that? Coast Guard Hydrofoil, they are so cool," Connie commented watching the ship scream past them and immediately go up on its planes and scream off. "They only built about five or six, said they were too expensive, but they are fast."

"That is cool, wonder where he is headed off to so fast; they normally wait until they get a few miles out before popping up," Davin stated looking at the U.S. Coast Guard Cutter (USCGC); she was seventy-three feet in length and as fast as his own cigarette boat, with a top speed of forty-five knots (fifty-two mph) and a normal crew of thirteen. She was designed to chase down drug runners and other criminal activities in the Florida Keys. Those men and women were dedicated to the job and performed rescues and arrests almost on a daily basis. The *U.S. Coast Guard Cutter Mystic* was equipped with two mounted M60 Machine guns and a three inch deck gun mounted on the bow. She could handle most any drug runner or illegal aliens attempting to cross over from Cuba or any other location. They also carried an assortment of small arms, handguns and M4 5.56mm assault rifles.

"You are right, honey. Why don't you pull up the anchor and let's cruise in that direction," she suggested. Her FBI training and inquisitive nature had started to come out again.

"Hey, you are not working today. We are on vacation, remember," Davin started to say but got up and walked to the bow and started to pull up the anchor, "Start the engines and you may want to put some clothes on, an FBI agent showing up at a crime scene in a tiny string bikini may cause more problems than we need, assuming it is a crime scene and not just a joy ride."

"Oh, yeah, guess you are right about that," she said and then got up, jumped into the cockpit, started the engines, ducked below deck, and grabbed a pair of shorts and shirt for herself and a shirt for Davin. Connie returned to the cockpit just as Davin hopped into the cockpit; she pushed the throttles forward and turned the boat in the direction of the cutter. "Here, slip this on," Connie said as she handed him his favorite Harley-Davidson t-shirt, the one he got in Stuart, Florida complete with the graphic of a pirate captain.

"Thanks. Did you grab your badge and gun too?" David asked.

"No, but they are in the glove box right beside you. I don't let them get too far from me; you know that." She paused, and then asked, "Where is your weapon?"

"In the bench seat," he replied, smiling. It was a beautiful day and all was right with his world, for the moment.

Minutes later, they saw the cutter on the horizon heading southeast towards Sand Key, a small island about ten miles southeast of Key West.

"They are slowing down; look, there is a small fishing boat just about a half mile in front of them," Connie said as she handed Davin the binoculars. "Let's stop here and watch," she said as they approached to within two miles of the cutter.

"They are stopping about one hundred yards from the fishing boat; looks like they are dropping a large rubber boat and heading over. We will watch from here. Don't want to get in the way," Davin commented as he watched through the binoculars. Connie reached down, picked up a second pair of binoculars, and they watched the drama unfolding. The rubber boat reached the fishing boat and two men climbed onboard as two more stayed with the rubber boat. As they watched, they saw a flash which grew in size until it completely blocked their view of both boats, and then the concussion knocked both of them to the deck. Seconds later, the ocean below them swelled into a mini roller coaster pitching Davin's fifty foot boat like a toy. The sound from the explosion was almost unbearable.

"What the hell was that?" Connie yelled over the explosion.

"I don't know, but I think we just witnessed a terrorist attack on our country," Davin yelled back after the ocean and sound finally died down enough to be able to be heard. Standing on wobbly legs, both he and Connie had pulled themselves up off the deck and looked around at the horizon hoping to see the cutter. The cutter was still floating but listing badly to starboard and they could see several fires on deck. Reaching over Davin turned the engine keys off and then back on to see if his engines would start. "No luck, it won't start."

Getting down on his knees Davin pulled open the engine compartment hatch. "Damn!" he exclaimed as he examined the engine, "Looks like they are flooded, should be able to start in a minute or two."

Five minutes later, the left engine finally caught and they were able to move toward the damaged cutter. The fires onboard looked as if they were being extinguished, which was a good sign; but the list had increased. Within minutes, the right engine started and Davin was able to increase his speed toward the cutter. Closing the distance to the cutter only took a couple of minutes on the now calm ocean. Pulling to within fifty feet of the cutter, Davin picked up his microphone and switched his radio to use the loud speaker mode.

"Attention Coast Guard Cutter, can we offer assistance!" Davin yelled across to the cutter and immediately got a response.

"Fifty foot powerboat, this is Lt. Commander Frost, can you take injured?" a strained female voice came over the radio. Davin immediately switched to the frequency they transmitted on and answered.

"Yes, we can take up to ten if need be. What is your condition over there? We are on your port side; can we get closer to tie on?"

"We are stable for now; the pumps are working overtime to keep us afloat. The Captain is dead, and we have at least five dead and nine injured. We only have a crew of thirteen but two are civilians. We have called for assistance; a helo is on the way. But I want some of the injured off the boat, in case she goes under," Frost stated, paused for a second, and grimaced in pain, which Davin heard over the radio.

"Commander, are you okay?" Davin asked as he pulled his boat over to the port side of the cutter and had Connie catch the line being thrown down to them.

"Not exactly, but I will survive. We are getting the seriously injured on the fantail for the chopper and the minor injured are going to come over to your boat. Take them to Boca Chica Naval base as fast as possible. Senior Chief and I will remain onboard until we can get a tow. My boat is dead in the water, but we will not abandon her, at least not yet."

Chapter 4 Fort Bragg, North Carolina

The morning started out as quietly as expected at Fort Bragg, a large Army training facility. Sergeant First Class Eric Clark got up from bed at his normal time of five a.m., finished his run, showered and headed into his office at the base in-processing center. He was expecting a busy day, as usual; today was the day six new reserve units were processing in and preparing to be deployed to the Middle East. They would only be here for three weeks, going through some specialized training and receiving new equipment.

The morning was cold and there was a light dusting of snow on the ground. The weather station had predicted more snow before the day was out and it looked like another beautiful day in North Carolina.

Clark arrived at his office at six thirty in the morning, unlocked his office and entered; he grabbed a cup of coffee from the refreshment center as he came in. The morning went by slowly; he caught up on paperwork and readied for the afternoon of new arrivals. At eleven thirty that morning Sergeant Bettes came in with a concerned look and a message in hand. The morning had passed quickly since Clark had a lot of paperwork to catch up on and with the new recruits showing up this afternoon he was busy getting everything ready.

"What's up Bettes?" Clark asked as he sat behind his desk, took a big gulp from his coffee cup, found it cold, and then looked up at the unsmiling Bettes.

"Not much, but we just got an urgent message in from command, which you and the commander need to see," Bettes said and handed him the message.

"Is this true?" he asked, knowing it was. "Has the Captain come in yet?"

"Not yet, got a call from him; said he had to stop at Headquarters for a briefing," Bettes stated.

"Must be because of this; okay, get everyone in the conference room. I will brief them," Clark ordered. He then picked up his phone and dialed a number to reach the office of the Provost Marshall; there were a couple of rings before it was answered.

"Provost Marshall, how can I help you?" the person on the line answered.

"This is SFC Clark over at the In-processing center. Did your office receive the latest message? Yes, good. Not that we expect trouble, but can you dispatch a couple of MPs over here. We have several large groups coming in today and may need a bit of assistance." After pausing to hear an answer, he said, "Good, have them here by thirteen hundred; thanks!"

Clark left his office and headed for the conference room to brief his troops. As he walked toward the conference room, he saw Lieutenant Goodman entering through the back door.

"EL Tee, good morning; would you come into the conference room? You need to know what is going on. And it isn't good, sir," Clark stated as he stopped in front of the Lieutenant.

" Okay, can I get a cup of coffee first?"

"Yeah, but you may want something stronger after you hear this," Clark acknowledged then turned and headed for the conference room. LT. Goodman decided not to get coffee and followed Clark.

"Atten-HUT!" yelled Staff Sergeant Andrews, which immediately got all soldiers in the room on their feet and standing at attention.

"At Ease," LT. Goodman ordered and then took a seat in the front row. "This meeting is SFC Clark's; you need to pay attention to him."

"The Commander is at headquarters and will be in shortly to issue any orders, but in the mean time, pay attention. At oh seven forty-five this morning, there was an attack on the *Coast Guard Cutter Mystic* off the Florida Keys. Several sailors were killed and more injured. The ship was severely damaged, but salvageable. This has been determined to be a terrorist attack and all bases have been put on high alert, which as you know means a total lock down of the base. I have requested extra MPs to be dispatched to assist here. El Tee, do you want to issue weapons to anyone?" Clark reported and asked, already knowing the answer; but the Lieutenant was the ranking man on site, and he had to give the order.

"Yes, side arms to Staff Sergeants and above; and pick three others and issue M-16s to them; they will assist the MPs to cover the exits," Lieutenant Goodman ordered. "And of course, give them bullets this time," he continued trying to put a little smile on the men and women to ease the tension, knowing that in practice drills no ammo was issued, just empty magazines.

****

Fort Bragg, Officer Billeting area

It was noon and two miles away a young Major was preparing for his final mission. Before leaving his home, he opened his safe and pulled out his personal weapon. A weapon that was not supposed to be on base; a 9 millimeter Chinese built copy of a Berretta 92F. It was a federal offense to have unregistered personal weapons on any military base. He checked the magazine to ensure it was fully loaded with hollow point bullets, which it was, fifteen rounds of death.

Walking into the living room, he looked down at the prayer rug, stopped, stood behind the rug, knelt down and said his afternoon prayer. Carefully he rolled up his rug and placed it in the corner. Minutes later he left his home, but not before he grabbed two more fully loaded magazines that were lying on the kitchen table. He slowly walked out of his home; got into his car and drove out of the officers billeting area.

Within a few minutes, he pulled his car into the parking lot of the base hospital and sat looking at the front of the building. He looked at the door and then down to his weapon lying on the seat beside him. Undecided as to his next move, he started to breathe heavily, then lowered his head and said a prayer. Even though he despised the Americans, the uniform he was wearing and all it stood for, he could not bring himself to kill men and women dedicated to helping others in need. He was first and foremost a soldier, and soldiers no matter what military they were with killed only soldiers. His religion had taught him that there were no differences; infidels were infidels no matter who they were. But he had some pride and principals left and would not go against them, he would kill only soldiers, fighters, whether they were armed or not; they represented the enemy and had to die. He had received his command from Calib last night, it was time to act; he along with other sleeper cells were ordered to complete their missions. It was time to kill infidels.

Starting the car again, the Major shifted in gear and pulled out of the hospital parking lot. He drove another mile toward the main In-processing area located near the Base Exchange. It took him ten minutes to travel that final mile. As he pulled into the parking lot, he spied an empty parking space up close to the building and headed toward it. He noticed the name on the head stone as being the Commander of the In-processing center, a Captain McGee. He won't be in for a while; the attacks have begun and the good Captain would be at Headquarters getting briefed on the current situation and making plans on how to protect Fort Bragg and the civilian population that lived around it.

The major looked at the door and saw a bus pull up and stop in front. *'Must be the newbie's coming in; they will not be armed. Targets of opportunity, the enemy await death,'* he said to himself as he opened the door and slid out of the car, putting his weapon in his belt at the small of his back. He placed his hat on his head so he would not attract attention until he wanted to. He walked swiftly toward the door, but had to stop short as the door of the first bus opened and the newbies started to march toward the door only to be stopped by a young MP with an M-16.

"Please form a single line and have your IDs out. Sergeant Clark will be here in a moment to escort you to the conference room," the MP stated then looked over to the Major and saluted. "Atten-HUT!" he yelled.

The Major stopped ten feet from the MP and the other soldiers, returned the salute and then reached behind and pulled his weapon from his belt, swung it around and shot the MP in the chest. He then turned and fired at the other soldiers standing at attention less than ten feet from him. He killed or wounded the first fifteen men and women in line, dropped his first magazine and slid in a second but not fast enough. He was out of practice and clumsy, missed the ejection button and then wasn't able to get the new magazine in quickly. Three soldiers jumped him and forced him to the ground, pinning his arms to the ground; a young female Staff Sergeant grabbed the M-16 from the downed MP, jacked a new round into the chamber, clicked off the safety placing it on full automatic, and raced over to where the others had tackled the Major. After pointing the M-16 at the Major's head, she said quietly, "Give me an excuse!" Her finger was held lightly on the trigger.

The Major struggled; he twisted and attempted to push off the three soldiers that held him down. He pushed off one of the troops, freed his gun hand, swung his weapon toward one of the soldiers and pulled the trigger. The bullet went wide and missed the soldier, but that was all she needed to pull the trigger of the M-16 putting three quick shots into the Major, killing him instantly.

"What the hell?" yelled one of the soldiers that had tackled him and then immediately followed by saying, "Nice shooting, Tex!" He stood up and looked down at his blood stained uniform.

Seconds later another MP, SFC Clark, LT. Goodman and several others burst out the door with weapons drawn; but it was all over.

"Call for medics," Goodman ordered to the nearest soldier. SFC Clark and Sergeant Bette bent over several of the bodies to see who was still breathing and who wasn't.

"Damn it to hell. Who the hell is that man?" Clark yelled. "Did he say anything before you shot him?"

"He was yelling something in Farsi, Arabic or one of those Middle Eastern languages," the Corporal that tackled him reported as he dabbed a handkerchief on his face to remove some of the blood he thought was his own but wasn't.

"Arabic, are you sure?" Goodman inquired.

"Yes sir, he was yelling 'Allahu Akbar' Muslim prayer," Staff Sergeant Holly Redman stated. "I am an Arabic linguist and he was saying his death prayer, now he is going to get his seventy-two virgins." She then slowly put her acquired M-16's safety in the safe position and shouldered the weapon.

"Don't you mean, seventy-two Virginians?" Bette humorously commented, not getting a laugh out of anyone.

"Enough, Bette, go see to the injured," Sergeant First Class Clark ordered, mostly to get Bette out of the way and doing something productive. "Redman, why not give that weapon to Corporal Henderson and let's get everyone inside." He then looked at the MP and said, "Do a quick walk around to see if there are any more of his friends and then you and Henderson guard the perimeter. I will get the Provost Marshall over here to interview all the witnesses. Move."

Minutes later, the first ambulance pulled up along with three Military Police vehicles.

"Good, reinforcements," Goodman said and then directed the medics to the wounded. He then met with the lead MP and gave instructions. .

Chapter 5 Electronic Warfare

Fort Meade, Maryland, home of the National Security Agency (NSA) is where numerous civilian and members of the military work twenty-four hours a day every day of the year, including Christmas and all other holidays. The morning had started quietly at the NSA, but shortly after lunch all hell broke loose. Reports were coming in from all over the country of attacks. Fort Bragg just sent a report that eight soldiers were killed and seven wounded in an early afternoon shooting. The shooter had been killed, but his motive was still unclear; he was reported as speaking Arabic and saying a Muslim prayer, before being killed. The shooting was classified as a terrorist attack, but none had laid claim to the attack.

"We need to brief the President. Get everything together on what has happened and anything on possible targets. I will call the Director and brief him so he can go over to the White House," Department head Matthew 'Matt' Harmon said and started to head out of the collection room.

"Sir, they are not using normal channels to order the attacks and, well, we don't have any way of telling where they will attack next. Since we started *Operation Blindfold*, they have started using their cell phones and must be using a code because we have not been able to identify any clues as to where or when the attacks will happen."

"What, we are the best intelligence agency in the world and we have no way of finding out when and where they will hit us," Director Harmon commented. "What are we going to tell the President?"

"Tell him, ah, we don't know," replied the head analyst.

****

South of Key West, Florida

Twelve hundred miles away off the coast of Key West, a fifty foot Scarab powerboat sped across the open water carrying three injured sailors. The water was glassy smooth and there was a light wind blowing out of the southwest; the conditions were perfect to be lying around doing nothing. If it hadn't been for the terrorist attack on a United States Coast Guard vessel, it would have been a perfect day. It certainly wasn't perfect for the men and women on the cutter.

Today was not a day to relax; it was a day to start the hunt, a hunt that would result in multiple deaths and hopefully not much destruction. But that might not be the case. Unknown to the powers in the White House, NSA, CIA and the other intelligence gathering organizations within the United States, the terrorists were very well organized and well funded. They had trained and were working without known communication, no cell talked to any other cell. Many did not even know what their leaders looked like or even their names. Once they received their orders, they were on their own, completing their mission at all costs including dying for their cause. Some of the missions were suicide bombers and they would give their life to receive a permanent place in heaven with their seventy-two virgins.

"How are our passengers holding up?" Davin asked Connie as she went from sailor to sailor checking their wounds and making sure they were comfortable.

"They are doing as well as can be expected. How soon do we get to Boca Chica Naval Station?"

"Half hour, plus or minus. Let's see if I can get a few more revs out of these engines," Davin replied. "I called ahead and they will have ambulances waiting at the dock."

Watching the horizon, Davin did not see the smoke bellowing up over Key West, until he turned his head to look west. "What the hell is going on over there?"

Connie grabbed the binoculars and looked, "Looks like a large fire at one of the hotels."

"Do you think it is related?" Davin asked and then pushed the throttles full forward; his boat gained another ten miles per hour and nearly jumped out of the water. "Hang on boys; this is going to get rougher before it gets smoother."

"Maybe," is all she said and continued to watch the fire.

Twenty minutes later, Davin cut the throttles back to nearly idle so they could enter the channel safely. He could see the line of medical people and vehicles lined up beside the dock. Within twenty-five minutes, all the injured were moved from the boat to the dock and then to the waiting vehicles.

"Connie, I think we need to go back to Palm Beach; see if you can reach Josh and tell him to meet us at the resort and to pack. We are leaving. I have a real bad feeling about what is happening," Davin stated even though he had no solid information about what was happening to the country.

"Let me finish hosing the blood off the cushions first," Connie said as she sprayed the fresh water hose over the boat.

A young sailor ran up the dock, stopping short of Davin's boat. "Sir, Mr. Pierce, I have been asked by the Base Commander to ask you to wait, he wishes to talk with you. He will be right here."

"Base Commander, wonder what he wants?" Davin said quietly.

"He said it will not take long but he needs to see both of you, sir."

****

Washington Navy Yard

Several miles from the White House stood the Washington Navy Yard which employed about thirty-five hundred civilian and military personnel. The weather in Washington was clear with a chance of snow in the afternoon. Each morning and afternoon, employees drove in the various gates located around the compound, and passed by armed Navy guards who had not seen any trouble at the yard in over fifty years. Today was going to be different. The base had been on lock down since the Coast Guard Cutter was attacked; it was four thirty and the evening shifts of employees were still coming on base. The gate guards were doing their job and checking each Identification card, as another guard ran a mirror under the vehicle checking for explosives. A third guard had the drivers open the trunk and viewed into the vehicle from all sides.

Henry James and Marvin Gibson entered the compound from different gates as they had been doing for the past six weeks. The guards recognized each man as they stopped and showed their identification badge. After inspection of the vehicles, they were both passed through without incident.

Driving to their work areas each afternoon on the same route did not cause the guards to suspect anything was amiss with either man. Both men had been hired as janitorial employees using fake IDs and backgrounds. Both men were soldiers of Calib Mohammed and fighters for ISIS. Islamic State (ISIS) had declared Jihad on infidels around the world and James and Gibson were sleeper members of ISIS and were now ready to die for their cause. They had received orders last night to complete their mission; kill as many infidels as they could as quickly as possible.

At five o'clock the men returned to their cars and removed two nine millimeter pistols they had hidden under the floor boards of their cars. They walked back into the building they worked in. Once inside, they started to shoot their coworkers, one at a time. After shooting and killing the men in the front office, they each moved deeper into the building and continued their killing spree. Reloading several times, they continued until the Naval Shore Patrol showed up and rushed into the building. This was a mistake for the first two SPs; they were caught in a cross fire and were killed instantly. The second group of SPs were a little more careful and were able to shoot and kill Henry James. Gibson escaped out the back of the building, but was met by six armed Shore Patrol officers. He was shot and killed before he had a chance to react.

His last words were *'Allahu Akbar'*.

Calls went out to the Metropolitan Police Department and FBI.

****

Dallas, Texas

At five fifteen in the afternoon, four men walked into City Hall and opened fire on the guards and anyone who happened to be standing in and or around the entrance. Twenty minutes after the shooting started with the police surrounding the building, a single man walked out the front door and stood quietly looking at the police and fireman surrounding the building and smiled.

"Do not go back in the building, lay down your weapon and put your hands behind your head," the chief of police spoke into the megaphone.

"We are members of ISIS and have taken control of this building. You are infidels and we will give you one chance to renounce your religion and join us, or die," the man yelled back.

"We are Americans and have a choice in our religious and political beliefs. We need you to surrender and tell your buddies to come out, NOW!"

"You have ten seconds to renounce your religion and join us, or die!" was the response. "We have hostages and they will die a horrible death in ten seconds."

"Don't do anything you will be sorry you did. Surrender..." the Chief yelled back, but did not get to finish his ultimatum. The building exploded, killing everyone inside and injuring several of the police and by standers outside that were too close to the building. The chief was thrown to the ground, but was able to recover within a few minutes.

"Holy crap," the chief said as he picked himself up off the ground and dusted himself off. "Sergeant, see who needs medical help. I need to call the FBI."

****

Oval Office

"President Mitchell, we have had over eighty attacks around the country in the past twenty-four hours, over eighteen hundred known killed. Intelligence has not been able to nail down when or where the attacks are going to happen. We are flying blind, sir. What we do know is each attacker has yelled in Arabic two words, *'Allahu Akbar'* and is possibly a member of an Islamic State Group. The group that blew up the court house in Texas stated they were ISIS, just before detonation," Director of National Security Agency (NSA) Eric Fredericks stated as he looked at Ashley Peterson. "From what we gather, it is like a final prayer meaning 'God is Great'; Ms. Peterson does the CIA have any insight on these attacks?"

"Mr. President and Mr. Fredericks, I only wish we had information to provide to you, but the CIA is just as stumped as you. I have agents working twenty-four/seven trying to gather information to stop these attacks," Ashley Peterson responded.

"Mr. President we may be looking at this the wrong way. You recently ordered NSA to initiate *'Operation Blindfold'* which was designed to target the Internet, and monitor specific servers to locate transmissions concerning terrorist activity", Eric Fredericks stated. After pausing for a second, he continued, "We have been operating this way for several days and have not been able to recover much over the Internet and we are also monitoring cell phone activity."

"What's your point, Eric?" Darrell Mitchell asked.

"Okay, Mr. President, I feel we need to take *Blindfold* a little further. We have a scenario in place that NSA has been working on for months; it is code named *'Witchhunt'*. The program is to target specific web servers and cause them to go off line, or we can just take over the server and only allow traffic to flow that we want to flow. Once we have control, we can also input dis-information, just like we used to do with radio signals in the past. The Air Force and Navy Cyber Commands are already on board, just waiting for targets. You know under U.S. Law, Title 10 does not permit NSA from war fighting; we are an intelligence organization and will provide the targets and control what the Cyber teams do. They also may be using the Internet with voice over IP. Like the one advertised on TV," Eric Fredericks stated.

"Can you do that?" After pausing for a second, the President continued, "I guess you can; otherwise you wouldn't have offered."

"Yes, sir, with today's technology, we can do a lot of things that were only dreamed of a few years ago," Eric confirmed. "We have been working on a minor level with your *'Operation Blindfold'* with some success but we do need to take it up a level."

"That sounds good, make it happen, immediately. Let's take control of their Internet communication. Since they are not using radio or phone, it must be the way they communicate. Maybe that will help flush them out," Mitchell ordered and then continued, "We need to stop this, the country is in danger and we can't protect our people when we don't know who and where they are going to attack. Double your efforts, we need to get a handle on this. Tony, when we are done here order up the National Guard and activate the Reserves; tell them orders are on the way. Get them in place," Mitchell ordered. "Fredericks and Peterson get back to work; Doug and Tony stay, we need to talk." Mitchell paused for a second as Fredericks and Peterson left the room.

"Yes sir," Doug Williams, Director of the Secret Service for the White House replied.

"Yes sir," Tony Sanford answered and returned to his seat.

"Doug, Tony, I do believe we are about to start World War III. The country is under attack from forces that are well organized and secretive. We are vulnerable and need to stop this now. I don't want to lay blame on anyone for this, but our previous administration really screwed the country by cutting defense and home protection services. Money was wasted on trivial things and not where it should have been spent. But that is now water under the bridge. At least he didn't cut everything."

"Shouldn't you be discussing this with your Secretary of Defense and the other members of your staff instead of me, sir?"

"Yes and no, you are the National Security Advisor and Doug needs to be read on to this because he will be here with me and needs to know why we have drones flying over the White House," Darrell said. "Under the War Powers Act, I can issue Executive Order 6, dated today. How many drones do we have available? Armed and passive. And I would discuss this with our Secretary of Defense but I have not appointed one yet."

"I had a feeling you were going to ask, so I got the latest count this morning. At last count, we had twenty-five ready on the east coast, thirty on the west coast and about fifteen in St. Louis. But before we get carried away with that, may I give you my opinion?" Doug questioned but continued without waiting for a response from the President. "Well, I think you are right, but without targets how are you going to get it started?"

"But Doug we have a target, at least a suspected target; and with a little more research, we will confirm it. I do need your opinion and support. Things will get real dicey around here and I need you to beef up security. For now we need to have armed drones over our most important assets, Washington D.C., New York, major infrastructure points such as dams, nuclear plants, military bases, you get the idea. I also want armed fighters in the air around the clock, jets, helicopters, anything and everything that can fly armed; I want them in the air on a rotating basis to prevent another 9-11 attack. Place them over major metro areas, areas of commerce, everywhere. All commercial traffic is to be advised of the situation and to maintain contact with airport control at all times. Yes, it is going to be an air traffic control nightmare, but they can handle it. Make it happen. " Darrell commented. He paused for a second to think before continuing. "Doug, your section head on the day shift, Polson, is a good man and I want him along with one other of your choice to work with me on a special assignment. Tony go on and get started I have something I need to discuss with Doug."

"Okay sir, I will check in later today; it's going to take a while to get this moving," Tony acknowledged and left the Oval Office.

"I want the drones up within the next couple of hours," Mitchell stated as Tony started out the door.

"You got it, sir," Tony yelled back as the door closed behind him.

"Special assignment, it will be me and Polson," Doug answered after Tony left.

"No, not you, I need you here," Mitchell said and then walked around behind his desk and sat down. "First, I need you to double the protection around here and then get Polson and another of your special swat team trained men and send them to me. I will brief them on what I need; you can sit in if you like. Get me Polson and his partner now."

"I will have them here in ten minutes," Doug said as he hurried out the door.

"Good, now go, I have a couple of things to complete before they get here," Darrell ordered and then sat down at his desk. He picked up a correspondence he had received earlier and started to read it again.

Chapter 6 Key West Naval Air Station

"Thank you for staying for a few extra minutes; I am Admiral Huntington, base commander here at Boca Chica. I appreciate what you have done for the Navy and Coast Guard in this attack. But I need to ask you why you were so close to a Coast Guard vessel while they were in the process of stopping an illegal fishing boat?"

"Captain, we witnessed the attack. The explosion was massive, it almost capsized us and we were a couple of miles away when it went off," Connie told the base commander, "If we had been closer, we would not be here. How are those sailors doing? We were cruising down there and saw the cutter stop beside the fishing boat. We were curious and watched; we were about two miles away and it almost capsized our boat."

"They were lucky you were close. We just got word that out of a crew of thirteen plus two civilians, six were killed and the rest of the crew had various injuries but will survive. Most have some or complete hearing loss. The helos arrived about ten minutes after you left with the injured sailors, bringing the critically injured directly to the hospital. The two civilians were there filming a documentary for the Discovery Channel about the work the Coast Guard was doing in the Keys. They were pretty banged up and probably have one hell of a story on film, if they survive. At least they are alive; we can heal their wounds, for the most part anyway. The boat, well, may not be salvageable, but we will see when we get her back to the dock. There is a sea tug on its way out there now. Her Captain died in the attack, but the XO and Senior Chief are still on board, waiting for the tug. A medic is there treating their injuries, both will survive but be on medical leave for a while. But again why were you so close?"

"Sir, we are down here on vacation and cruising; now, I think if we identify ourselves, it will make it easier for you to understand why we were so close to the cutter. Connie is with the FBI and I am, well, for now anyway, I work with one of the other three letter groups."

"Whoa, thought that was you two; I read the report about you and Mr. Randal and that Soviet sub that was destined to destroy the world. Hell of a job. Thank you! You saved a lot of lives; it looks like you saved the world. So you followed the cutter and stopped a short distance away because you are both inquisitive super agents that just happened to be in the area when a terrorist attack was staged."

"Yes, I guess you can look at it that way," Connie commented wondering where this conversation was going. "And by the way it was a team effort that saved the world, not just us; we had a lot of support and help from a great many people, both civilian and military."

"Sorry, I did not mean for it to come out that way but from all the reports I have seen, it almost seems as though trouble looks for you two and finds you most of the time. But..." Huntington said, then paused and looked intently at Connie and Davin. "But, I appreciate the fact that you two were in the area and were able to help. Thank you. Now I need to let you go and I need to get my base locked down. Hopefully, there will be no more attacks and this was only an isolated incident."

"Let's hope so, but from what we were told it may not be. Now we are needed back up north, Captain. We got a call from our boss just before we docked," Davin said as he stood and started for the door of the small office located on the dock. It was usually used by the boat captains to check weather and make phone calls prior to taking out their boats. "Take care of those sailors Captain."

"They will get the best we can offer. I don't want to hold you up any longer; when the boss calls you have to run. I just wanted to thank you personally for bringing those injured in as quickly as you did. If there is anything my base can do for you just call me directly. Here is my card, with my personal cell number."

"Thank you, sir. Hopefully the next time we meet, it is for a steak and a few drinks, not a national disaster."

"Me too, now we have to go; can't keep the boss waiting."

Five minutes later, Davin and Connie were back at their boat and pushing away from the dock.

"Try to reach Josh again and tell him we will arrive at the Key West dock in about thirty minutes. Tell them to be ready to leave; we have a long way to run and no time to do it," Davin asked Connie as he steered his boat out of the harbor and headed for open water at slow idle. It would take about ten minutes to reach open water while maintaining a no wake speed until he reached the last marker, at which time he could open up the twin engines and go to max speed, at least until they reached the marker to enter the Key West harbor.

"Have you checked the weather for the next few days?" Connie asked as they cruised out of the harbor, removing her shirt and bikini top which were covered in sailor's blood and shorts to expose her tiny white bikini bottom she was still wearing. She tossed them into the sink in the galley. She stood at the wheel in only her bikini bottom, not thinking about putting on a shirt or bikini top at the moment; she had other things on her mind.

"No, guess we better check to see if we will have smooth sailing going home. And I will call Ashley and let her know when we should arrive in Annapolis," Davin commented and then said, "Take the wheel while I check the weather."

"Got her, go check the weather and bring me a bottle of water," Connie said and sat behind the wheel and steered the boat gracefully though the channel. Davin returned and handed her a shirt to put on before they reached the dock.

"Ashley said we need to find a faster way home. Did you call your boss?" Davin stated and also asked Connie about her work.

"Okay, no I did not get in touch with the boss, but was told by his secretary that I have to get back as quickly as possible. The boss is in a meeting with the Security Council."

"Did you reach Josh or Stephanie?"

"Yeah, they will meet us at the dock. Thanks for the water and clothes." She opened the bottle of water and poured some on herself to wash off more of the blood. When she looked down at her bare breasts and saw that the blood was gone, she slipped on the tee shirt. Smiling she looked at her husband with concern as to what was going to happen next. They were supposed to be on vacation; yet now, they were about to enter into harm's way again.

****

Naval Security Group, Key West, Florida

"Chief, I think you need to see this," Seaman Murphy yelled across the room to his Master Chief. "This is too much for so early in the day. First the Coast Guard cutter, now this, one hell of a day."

"What you got, Murpf?" Master Chief Damon responded and walked over to Murphy's console.

"They are done; I will rewind it, but I believe we have something that needs to go up the hill."

Damon put on a pair of headsets and listened to the conversation that was just recorded. "Replay that." After a minute Damon, looked intently at Murphy and said, "Transcribe that and let's send it up ASAP."

"Roger that, Chief, I will have it ready in a couple of minutes. But do you really think they kidnapped the President's daughter and are taking her to Mexico."

"If that message is correct, then they may have already kidnapped her and are transporting her out of the country. Who were the recipient and sender? I will call the commander and let him know what we have."

"The message originated in Germany, Berlin to be exact, and sent to a person in Mexico City."

"Interesting, get it transcribed," Damon ordered and quickly left the operations center.

Within ten minutes, Murphy had the conversation transcribed and ready for transmission. While he was doing that Damon called the commander and asked for him to come down to operations immediately.

"What's up Chief?" Commander Phelps asked as he walked into operations and confronted Chief Damon. After briefing the commander, Phelps said. "No time, let's make a call."

"Yes sir," Chief Damon said and they both walked over to the secure phone, the phone that was used only when the information needed to get to the President immediately. Once the phone call would be made then it would be followed up by a secure fax. Damon opened the safe to retrieve the code book while Phelps walked over to the hot line phone. Within two minutes, Commander Phelps was talking to the head of Secret Service, White House Detachment, Doug Williams.

****

Oval Office

"Sir, I just got a disturbing message from the Key West Naval Security Group. I ..." Doug said to Mitchell as he entered the Oval Office but was cut short by the President. Doug always answered the Red Phone if the President was not at his desk. This time President Mitchell was taking a short break in the President's private bathroom.

"Doug, I know what you are going to say, come in and take a seat. Is this Polson, and who is this young lady?" Darrell Mitchell said stopping Doug from saying anything more.

"This is Secret Service Agent Amber Miller," Doug replied. Amber was five foot six inches tall, brunette, twenty-eight years old and of average build; she was not unpleasant to look at but not your raving beauty either; in fact, she was the perfect agent, a lady that could blend into almost any situation.

"It is a pleasure to finally meet you, sir," she commented and then was directed to sit.

"I have asked Doug to bring you in because I have a problem that he was about to state as you came in. I want to keep this as quiet as possible. Doug was about to say that Tara, my daughter, has been kidnapped and is being held for ransom. What kind of ransom is not the problem. She was abducted a couple of hours ago. I got a call from the Governor of California about an hour ago. Both of her body guards were killed and she was taken."

"So you want us to find her and bring her home?" Doug asked before Polson could say anything.

"No, Doug, I want Polson and Miller to go to California and join with the FBI out there and find her. The FBI is to take lead but you two are to stay close and bring her home. Don't come back without her. Doug would you tell them about the chip, our little technological miracle."

"What I am about to tell you is not to be discussed with anyone outside of this office. It is classified Top Secret. In short, a previous administration had a brilliant idea to use GPS tracking to keep track of key personnel within the government, including family members of the top four members. Along with being able to keep track of their location, we can monitor their health, which is a side benefit to the chip. The chip is embedded under the skin usually near the heart on the back of each member. Once embedded, the chip uses the electricity our bodies generate to transmit the health and location of each member. We are able to track them, monitor their health and if need be, turn the chip off, once they leave office or are no longer required to be monitored. There are some minor problems with the chip. The primary one is that it cannot be detected when the subject is in a subway, under water or within an area designed to prevent emissions to escape such as a secure facility. The President's bunker and most high level secure facilities such as Mount Weather have an internal monitoring system that will pick up the chips' signals," Doug concluded after getting an indication from Darrell Mitchell to stop for a second.

"The system works great most of the time," Mitchell commented holding up a finger to indicate to hold on for a minute. "It was used to locate me in Iran and bring me home; it is a good system; maybe we should let the CIA have more access to it. The system is not perfect; using GPS we can almost pin point each member, but only to about a fifteen foot radius. Once we get close, we can switch to a hand-held device that can narrow the location down to a few inches; but we have to be within three miles for it to work." Mitchell nodded to Doug to continue.

"Yes, as the President says, it works most of the time. Presently we are tracking Tara and she is in Southern California and moving south. The signal has been intermittent, and the FBI is getting closer; but they do not know about the chip and will not be able to catch them without your help. We are giving you the equipment to be able to pinpoint her location and be able to pick a place to close in without tipping our hand as to how you know. We do believe her kidnappers will not harm her, but be fully prepared to move in as soon as you are sure of her safety."

"Okay, so our job is to just follow the FBI around and track her on this equipment but do not do anything until we are sure we don't give away your little secret?" Agent Amber Miller asked being a little confused. "Can we give them hints as to which way to go?"

"Yes and no, if you get the opportunity to rescue her then you need to do it. You are not to inform anyone in the FBI of the equipment you will be using," Mitchell stated. He paused, and then continued, "I want my daughter back, alive. Moving in too soon could get you and her killed."

"Understood, sir," Miller acknowledged, looking over at her partner and getting a nod of acceptance.

Chapter 7 Cyber Warriors

The United Air Force Cyber Command Center is located at McDill Air Force Base outside of Tampa Florida, in a large concrete building just off the runway. The building used to be the Strategic Air Command (SAC) headquarters which was the command center for the east coast B-52 and support teams for many years. The Center commanded the Air Force Squadrons located in McCoy, Patrick, Eglin and Robins AFBs. All are still active Air Force Bases except McCoy which is now Orlando International Airport. Their missions changed after the end of the Cold War.

The Air Force Cyber Command was formed in a provisional status and planned on drawing on personnel resources from the 67th Network Warfare wing and other resources of the Eighth Air Force Centers. The Joint Forces Command issued a statement: Cyberspace technology is emerging and along with Navy Cyber Forces, the Twenty-fourth Air Force is the first pillar to recognize that the new domain for warfare is cyberspace. On October 1, 2013 the Air Force Cyber took on the role of Joint Force Headquarters and operations center controlled from Cyber Command at Fort George G. Meade, Maryland.

McDill was in constant communication with NSA at Fort George G. Meade, Maryland to receive updated intelligence on targets of opportunity and they were taking orders from NSA about when and where to launch an attack. Early in the day, Cyber Command was given authority to initiate an all out cyber attack against known enemies, known as *Operation Witchhunt*.

Each team had twenty-four of the best computer geeks and hackers the United States Air Force could find and convince to join their team. The teams also included eight civilian hackers on contract that worked along with the military. There were four teams, giving them enough to operate twenty-four hours a day and seven days a week if need be. It was 16:30, just near the beginning of the swing shift; and today, six of the swing shift worked as fast as they could to find out who and how the California Electric grid was hacked. They needed to fix the problem before North America froze to death.

"Any luck in here with the new tasking?" the shift supervisor, Air Force Major Amanda Sorenson, call-sign '*Spooky*' asked the room of experts. She was a graduate from MIT with a doctorate degree in computers and a minor in languages. She was top in her class and was presently working on another doctorial degree in psychology. At the age of thirty-eight, five foot six inches tall, and red headed, she posed a striking figure. Amanda had never married, but she attracted many men who wished they could get close to her. However, her work and studies came first, and right now, her work at Cyber Command was taking up all her spare time.

"A little, sir, we have discovered that the hacker is damn good, but not as good as we are. He, or she, is in Beijing, China. Well, at least the first server that they went through is located in Beijing. We will get a bit closer soon and hopefully Dusty over there will be able to crack the code and turn California back on. Give us another hour or two." Dusty was one of the best at this game, she was not your normal Air Force geek. She came into the Air Force just over a year ago at the personal request of Darrell Mitchell, the President of the United States. Dusty was her call sign, every one of the cyber warriors had a call sign; her real name was Jessica Angela Moore and she was nicknamed JAM before she joined the Air Force. After she completed basic training, she was immediately entered into the Officer Candidate School. She graduated top of her class and was sent to McDill to join the newly formed Cyber Command Center. As a young computer wiz wearing short skirts, multi-colored hair, pig tails and dog collar she helped to save the world when she assisted in cracking the code on a Soviet nuclear submarine. The code was embedded in the launch and detonation system on board the Russian nuclear missile boat, set to detonate all of its warheads and destroy the east coast of the United States. She, with the help of a best friend William J Savage, was able to crack the code and stop the detonation of the warheads and the reactor on board the *Terminator*. She no longer wore the short miniskirts, except while off duty, and had her hair in multi-color; now she was a respected officer wearing the uniform of a Lieutenant in the United States Air Force, working in the Cyber War Command Center and very proud she was here. William Savage, call sign Mr. Data, was sitting two computers to her left. He was no longer a Seaman, but had been given the opportunity to attend the Navy Officer Candidate program; and upon completion, he was promoted to Ensign Junior Grade (JG) and reassigned to the Cyber Command. Savage held a Masters degree in computer engineering and was almost through his doctorial. The Navy had previously decided it would be in their best interests to send him through Officer Candidate School and get him a commission.

"Keep me posted on that. I will be back in a couple of minutes; going to check on what is going on in Iran," Spooky said and then turned and left the room, heading across the hall to where the cyber warriors were waiting for the order to proceed with their own cyber war attack plan.

"Master Sergeant, is everything in place?" Spooky asked as she entered the room. All was dead quiet; all the operators were sitting at their computers waiting, sipping coffee or energy drinks.

"All is set, the code is in place and all is ready, just waiting for the order," Master Sergeant Wiggins replied. This command was a mix of members from the Army, Navy, Air Force, and civilians. The Air Force provided the command staff with several of the senior NCOs such as Master Sergeant Todd Wiggins, twenty-four year veteran of Army Military Intelligence. He reported directly to Major Sorenson, who in turn reported to the base commander for logistical support, but took tasking from NSA and the President directly. Today, they were about to initiate a bit of cyber warfare against three nations at the same time: China, North Korea and Iran. They had done this many times in simulation and they were not sure if the real thing would react like the computer simulations predicted. But the country was under attack by forces of evil out of all three third world countries and they had to be stopped. Most of the country west of the Mississippi River had gone dark, the infrastructure, electrical grid, telephone systems, mass transit, and well, everything that relied on electricity was not functioning unless it had a backup generator. Luckily hospitals, specific critical facilities on military bases, police, FBI and other government facilities did have generators and were using them to maintain a modified state of functionality. But this would not last long. Once the fuel ran out, which could be hours, days or weeks depending on the amount of fuel on hand, then those would go silent as well. Most had fuel storage for at least a week, some much longer. The military had dispatched fuel trucks from the east coast to assist in keeping vital components operational.

"Master Sergeant, we just got the go ahead with *Operation Witchhunt*. Make it so!" Major Sorenson ordered. "Let's hope this works; the west coast is getting very cold."

"I assume the White House knows this could start World War III," Wiggins stated with a laugh.

"Yes they do. Has anyone broken into the hacker's site yet?" Sorenson asked.

"Yes, about ten minutes ago, Dusty got in and sent in a little spyware to do some digging. Don't know what she got back yet; but once we start *Witchhunt*, we will lose contact with anyone over there," Wiggins commented, "Why don't we check in with Dusty first, then start; she may have discovered something that would help us shut them down for good."

"Good idea, we can hold up for fifteen minutes, but no longer," Sorenson said and turned to leave the room and headed over to the room across the hall where Dusty and Savage were working.

"Dusty, Data, what have you come up with?" Sorenson asked as she and Wiggins entered the dimly lit room.

"We have a lot, sir. Once we got into their server, we were able to slip into their computers; they are running a UNIX based computer which made it a bit harder to break in, but we got past that. They are part of a group that call themselves, as best we can tell, 'Zero Fighters', that is what it translates into anyway. They were able to hack into the California electrical grid first, with a program that looks like they downloaded online from a source in Northern California. They used a program developed by an American to attack us. The program was not developed for that purpose; but once they got it, they modified it to do what they are doing. The program was designed to locate flaws in Windows software and to automatically patch them, plug the hole in other words. Microsoft is a closed system, propriety and the code is very well protected. But these hackers are damn good. How they got the program, we are not sure; but they got it anyhow. According to the information we have been able to flush out of their computer, we know their names, ages, and bank account numbers; it looks like they are using their own personal computers to do this. It only takes one computer with a good hacker to do what they are doing," Dusty reported in between typing on the keyboard.

"Wow, you said she was good, Master Sergeant, but I didn't realize how good," Sorenson commented. "Anything else you wish to tell me, before we shut him down."

"Yes, sir, if you would don't shut him down just yet. I can bring back the power grid and restore the systems if you give me permission to do so. And after that I can gather more intel about him and maybe even cause him some problems."

"Make it so, Dusty. And give him a taste of his own medicine." After pausing, she turned to Wiggins and said, "Go turn on North Korea and Iran *Witchhunt,* and we will hold on China for a bit."

"Major, I have Iran covered. Actually I have already taken control of three of the major servers that support Iran and am about to take control of four more. Instead of shutting them down, let's play war with them," Ensign Savage reported.

"I need to report our progress and tell them we have delayed implementation of *Witchhunt* because we have taken control of their Internet."

Twelve minutes later, the electrical grids started to come back online in California and Arizona. Within an hour, most of the electrical infrastructure across the nation was back in operation; and as systems came up and the lights came back on, the phones started to ring in every police station west of the Mississippi.

Chapter 8 Orders from the Desert

Earlier that day half way around the world

Somewhere in the middle of the Iranian desert a hundred miles from the nearest town of any size, the temperature was reaching fifty degrees at six in the morning; by noon it would be well over eighty; and by five that evening, the ninety-five mark would be hit and held until the sun finally set later that day, which is when the temperature would drop rapidly back to about forty degrees. This was the desert, and it was November; temperature swings this time of year were brutal with as much as a sixty degree temperature difference between night and day.

Calib was sitting in his hut typing on his computer, sending encrypted orders to his men and women via the Internet to the United States. He was unaware that much of his email would never make it to the intended receiver. It had been blocked or intercepted by NSA since they started *Operation Blindfold*; the servers that handled the traffic from Iran were under United States control. The next email would be to several of the major news media in New York claiming his group was responsible for the attacks and that there were many more coming.

"Calib, we have a problem," his lieutenant said as he entered the hut.

"No, Savon Hussain Laden, the United States has a problem and that problem is us," Calib Abdul Mohammed remarked with a smile. "Just think, here we are over one hundred miles from the nearest big city with any kind of Internet service; yet we can communicate like we are sitting in New York City and we are using the satellites built by the United States. Ironic in a way, we are using satellites built by our enemy so we can destroy them. We are using their own technology to bring them down."

"Yes it is, Calib. We have a big problem."

"Well, what is the problem that is bothering you? We are about to bring down the most powerful nation in the world and complete the destruction of President Mitchell by kidnapping his daughter. And you say we have a problem."

"I just received a call from one of our contacts in the United States and was told that they are experiencing computer trouble. Your emails are not getting through at the appointed times, and the most recent ones were garbled, unreadable. Like they have been intercepted and purposely scrambled. And the United States has put a ten million dollar bounty on the leaders of the group that have attacked their country."

"That is not a problem. It tells me that we have their attention and they are scared. Just what we want, so we continue until they meet our demands. As for the email commands not getting through, we will just have to start calling each cell to pass out their orders," Calib acknowledged smiling.

"What are our demands?"

"That is a good question, my friend. I really have no demands except for the complete destruction of the United States and all her allies, rid the world of all the infidels once and for all."

"Our little group does not have the resources and people to do that, we are small, remember, and already have lost twenty-two of our freedom fighters when they became human bombs. We only have…"

"Stop Savon, I know what we have, but we can cause a lot of damage before we are stopped. And they will stop us, sooner or later; let us hope it is much later," Calib commented, then looked back at the map over his computer and then back to the computer screen. "Now get the men together, I want to talk to them before we start the next phase of our operation. I need to send two more emails, no, I guess I need to make two more phone calls, then I will be there, get the men ready. Did you know you can track almost anyone on this Facebook website; people are so open and unaware as to who is watching them. Even the President of the United States' daughter has a page and is on it almost daily. Between that and Twitter, I know her movements and schedule. Her abduction was easy, thanks again to American satellites, Facebook and other social sites. All come from America and all leave them very vulnerable. Our men were in place and took her during her lunch time. She is being moved to Mexico as we speak. The German will pay us handsomely for our part in this."

"Yes sir," Savon said and left the hut in a huff, not understanding his leader; and he really did not want to either.

"Okay, that's done for now," Calib acknowledged to himself and then headed off to meet with his men. "We have her now and her father will bow to my wishes or she will die. Maybe she will die anyway, depends on how much trouble she is."

****

London, England

"Mr. President, how are you today, my old friend?" the Prime Minister asked when he was informed that President Darrell Mitchell was on the secure line.

"As well as can be expected; I understand you have had a few incidents. Have you any clues as to whom, or even, why our countries are under attack?" Mitchell asked without going into any small talk.

"Not as many attacks as you, we do have a few leads as to who and where they are. When do you want to eliminate this threat?"

"We have called out all our military, both National Guard and Reserves. We received a video a few minutes ago from a group that is claiming they are responsible. It was sent to the New York Times, by FedEx overnight delivery, and they forwarded it to the FBI immediately. They identified themselves as ISIS, an Islamic State Group. But the video doesn't really tell us much except that more attacks are coming and the destruction of the United States and her allies is their goal. They are not asking for anything. Just that we give up and die, because they are persistent and will not stop until they have destroyed all of us," Mitchell reported.

"That sounds pretty serious, but Hitler tried it and he had thousands of followers, how many do you think this group has, ah maybe a couple hundred, or a thousand. He has declared war on the world and will lose. Will you send me a copy of that video? I would like MI-6 to take a look at it."

"I will have our guys send it over. May I ask a favor?" Mitchell asked.

"What can England do for the United States?"

"Just this," President Mitchell started and then outlined his plan with the Prime Minister.

****

Key West, Florida

"Davin, how long is it going to take to get back to Virginia?" Connie asked as she pulled the boat into the slip at the marina in Key West.

"That depends on Josh and Stephanie, they are not here. Where the hell are they?" Davin said as he grew more pissed off. He had asked Josh to be at the dock ready to leave when he called.

"They will be here, give them a break," Connie stated as she tied the line to the dock. Davin tied the stern line and stood looking up toward the marina office, seeing Josh coming out of the door. Seconds later Josh and Stephanie walked up to the boat and tossed their bags on to the dock.

"What the hell is going on? The news is stating we are under attack. I just got a call from our new boss wanting us back as quickly as possible. I tried to get us some seats on a flight out, but everything is full; so I chartered us a plane. We can leave as soon as you two are ready," Josh commented as he and Stephanie jumped down onto the deck of the boat. "We packed your clothes and checked out of the condo. So let's secure the boat and get out of here; the weather is good for the trip home."

"Good idea, Josh. I guess we have to get the hell out of Dodge, as they say," Davin said as he looked around his boat.

"Well, old buddy, I guess it's time to save the world again," Josh said kidding his friend.

"You know Josh, we are almost ready to retire again; the mandatory retirement age for an agent is sixty, or at least to quit field work. And hell what are you now, fifty-eight, fifty-nine?" Davin jabbed back at Josh.

"You know they say the memory is the second thing to go, ole buddy; you know I am two years younger than you, so that would make me, let's see, you are fifty-eight so that makes me fifty-six, right, I am fifty-six."

Twenty minutes later, the four of them were in the taxi heading for the airport. The boat was locked and secure. They would pick it up when this operation was completed, if they survived.

Chapter 9 New Appointments, Later That Day

"Good afternoon, ladies and gentlemen, please come in and sit, we have a lot to talk about," newly appointed CIA Director Ashley Peterson said as Davin, Josh, Connie and Stephanie entered her office on the second floor of CIA headquarters. "Please excuse the mess; I just moved in today and have not had the chance to unpack. But before we start, I need to point out a few things that you may or may not be aware of," she stated and then sat behind her new desk and leaned forward to look closely at her four guests. "Before you start asking questions, allow me first; Mrs. Randal, you have been part of this motley crew from the get go and have never been officially sanctioned, appointed, or otherwise named as a member of any of our paid agencies, yet you still hang out with these three. Why?"

"Ahh, I may not be a trained agent by your standards but both I..." Stephanie started to say but was cut off by Ashley.

Stephanie was blonde, blue eyes, five foot six inches tall and as beautiful today as she was when she turned twenty-one, a bit over twenty years ago.

"Yes, we know the training these three misfits have been giving you; and when this operation you are about to embark on is completed, I expect you to report to Quantico for a more formal training. Mrs. Randal, we have done a little research on your background. Our files indicate you were with Miami Police Department for six years. You worked vice and were promoted to detective, the youngest female to do that in Miami. Impressive! And our records also indicate that you were assigned to work undercover until there was an incident with the death of a suspect, with whom you were involved. The report says you were undercover as ahh, prostitute and the, well, you know the details, and I will not go into them. After that you were assigned to work as secretary for Mr. Pierce to see if he was doing anything illegal, only to find out he was really working as a CIA operative and the insurance office was just his cover. Well, well, you have been a busy little lady, working vice undercover, infiltrating a drug ring; wow you are a gutsy lady. Okay, you know the rest of the story, and here you are. You are still assigned to the Miami PD, well up until a few minutes ago. They have agreed to release you, if you want to work for us. And you can fill your husband in with all the details, if you haven't already. But, as for now, you are officially working for the CIA; we already have a file on you and documentation stating you are willing to join our forces and defend our great country from enemies, both foreign and domestic. Say you will and sign on the bottom line, please," Ashley asked and passed a single sheet of paper over to her.

"I will," Stephanie stated, confused but willing, "Thank you." Looking over at her husband and best friends, she whispered, *"Wow!"*.

"Now we also have a problem with Mrs. Pierce, what should we do with you? You don't work for us, but are married to a Senior CIA Field Specialist and have been working with him on several of his operations, whether you wanted to or not and most likely without full approval of your boss. So I cannot just take you from the FBI, like I can with the Miami PD. But since I have the blessing of our President, I have the authority to appoint you as the official liaison between the FBI and CIA for the unforeseeable future. There are many reasons for bringing you into the fold and we may do that in the future, but for now, you are to remain with the FBI. And we have already informed your office that this is happening and they agreed you are going to be in the right place, for now anyway. Now saying all that, I also have to appoint one of you three as the lead on your next assignment, " Ashley stopped, placing her finger up to her lips and took a small breath before continuing, "I almost forgot, for this op you will need all your security clearances raised to a much higher level... Oh, I already did that, you are now cleared for and have the need to know at a level that is not commonly given to field agents. And as soon as this op is done, if we still exist, then we will revoke that level and bring you back down to earth."

"Let's make this easy for you, Ms. Peterson; I want Josh to be the lead. He has the most experience with the company and frankly I just am tired of being the lead of anything."

"Okay then, it is settled; Mr. Pierce you will be lead on this op," Peterson stated with a smile.

"No, no way, Josh is the lead, not me," Davin protested.

"Mr. Pierce, you are lead, like it or not," Peterson stated firmly.

"I tried Josh, really I did," Davin stated, "Okay, what are we up against now. We see that there have been several attacks and one of our Coast Guard Cutters was almost destroyed. Have we gotten any leads as to whom, or why, we are being targeted?"

"The answer right now is we know who and where they are, with just possibilities as to when or where the next attack will be. As to the why, you just need to look at the people attacking us; they hate us and are terrorists; no matter what country they come from. That is all we know right now. And they need to be stopped. But that is not why you are in here. Your assignment does not have anything to do with the attacks, not directly anyway, but something more important."

"How can it be more important than saving our country?" Stephanie asked.

"We need you to retrieve an item that has been stolen and return it. This item, if gotten in the wrong hands, can start World War III and we will be the target of every nation on this planet."

"Wait, the Lost Ark was already recovered by Harrison Ford back in 1936 or was it '34. And didn't he also get that crystal skull back in the alien's hands later on," Davin started to joke around.

"Yeah, and the Roswell spaceship is in Hanger 19 out at Area 51. Amelia Earhart is still missing; maybe we can find her. That would set history a new one," Josh added as he picked up on it.

"Okay, gentlemen, that is enough; it is true that those may have happened, but only in the movies, and Amelia has yet to be found. But that is not what we need you for. And as far as I know, the Ark is in Warehouse 13 out in the southwest. But that is another topic which we will not get into right now. What we need you to recover is a document, or rather a computer hard drive, one that disappeared a few days ago from a lab in Virginia. This drive is classified Top Secret and when it is decrypted could cause a total melt down of our nuclear defense and space program and the possibility of the exposure of many of our field agents, including you. The information on the drive is in a high level encryption and hopefully cannot be opened and read. But the people that took it may know the code to decrypt it. We are not sure. And there are a lot of very good hackers out there. With enough computer power, time and money, they could crack the encryption, hopefully never, but no encryption is completely unbreakable. We need you to recover the drive or destroy it before it is cracked. We estimate we have about eight days before the encryption is broken and then all hell comes loose."

"Wow! That does sound important. I guess we will just have to go and get it. Where is it supposed to be now?" Connie asked, cutting in before the boys had a chance to make another comment.

"I knew it would involve aliens somehow," Davin stated to slip in another jibe, and then seriously he asked, "Do you have any idea about who may have taken it and how they got it out of the building?"

"That is a good question. We only know that there was a system failure for about twenty minutes at the lab, at which time they may have been able to get out without detection. It is your job to find out where it is and get it back or destroy it. Preferably, not destroy, but there are other copies in a secure location. We can give you the files on the two missing scientists but beyond that we don't have much," Peterson replied. She paused for a second and then answered Davin, "Sorry, we don't have much in the way of leads, except one, we got a call from the FBI office out at the Presidio saying they were recently contacted by an Army crypto officer saying he was contacted by a rather shady character that had some encryption he wanted him to crack. He agreed to meet the gentlemen and let them know what he found out. They have not heard from him since."

"Why did the FBI call the CIA? Couldn't they handle it?" Josh asked, thought for a second and answered his own question, "Oh, yeah, we are spies and use crypto stuff, but wouldn't it have been better to call the Puzzle Palace, the NSA?"

"They did and were asked to call us too, in case we knew anything about missing crypto stuff," Ashley Peterson commented, "Now let's get down to why you are here."

"What really would happen if the code was cracked?" Josh asked out of curiosity.

"As I said earlier... World War III," Ashley commented without smiling.

"What! You are kidding, right?" Davin and Josh asked at the same time.

"Yes, you need to know what we are up against. First of all, the drive holds information as to the exact location of every nuclear weapon we have, even the ones we are not supposed to have, which is a direct violation to the treaty. Second, it describes in detail our nuclear and laser space defense program, *Star Wars*. There is a lot more on the drive that confirms that we as a country are in direct violation with the nuclear treaty which we proposed, pushed through and got other countries to sign up to, yet we are in violation of. So you see some of our former administration talked a good game but did not play fair when it came to implementation of the rules. Our present administration has been in the process of fixing it, but it takes time. We are in a serious pickle; and if the information gets in the wrong hands, it could mean World War III; or at the very least extreme embarrassment for the country. A possible outcome would be a lot of nuclear warheads detonated around the world, possibly ending the life as we know it."

"How the hell did they get it out of wherever it was and who would know which drive to steal in the first place? And whose bright idea was it to have all that information in a place where it could be stolen?" Davin asked.

"Inside job, we have found two bodies, men that were working on the clean up that needed to be done and two more are still missing; so we figure at least one of the two took the drive and possibly killed the two we found and the fourth is still an unknown. We also have two company operatives missing. Yes, we will provide you with names, pictures and anything else you need to track them down," Ashley said ignoring Davin's question.

"Anything else you wish to tell us?" Josh questioned. "What about company agents?"

"Yes, the two missing agents are Hamilton Bradley Jones and the other is Valerie Marie Sikes. We have issued a bulletin to the local police and all transportation outlets but no results yet." Ashley just ignored the repeated question.

"Well, let's get started. We have a cold trail and minimal leads, but at least we have names and pictures," Davin said and started to stand, but got a hand from Ashley to remain seated. "Okay, question, Ms. Peterson, can we start in the Lab?"

"What?" Josh asked. "I want to review the files on the two missing scientists and, well, can we hit the head before we go?"

"I must over emphasize that we must get the drive back or it could mean war," Peterson stated. "The terrorist attacks are being handled. President Mitchell has a plan which he is putting into motion to curtail the attacks and stop the terrorists permanently. At least that is the plan. Keep in mind that the CIA does not have authority to operate in U.S. soil, which is why Mrs. Pierce is going with you. She has authority where you don't and doesn't where you do. Keep that in mind. Okay, as for the agent files, someone also hacked in and downloaded a complete list of all the company's employees, field agents, secretaries, everyone. And it isn't encrypted but we assume it is on that hard drive also," Ashley stated completely ignoring Josh's question.

"No! We are not leaving until you tell us about the two missing agents. Are they dead or just missing?" Davin questioned, being a bit sterner than he meant to be.

"Okay, Bradley and Sikes were assigned to track down the two missing scientists. They last reported from San Francisco yesterday morning. We don't know if they are alive or dead; we have not located bodies, and they have not checked in or returned to their hotel. Satisfied?"

"We need their pictures and anything else you have on them. We will head to S.F. and start our search there," Davin commented and then stood to leave.

"You want to start at the lab, right?" Ashley asked. "Well, have you got good walking shoes on?"

"Yes, why?" Connie asked.

"You will see."

"Okay, give us the address and a name of a contact person and we will head right over," Josh acknowledged.

"I will take you there, why don't you go out. The restroom is down the hall on the left Mr. Randal. Please wait in my outer office for a minute while I make the arrangements," Ashley ordered; as they stood and walked out of the office, she picked up her phone and punched in a four digit number, waited and when the door was closed, she said. "This is Director Peterson; I will be bringing four agents to the mountain. Make the arrangements for transport and we may as well stay for lunch in the Blue Room. Names are Davin and Connie Pierce and Josh and Stephanie Randal." After pausing to listen, she replied, "Thank you, we will see you in thirty." She hung up the phone, grabbed her jacket, weapon and the four special access badges she had in her desk as she prepared to exit her office.

"Ladies and gentlemen, are you ready?" Ashley said as she exited her office. "You will need these," she said handing the four badges to the team.

"Let's go," Davin responded.

Walking from her office, they headed to the bank of elevators located down the hall.

"For the foreseeable future, if you are to go to the lab from this building, you will need to use elevator number 5; the others will not take you to the proper floor," Ashley said as they entered elevator 5 and inserted her badge in a slot under the floor buttons. When a door popped open, she pushed the button marked B-5. Immediately the doors closed and the lights dimmed and turned red.

"Wow, where the hell are we going that requires red lights?" Stephanie questioned.

"Most people know Ft. Meade as the *Puzzle Palace* and our building as the *House of Secrets*; you are now going to the *Emerald City*."

What seemed like forever but really was only about three minutes, the elevator stopped and the doors slid open to expose a long hallway lighted with low level lights. Off to the left of the hall was a platform like you would find in a subway.

"Is that a subway?" Davin asked.

"Not exactly, we have a few minutes wait, so let's go over to those tables and I will explain. This area is secure; I can let you in on some of what is going on, but only to the Secret level, so listen up. I will only say this once," Ashley said as they exited the elevator. After sitting at the table in over stuffed lounge chairs, Ashley continued, "That is not your ordinary subway. It is actually a prototype MagLev train. She can exceed speeds of one hundred twenty miles per hour; we will board and be at our destination within minutes instead of the hours it would take to drive there. You will need to keep those badges with you at all times while down here; they are encoded and your movements will be recorded by the sensors located throughout the facility. If you are caught without the badges, you could be shot as an intruder. The guards down here do not play games; they shoot first and then ask questions. But what you are about to see is way above your pay grade; and with the consent of the President, we raised your clearance level and need to know to complete this mission. When we get on the train, there will be a box marked 'Phones'. You are to remove your phones and any other recording devices and place them in the box, and this includes cameras, tape recorders and any electronic device."

Chapter 10 Death under the Bridge

Sergeant Scott Lascell and Officer Harry Snow had showed up to work at six in the morning, as they always did. The morning was cold with a layer of fog hanging over the bay, slowly burning off as the sun came up. They always made a stop at their favorite Dunkin' Donut for coffee and a bit of cop food, glazed donuts, after leaving the station house. Traditions ran deep within the department; they would meet the two officers they were relieving to get updates as to what was going on in their area of coverage. This morning was no different from any other, at least not yet.

"Good morning Sue and Richard, how was the graveyard shift?" Lascell asked as he and Snow walked over to the table where Officers Sue Ridgeman and Richard White were sitting drinking coffee.

"Actually pretty quiet night, only one B and E, which turned out to be the dad coming home late from a night of drinking with his buddies. He tried to sneak into his own home without disturbing his wife, but she was awake and almost shot him as an intruder," Ridgeman commented between sips of coffee.

"Really just a lot of cruising and watching the fog roll in. We did run by the Presidio and talked to the gate guard for a few minutes. Pretty quiet night for them too, just a couple of students returning back to the barracks after hours; he let them slide. They said they had caught the late movie at the Paramount and thought they would be back before curfew."

"Let's hope the day will remain as quiet, two years from today, my young friends, two years from today," Lascell stated smiling.

"Two years?" White questioned.

"Two years, exactly two years from today, unless I make Lieutenant or Captain, I will retire and then it is fishing and beer every day until I die," Lascell responded as he and Snow sat down opposite their teammates.

"You will never retire, Scott. You love it too much. And I did hear through the grapevine that there is a Captain slot coming open in Precinct 9. And they are looking at you to take it," White commented and then took a bite from his Bear Claw.

"Precinct 9, down by the wharf; rough area, not sure if I would take it," Lascell said smiling. "I did hear that, and they did offer it already."

"Cool, are you going to take it?" Ridgeman asked.

"Not sure, they asked me to let them know by the end of the month. And if I did take it, I would move over on the first of the year. I am considering it, seriously. Big jump, but it would be my swan song; I'd work that until I could really retire in twelve years," Lascell said stopping to listen to the radio call.

"Shots fired, north east side under the bridge," the radio call announced.

"We have to get going, duty calls," Lascell said. He stood, reached for his radio, and answered. "Car 18 responding, on site in fifteen, over."

"Roger Car 18," the radio barked.

Fifteen minutes later, Lascell and Snow pulled up under the Golden Gate Bridge and scanned the area. Not seeing any movement, they slowly exited their patrol car; and with weapons drawn, they started to slowly walk the area. Seconds behind them were Ridgeman and Snow, performing backup, just in case. They really didn't want to miss any of the excitement if it turned out to be more than a few shots fired. Within a few minutes, they came across a body lying in the snow down close to the water's edge.

"Ah, crap. This day is not starting off very good my young Padawan," Lascell said as he approached the body, referring to Snow as a Jedi Knight learner, also known as a Padawan.

"I think we need to call this one in, Obi Wan," Police officer Harry Snow said looking at the body lying in the snow at the foot of the Golden Gate Bridge, referencing Obi Wan Kenobi from Star Wars. "This is definitely a job for ARMY CID."

"What do we have?" Ridgeman asked as she walked up, "Oh, guess you are starting your day off with a bang, we will check the area for the attacker. Come on Snow, they have the body, we need to secure the area."

"Yeah, right again rookie. I will call the chief and then those boys over at Army CID," Police Sergeant Scott Lascell said. She then walked over to their patrol car where she picked up the radio microphone and proceeded to call in to the station about the body they just discovered laying on the rocks at the base of the bridge. *'Damn, it had to be on a cold wet day, why couldn't they have waited until summer?'* Lascell said to himself.

"Go ahead; the chief is on the line," the radio dispatcher replied after receiving the initial call.

"Chief, Sergeant Lascell here; we have a body, male, about thirty years, dark hair and two bullet holes in the back. The body is dressed as a Major in the Army. We need ARMY CID here to take over. Do you want to make the call?"

"I will call; keep the area clear and stay on the scene until relieved by me," the chief ordered. "Is Snow and Ridgeman there?"

"Yeah, they volunteered to help secure the area until CID arrives."

"Good, I will get in touch with Army CID," the chief said and then disconnected.

"Yes sir, consider it done," Sergeant Lascell acknowledged, with over eighteen years on the force, he had thought he had seen it all; but today was going to be different, he just knew it, deep in his heart. He knew there was something different about this murder; his gut told him to watch out.

Twenty minutes after making the call, a large Army CID (Criminal Investigation Division) van and two Army green Humvees pulled up and four agents and the medical examiner with her assistant climbed out and walked over to Sergeant Lascell. There were two other patrol cars with four more officers on the scene keeping a sharp eye on the area so it would not be tampered with by anyone.

"Colonel Monica Blair, this is Sergeants Donald, Sandlewood, Captain Parks, and my Medical Examiner is Doctor Mackey; what do we have, Sergeant," Blair stated, flashing her badge and identification to the Sergeant.

"We got a call about a half hour ago reporting shots fired around the bridge. Came to check it out and he is what we found," Sergeant Lascell said pointing to the body laying face down on the rocks at the base of the bridge. We did a quick search of the area but found no shooter, weapon or spent bullet cases. Decided it would be best to call you in, since he is in uniform."

"Thanks for the call, can your men stick around for a bit longer, at least until we can secure the body?"

"Sure, no problem just let me know if there is anything else we can help with."

"What have you got, Mac?" Blair asked as she walked up to where she was examining the body.

"Give me a minute and I will have something for you," Mackey replied.

"Parks and Sandlewood, photos. Donald you know the drill, get moving," Blair barked out orders.

" Okay, looks like time of death was about an hour ago. But not from the bullets, look at this," she said pointing to the side of his skull where it was obvious that someone had used something to smash in his skull. "Blunt force trauma with a couple of bullets to the back to make sure he was dead. A bit of over kill for sure."

"Boss, that is Major Frederick Hanson, stationed at the Presidio, Defense Language Training Center," Donald responded after running the victims prints through the military database. "Says he has been here for the past two years as an instructor teaching Farsi and cryptology."

"Any next of kin?" Blair asked.

"Yes, daughter in Baltimore and wife is deceased," Ricky Donald answered reading the rest of the report he received from the Army CID database.

"Blair, looks like small caliber bullets, possibly 380s or 32s; when we get them out, I will send them up to Spock. He will be able to tell pretty quick," Mac stated referring to their forensic scientist Jonathan 'Spock' Nimoy, picking up the nickname while in high school because of his famous uncle, Leonard Nimoy; who played Dr. Spock in the TV series and movies, *Star Trek* and also for his complete reliance on pure logic in everything he did with one exception, women. When it came to women, he was totally lost.

"Angel, find anything of interest?" Blair asked as he looked over at her and Parks.

"No, sir, the area has nothing but… wait… what's this," Angela 'Angel' Parks said as she leaned over to pick up an empty shell casing that was lying between several rocks and an old beer can. "Looks new and recently fired, possibly one of the cases that housed at least one of the bullets that killed him, it's a 380. Maybe the other one is here too," she finished and bagged the case.

"There's the other one," Todd Sandlewood said and leaned down into the ice cold water to retrieve the second case, "Yep, 380."

"Bag and tag it. Mac almost has the body ready for transport," Blair said looking around at the area and not seeing anything out of place. Nobody hanging around to see what they were doing, at least nobody they could see.

"Sergeant Lascell, thanks for your help, I think we can handle it from here," Blair told the officer and then turned back to her team. "Let's wrap it up; it's starting to snow again."

Sergeant Lascell gathered his officers and after checking in with his chief, they headed off to their assigned duties.

Two hours later, Blair and her team headed back to the office located on the north end of the Presidio, about four miles from where the Major was killed. Dr. Mackey took the body to autopsy, the bullet cases and other possible evidence were headed for the lab of Forensic Scientist Spock and the rest of the team assembled in the conference room to discuss the case and decide what was to happen next.

Chapter 11 History Revisited

Berlin, Germany was a divided city for many years; and during the Nixon administration, the wall that divided the city finally came tumbling down. A free market started to bloom and along with the good side of the rebuilding of a city that was still in 1945 came a very strong underground know as the German Mafia. This mafia was just as dangerous as the mafia that plagued the United States in the early 1900s. There was murder, corruption and a world that most decent people hoped to never become aware of. But it was there, none the less. Within this world were four families, kind of like the Italian Mafia, but much worse. It was run by leaders of families with huge armies of men and women working for them, doing the dirty work, running the drugs, money, weapons and sex throughout the city. They operated above the law in most cases, and the wall between the cities did not stop them; they operated on both sides, although a bit more difficult in West Berlin because of the restrictions on travel between the two cities. This, however, became less of a problem when the wall fell. The largest and strongest group was not known as Mafia but as Nazis.

Gregory Dietrich was the grandson of SS Colonel General Josef "Sepp" Dietrich (1892-1966). 'Sepp', as he was known, in 1933, was the commander of the Life Guard SS (Leibstrandarte), Judge of the Supreme & Disciplinary Court of Honor of the German Labor Front and close confidant with Adolf Hitler. He was appointed by Hitler in August of 1926 to Sturmbannfuhrer of the SS; he became Hitler's confident and protégé and in 1930 appointed Oberfuhrer and elected to the Reichstag. He was a cold-blooded killer totally devoted to his Fuhrer. In the winter of 1941 and early into 1942, he led the 1st Panzer Group attacking Tostov in temperatures of -30C, took possession in November but had to retreat to the river Mius where they finally stood ground. He had given orders to his troops to take no prisoners.

Although he never married, he did father several children, who luckily survived the war. Sepp was taken prisoner in May of 1945, judged by a military tribunal in 1946, and sentenced to life in prison on charges of "offenses against ethics of war" for alleged massacre of U.S. Soldiers during the Battle of the Bulge. Historically the charges were unfounded, but the Allies did not care and wanted to set an example which they did. In 1951, his sentence was commuted to twenty-five years and he was finally released in 1955 on parole. But his time in prison was not over; in 1957, he was accused, tried and sentenced to eighteen months for being an accomplish to a manslaughter, in the execution of SA leaders in 1934 even though he was not directly involved. When he was released in 1958, his friends of the former Waffen SS and Army officers converged on Landsberg prison to welcome him. He died in 1966 from a heart attack at the age of seventy-four. His grandson Gregory, age twelve, attended the funeral along with his sister, Michelle, age ten and their father. Gregory's father was killed ten years later in a shoot out with a rival group. When Sepp died, he knew nothing of his son's business dealings or how the family had survived since the war. At the early age of twenty-two, Gregory was now in charge of the family business; Michelle aspired to become a model and actress and go to Hollywood. She wanted nothing to do with the family business which was fine with Gregory.

Gregory grew up hearing the stories about Sepp and the mold was caste; he was going to be like his Grandfather and follow his long dead Fuhrer, Adolf Hitler. His family only dressed in the traditional Nazi uniform during rallies and the rest of the time when out in public each member dressed in current civilian attire. They blended in as best they could and did not attract attention. Each member was tasked to secretly carry out missions for Gregory to attain domination of areas around the world. Gregory was so obsessed with his grandfather he even took on being called 'Sepp' to keep his legend alive.

"Sepp!" Hans said as he entered the large office which Gregory occupied.

"Yes Hans, what is it?" Sepp responded not looking up from the report he was reading.

"Sir, we just received word that the information you wish to have has been located in San Francisco, in the United States. It is in the hands of a small time criminal element that is looking to sell it to the highest bidder."

"Interesting, do you have a name of this seller?" Sepp asked finally looking up at his assistant.

"No, not yet, but soon; it looks like he tried to get the computer hard drive decrypted, but the person he took it to decided to not betray his country and ended up dead for his loyalty."

"That's a shame, good cryptologists are difficult to find. How soon do you think it will be before we have a name and location of this seller?" Sepp questioned.

"Very soon, sir, we know he goes by the title, *Weasel* and are close to locating him. We have set a trap to bring him in. Should be any time now. The police are investigating the murder of the crypto expert along with a group known as Army CID. I have never heard of them, have you?"

"Yes, they are the Army Criminal Investigation Division, and are pretty good at solving crimes, especially the ones located in Washington D.C. But they are not our worry, Mr. Weasel is ours; we need that drive and Mr. Weasel needs to disappear."

"Understood, sir, we will make it happen very soon," Hans agreed and then turned to leave the room.

"Hans, I want you to take care of it personally."

"Yes, sir," Hans acknowledged and left the room to make arrangements to fly to California.

After pressing the button on his intercom, he waiting for his secretary to answer and then asked, "Greta have you seen my sister today?"

"No sir, she did call earlier and asked if you were going to be in the office today, said she would stop by and chat with you."

"Call her and ask her to come by for lunch," Gregory said.

"Yes, sir," Greta responded.

Gregory pulled his keys from his pocket and unlocked a file drawer behind his desk and extracted a blue binder. He placed it on his desk and opened it to the fourth tab and started to read. The binder outlined his plan for the destruction of the United States. He did not trust computers because they were easily hacked and files could be stolen. He did not trust hard copies either, but he trusted them more than computers. He could physically secure the paper copy in a class one fire proof safe behind multiple layers of defense, guards, and locked doors. The safe and alarms were connected to a top of the line security system, using lasers, pressure sensitive floor, biometrics and of course a combination which he changed once a week. His office was nearly as safe as the Vatican or White House.

His plan was simple, the continuation of where his grandfather and Adolf Hitler left off when the war ended; bring down the Allies starting with the United States, followed by England, and then the world.

Working with the North Koreans and Chinese, he would start World War III; and then sit back and control the pieces on the board, just like moving pieces on a chess board. He would use North Korea and China as pawns to start the attack, and then send in his own troops to mop up after bringing down the American infrastructure and killing their President. America was seriously damaged; their troops were widely dispersed, and the country poorly defended by weekend warriors and a weak police force. He could not lose; he had a North Korean General on his payroll that was going to make millions for his part, and the commanders of four Chinese ballistic missile submarines ready to launch against the United States and England on his command. He had also been financing the ISIS group in Iran to go in and start killing infidels, as they liked to call all those that did not believe in their ideology. They were doing a great job.

Three coordinated frontal attacks from countries other than his; he could not be implicated in any of what was to become World War III. But when the dust cleared, he would be there to pick up the pieces. The new world would be ruled from Berlin by the grandson of one of the greatest German leaders.

A knock on his door broke his concentration. He closed his binder, placed it back in the safe, and after locking the safe door, he yelled, "Come in."

The door opened and his sister, Michelle Dietrich, walked in. "Is it time for lunch Gregory?" she asked as she walked across the room.

"Yes, Michelle, I will be right with you. But first I have something that you may be interested in."

"What might that be my dear brother?" Michelle asked sitting across from him.

"A close friend of mine called this morning and asked if you were in town," Gregory started to say; after pausing for a second, he continued, "He is a producer of plays and movies. He asked me if you were available to audition for a part in a movie he is producing."

"You know my schedule almost as well as I do, Gregory, I just finished my last stage performance last night, got a standing ovation by the way. So I guess I am available. What movie is he producing?"

"He wants to do a remake of <u>Beauty and the Beast</u> and thought you might be perfect for the lead."

"When does he want me to audition?"

"Here is the script; he faxed it over this morning after our call. Read it and then call him; his number is on the cover." Gregory smiled; he loved his sister and wanted her to succeed in her quest to become a great actress. This might just give her the break she needed; he did not feel bad about paying his producer friend to give her the part. Backing a film was good business and if it was successful he could make millions. And since the film was going to be made in Italy, she would be safe from the killing and destruction in the United States.

"Where would you like to go for lunch, maybe that new bistro across the street?" Michelle asked.

"Sure, let's go. I have a lot of work to do," he agreed and then stood and started for the door with Michelle following close behind.

Chapter 12 Don't Shoot the Messenger

The trip to *Emerald City* took approximately thirty minutes in the ultra plush fast MagLev train. After reaching the Emerald City, they were greeted by a team of armed guards who checked each badge and had all four pass through a special scanner. After walking down the dimly lit hallway for what seemed like a mile but was only about one hundred yards, they stepped onto a moving sidewalk and rode for fifteen minutes before stepping off.

"Are we there yet?" Josh asked, looking around at the bare walls with a door about every twenty feet.

"Almost, Mr. Randal, almost," Ashley commented as she turned down a side hallway and stopped in front of a pair of double doors. "This is the lab. Before we go in, you must understand that what you see and do in here is only to be reported to me or the President; do not tell anyone about anything in this facility unless you are in this facility talking to someone with the same colored badge. Is that completely understood? Failure to comply will be treated as treason and you know the penalty for that. Here is the only copy of the investigation report that was completed by our internal security force. Now let's go in."

Once inside the lab, they started to look around for anything that could help them discover who killed the two technicians and supposedly copy and take highly classified information from the building. Davin scanned the report while Connie, Josh and Stephanie searched the lab. They were not able to find anything to add to the investigation report.

"This report is pretty complete; your people are damn good," Davin commented after he finished reading the report. The only fingerprints are the ones that should be here. All drives, discs and other recording devices are accounted for. There is nothing missing except for two technicians being unaccounted for and one twenty gigabyte drive.

"Kind of leaves us in a hole doesn't it," Connie commented as she scanned the lab. "Can we talk to the medical examiner?"

"They are not my people, they are the internal security force investigators; you are my people and you are the ones picking up this case from here. Now we have one stop before we go down to the morgue," Ashley stated as they left the lab.

"Where might that be?" Davin asked as he and his team looked down the long hallway.

"Well, you can't come to *Emerald City* without visiting the *Wizard*. So we are going to see her now. She has some information you may need to help with your investigation."

"Okay, I'll bite; who the heck is the wizard?" Stephanie piped in.

"General Margaret Hunt is in charge of this facility and would like to meet you. Your team is pretty famous around here. Her office is one level up, we can take the stairs. Follow me."

"Lead on El Commandante," Josh said sarcastically, getting a cold eye from Ashley.

They reached the top of the stairs and walked down a long hallway to an unmarked door. Ashley Peterson knocked on the door and they heard the door buzz and a faint voice that sounded like it was miles away say, "Enter."

"General Hunt, may I present Mr. & Mrs. Davin Pierce and Mr. & Mrs. Randal, the team that has been assigned to solve our mystery," Ashley said as she introduced the team to General Hunt as they entered the office; there was no secretary or outer office, just a large windowless room.

The room looked more like a large conference room but tastefully decorated with some classic art, photos and statues. She sat behind a large wooden desk, which looked very old. Across from her was a highly polished twenty foot wooden conference table with large over stuffed leather chairs surrounding it. In the corner was a fully stocked wet bar complete with bar stools and four draft beer taps. One other door was located on the left wall close to the center of the room. There were two eighty-inch flat screen televisions mounted on opposite walls, providing each side with optimal viewing during conferences.

"You can call me Marge, please have a seat. I will get right to the point. I have been in charge of this facility for the past six years and we have had a perfect record for safety and security until two days ago when someone killed two of my scientists and either kidnapped two others or they were the ones that killed my people. We need to find out where they are and quickly. As for the supposed stolen information, well, that drive, or whatever they used, should have been wiped clean before they got it out of the building. Anyone trying to decrypt it will only spend a lot of time and money to get garbage. There is no way that drive will be readable, but we can't let the thieves know that. We are asking you to recover it."

"Wiped, how?" Connie asked.

"Just like the badges you are required to carry so we are able to track your movements, within the system located at all the exits, tunnels, air vents, and any other opening that a rat could get out of are multi-level systems that will scramble any program, software or recording media, including cassette tapes, CDs or anything magnetic. That is why your cell phones were left upstairs, we wouldn't want you to take pictures or lose any of your data. But you may have been told; we had a twenty minute complete shutdown of the security system right about the time they were killed. We are not 100% positive it was wiped."

"Pretty sophisticated system, but I guess if you want to keep your secrets you have to have the best security. May I ask some questions about this place?" Davin asked.

"Sure. I may not be able to answer all of them because of security reasons, not that I don't know," General Hunt said.

"*Emerald City*, as we have been told, is actually in Virginia under a mountain. Right?"

"Yes, Mount Weather to be exact and you can find us on a map, but only the people that work here know the extent of the facility and what is here," she replied.

"The train goes to Headquarters CIA; does it go anyplace else?" Josh asked picking up on Davin's thought train.

"Yes it does, actually you will be using it again when you leave here, but you will not be going back to the CIA. From here you will head to San Francisco. We have received information that someone is trying to get a drive decrypted, and we have good reason to believe it is our missing drive. The train will drop Ms. Peterson off at her office and then continue toward Dulles International Airport and deposit you four there; we have a jet waiting on the tarmac to fly you to San Francisco. We are sorry but the train does not go to San Francisco. Do you have any other questions?"

"Yes, but I think we need to get to work on the case and hopefully get invited back to view the rest of the facility," Davin stated.

"One final question," Josh's curiosity was getting the best of him.

"Go ahead Mr. Randal. Ask away," General Hunt said.

"Is it true about the aliens from Roswell, New Mexico? Are they here?"

"Seriously Mr. Randal, aliens, you mean the ones that crashed in New Mexico back in the 50s. That is above my clearance level. So I guess my answer is I don't know, but I can truthfully say not in this facility. Our mission here does not concern space aliens."

"Okay that's enough questions; you have a plane to catch. Thank you for your time Marge. I will stop by tomorrow."

Minutes later, they were standing on the platform waiting for the train which came speeding to a stop about three minutes later.

"CIA building," Ashley said as they entered the train.

Once boarded, the train started to move slowly at first; but within about 40 seconds, the train had reached one hundred fifteen miles per hour and raced down the dark tunnel.

"We will arrive in twenty-nine minutes, please be seated and relax," a female voice said from a hidden speaker.

"The train is completely computer operated, even the voice is synthesized; just tell it where you want to go when you board and it will take you there. It was modeled after the turbo lifts on the Star Ship Enterprise from the TV series Star Trek. Pretty cool isn't it?" Ashley commented when she saw the bewildered looks on her four guests.

"What else can you tell us about the mountain?" Josh questioned.

"The information I am about to tell you is classified and shall not be discussed outside of the facility. This facility is mainly here for research and to produce prototypes of a great many things. I trust you all have seen the movie *'Men in Black'*; they show some interesting objects that are supposed to be provided by aliens. Well, we are working on developing some of those objects here; some are already out there being produced and used by almost everyone. As far as the nation knows, it is the home of Federal Emergency Management Association, FEMA. This is true, they occupy a small corner on B-4 and do not have access to the entire facility, but it is much more. The facility is so big we have multiple services based in there. The main entrance is located in the Blue Ridge Mountains in northern Virginia. Some of the technology that is used in everyday life has come from here, but the main reason this is here is because of the Star Wars program. It lives and breathes from here. This facility is also in charge of all the nuclear weapons in our arsenal," Ashley admitted. After pausing for a breath, she continued, "NORAD, North American Aerospace Defense Command located at Cheyenne Mountain, is actually a subordinate of Weather Mountain; it was founded May 12th, 1958 to control our missile silos and other Aerospace projects. It is the home of the 721st Mission Support Group which is part of the 21st Space Wing headquartered at Peterson Air Force Base. There are six underground facilities located around the country, besides *Cheyenne Mountain* and *Weather Mountain,* we have Deadwood, Wyoming known as the *'Crystal Palace'*, Flagstaff, Arizona has the *'Observatory'*, one on the big island of Hawaii, the *'Beach'* and the other in Alaska outside of Fairbanks, known as the *'Icebox'*".

"Cool, I can live with that," Josh said quietly. "I can get used to this. Are they all connected with this super fast train?"

"All are except the Hawaii facility; the Pacific Ocean is a bit too deep to dig a tunnel across, so we use a high speed submarine, nuclear powered of course and able to exceed speeds of, well, let's just say the cruise to the Hawaii facility doesn't take very long and they surface inside the facility or we just fly," Ashley answered and then smiled as the train came to a stop at the station under the CIA building. "Time to go, your plane is waiting at Dulles."

Chapter 13 San Francisco

"Ashley said to go to Concourse A, Gate 28," Josh stated as they exited the train on a level below Concourse A. Stepping out of the train, he looked around and saw a set of stairs going up, "Well I guess that is our exit."

"Yeah, doesn't seem to be any other way out except by train. As soon as all were out of the train, the doors closed and the train started to return to Mount Weather. The four of them walked up the stairs. They came to a door with a sign on it stating: *'This door exits onto Concourse A at Gate 28. Please ensure the door is fully closed after exiting.'*

"Wow, they really have this planned out," Connie commented as they pushed through the door. "Look," she said pointing out the window at the Gulfstream VI sitting on the tarmac.

"That must be our ride," Davin said as he glanced out at the shiny new jet airplane.

It is not often that the company would put the corporate jet at their disposal, but the circumstances were not normal.

"Good morning ladies and gentlemen, welcome," a young female attendant said as they exited the door. "I assume you are Mr. and Mrs. Pierce and Randal. Do you have your boarding passes?" she continued quietly.

"No," Davin replied looking at Josh and the ladies, "Did Ashley give you any boarding passes?" he asked them, only to get a puzzled look from all of them.

"No, she gave us nothing," Stephanie answered.

"Sorry, no boarding passes," Davin answered the attendant.

"No problem, do you have any form of identification?" she asked.

Three handed her their CIA issued identification and Connie passed over her FBI badge and credentials.

"Those will do just fine," she replied taking each one, scanning it and then returning each. The pilots are already on board, please follow me. Do you have any luggage?"

"No luggage," Josh replied as they followed her out the door to the air stairs, leading them into the cabin. "Please take a seat; we will depart in a few minutes. Would you care for a drink before we take off? I will serve a light lunch after departure."

"Beer for me," Josh ordered, "Any kind, just cold."

The rest of the team ordered drinks and sat back in the overstuffed leather seats.

"I can get used to this," Connie stated.

"Good morning, I am Captain John Mott; we will be closing the door in a moment. We have one more passenger that is going with us and she is running late. Sorry for the delay." He paused for a second and then said to the attendant, "I believe our other passenger has arrived."

"She's here sir, closing the door now," the attendant responded, and then to the new passenger said, "Please take a seat, we are backing out now. Would you care for a drink?"

"No, thank you. I will wait until we are airborne," the latest arriving passenger replied while taking a seat in the back of the plane. She did not say a word to anyone else. She was five foot four inches tall, had short black hair, wore dark sunglasses, and dressed in a tasteful pants suit, a white blouse and matching black blazer; she looked like a member of the *'Men in Black'*.

Minutes later, the Gulfstream was racing down the runway and breaking ground for their flight to San Francisco. As promised, the flight attendant came around after the plane leveled off at thirty-two thousand feet with a light lunch of baked chicken, salad and green beans.

"Good lunch, Josh. Are you going to eat that roll?" Stephanie asked eying his roll.

"No, you can have it," Josh replied as he handed it to her. He then quietly asked, "Who do you suppose our other rider is?"

"My guess is she is a new agent for one of our sister intel groups. But she needs to get a little more style in her choice of clothing, so *'Men in Black'* with that black suit."

"Yeah, I know..." then he stopped and smiled at Stephanie, "She's standing behind me, isn't she?"

Glancing over her shoulder, she saw the new passenger standing behind them smiling.

"Oops," was all that Josh could say.

"Now that we are in level flight and lunch has been served, I would like to introduce myself," the lady in black said as she walked up and sat across from Josh and Stephanie, "Mr. and Mrs. Pierce would you join us back here."

After they sat in the seats across from the three of them, she began to speak. "Yes, I am dressed like a *Woman in Black*, but I am not looking for aliens from outer space. My name is Joanne Morgan; I go by my Korean name when working, Mi-Cha Sang and I work for Ashley Peterson as a field agent. Sorry for the cloak and dagger routine, but I was on my way to a dinner theater rehearsal; I play the detective in a murder mystery. But anyway, Ms. Peterson got a tip that there is something hinky going on in Korea and she wanted me to go back over and do a little undercover work to see what I can find out. Sorry for intruding in your mission, but I'm telling you this because there is a link somewhere between your mission and mine. Korea is involved somehow and it is my job to find out how. She told me to catch your flight to San Francisco and then commercial out of there to South Korea. Here are my credentials," she said as she handed over her identification.

"Interesting, okay, Ms. Morgan, welcome to CIA Flight 28 to San Francisco," Davin acknowledged, smiling.

"Yeah, welcome," Connie said.

"I may need to contact you if I can't get through to Ms. Peterson, would that be alright?"

"Sure, no problem."

"I already have your numbers listed as friends on my phone," she said, "Now let's finish lunch."

"I will drink to that," Davin agreed.

After landing in San Francisco, they rented a car and headed over to the Presidio to meet with Blair and Takahashi. Ms. Morgan, after saying her goodbyes walked down the concourse to the International terminal to catch a flight to South Korea.

After arriving at the Army CID headquarters, they parked; and within a few minutes, they were being escorted into the conference room. Minutes later, Blair entered and offered drinks and the use of the facilities to her arrivals.

"I am senior agent Colonel Monica Blair; you can call me Monica. Tam will be here in a few minutes, please help yourself to coffee, water or anything at the bar and the facilities are down the hall to the left. You don't need an escort to go there, but please don't wander the building. Some of the guards don't understand you have a higher clearance than they do and can move around as you please; let me notify them first."

"Thanks, Colonel Blair, ah, Monica, but we really need to find out what has transpired," Davin stated as he picked up a bottle of water from the bar. Before Blair could answer there was a knock on the door. She reached over and opened the door. Takahashi walked into the room. She did not look at all what one would expect of a homicide detective, standing five foot six inches tall, with a perfect smile and a Playboy bunny body, wearing a designer cobalt blue pants suit, white blouse and jacket. It wasn't very obvious where she carried her weapon but Davin and Josh both did a double take as to where it might be.

"Welcome Detective Takahashi, this is Davin Pierce, Josh Randal and Stephanie Randal from the CIA and Connie Pierce from the Washington office of the FBI. May I present Detective Tamako Takahashi, but she likes to be called Tam. Come on in and take a seat, we have a lot to discuss and no time to waste," Blair introduced and then took a seat beside Tam near the head of the table.

"We were told that a cryptologist, a Major Frederick Hanson, from the Defense Language Institute was found dead yesterday and that his death may have an impact on national security. Is that right, Agent Blair?"

"Yes, we have found out that he was contacted by a known criminal element that goes by the name of Weasel. They were to meet to discuss some kind of encrypted software he had acquired," Blair commented.

"How did you find out about the meeting?" Josh asked.

"Major Hanson called the FBI field office; they called NSA and then called the CIA about an hour before it was to happen and told our night duty officer, who was unable to contact me or any of the agents on call. We got a call from SF police, who found the body. Of all nights for it to happen, the entire infrastructure in the San Francisco area went off line, no phones, no Internet, nothing worked. The city is still trying to locate the reason, but so far none has been provided," Blair stated obviously disturbed about not getting the call and Hanson being killed.

"Our office got a call from the FBI yesterday also. They told him to be careful and not take any chances. He was advised to wait for assistance to arrive, but obviously he didn't wait," Davin commented.

"We wish he had waited; he might still be alive," Monica stated.

"Some other developments have come up; this fellow that calls himself 'Weasel' is a low life criminal that has ties all over the underworld in the valley. He has a rap sheet as long as your arm, but we have not been able to make anything stick. He has a couple of high priced lawyers that find loop holes in everything we do and he walks," Tam added. "Actually that is all we have at the moment. As for a connection with your case Ms. Pierce, we are not sure how it connects; but as Monica said when Hanson called, he sounded scared and the person he was meeting said he had some software that needed decrypting. That's about it. Here is my card; please call if you need assistance. My cell number is on there, so I can be reached anytime, day or night."

After about a half hour of trading information, it was time to leave and Davin stood and said, "Thanks Tam and Monica, I guess we need to get checked in at our hotel; we will check with you in the morning for any further developments. And we need to get something to eat; breakfast was a long time ago."

"See you in the morning. Are you looking for seafood or meat for dinner?" Tam asked as she stood to leave.

"Well, steak is preferred?" Josh answered quickly before the ladies had a chance to ask for seafood.

"Try 5A5 Steak Lounge over on Jackson Street, they are rated by 'Gayot' as the best in the area," Tam offered. "Great atmosphere, awesome steaks, may be a bit pricey, but worth it."

"Why don't you join us Tam and Monica?" Stephanie offered.

"I can't make tonight, but thanks," Monica replied.

"What time, I would love to; they serve a wonderful Japanese Kobe steak. I can meet you there," Tam agreed.

"Okay, it's four thirty now, how about six," Stephanie answered after getting a nod of approval from everyone. "If you change your mind, Monica, please come on over."

"I will see what I can do. No promises."

"Okay, we better go," Davin added and they headed out the door.

Chapter 14 Dead Ends

"Okay gang what do we have, "asked Blair as she walked into the operations center the next morning.

"We have run into a dead end boss," Angel replied. She stood and walked over to the closest monitor.

"No dead ends allowed in this game. Talk to me," Blair continued and then took a sip from her bottle of water.

"Well, we tracked down a possible suspect from a fingerprint he left on one of the bullet casings. Spock has determined the weapon used was a Wather PPK in 380. Same weapon used in a robbery two months ago, which left two people wounded and one dead. Metro Police have been searching for the shooter but no luck until now. The suspect is a fellow by the name of Eric Schubert aka 'Weasel'."

" Okay, bring him in," Blair ordered.

"He is downstairs right now," Ricky Donald replied but did not get a chance to finish his comment.

"Have you talked to him? What does he tell us about our dead soldier?"

"Boss, he is not talking; he is in autopsy, found shot dead at three this morning six miles from the Presidio. His weapon had been fired and was empty, looks like a minor firefight and he lost. No identification on the body, just his weapon and a folded note," Angel continued. "There is a blood trail leading to the parking lot. The tire marks and blood are being analyzed."

"A note? What did it say?" Blair asked looking seriously at the picture on the screen.

"No words, just a swastika," Ricky said shyly, not really believing that the Nazi party was still in existence.

"Swastika, you mean like a Nazi Swastika?" Blair questioned. He looked surprised and confused at the same time.

"Yes, like Nazis have returned from the dead," Angel commented. She passed the evidence bag over with the note inside.

"Why the hell are the Nazis showing their hand now? I thought most of them were in jail, dead, or otherwise just living a cool life somewhere in Columbia," Blair asked and took the bag. He examined it closely, "Any finger prints?"

"That is a very good question, but we don't have a good answer," Ricky said. "And only one print, left thumb, running it through FBI and local database."

"Okay, got it. As soon as we get a name, I need to know. What else do we have?" Blair asked looking around at his team.

"Not much, but we checked with all incoming international flights and came up with a name," Angel stated, pausing for a moment.

"Well, who just raised the red flag?"

"Savon Hussain Laden, a known Al Qaida terrorist. He came in on a fake ID but was caught on at least four security cameras. He was able to get off the airport before facial recognition picked him up. Sorry sir," Angel finished her report and then picked up her phone as it started to ring; she answered, "Sergeant Parks." After listening for a few minutes without saying a word, she hung up the handset.

"What was that about, Angel?" Blair asked seeing the concerned look on her face.

"That was Spock; he got a hit on the thumb print and the blood, and both belong to a Hans Bormann, a known Nazi sympathizer."

"Holy Batman, who the hell is going to pop up next?" Blair questioned and then turned back to her team. "Do we have a picture of this Bormann guy?"

"No, but we have contacted Interpol to see if they do?" Rick commented, "Should have something soon on him."

****

Gila Bend, Arizona

At a small airport in the little town of Gila Bend, Arizona, located about forty miles southwest of Phoenix, this uncontrolled airport frequently saw air traffic coming and going at all hours of the day and night. Tonight was no different; a small twin engine Piper Seneca touched down and rolled to the end of the runway. The right engine shut down and the pilot sat there for a couple minutes, finally the door opened and two passengers climbed aboard.

There was no luggage for the man and young woman; the pilot noticed that she really did not want to get on the airplane, but he dismissed it to the fact that she might not like to fly. Waiting until the man had her buckled in and he was buckled, the pilot started the engine and taxied to the end of the runway; minutes later the plane climbed in the cool crisp air of southern Arizona to one thousand feet and headed south toward the border. The pilot flew without lights. Since he knew that the Goldwater Range was not in operation on this evening, Savon Hussain Laden did not worry about being accidentally shot down by an Air Force F-16 or Marine A-10 doing their live fire training on the range. His contacts in Mexico assured him the range was closed. This short flight to Mexico was to meet with transportation to Germany, no questions asked. Mohammed had paid lots of money to the Guzman Cartel to ensure safe passage to Germany for Laden and his guest. No one spoke on the plane, the passengers just sat and watched the terrain fly by in between mountains that peaked above them.

****

"We have a bogie heading south, looks like he just left Gila Bend," the border patrol drone operator yelled to his supervisor. "No flight plan and he thinks he is below our radar, but he doesn't know we have updated our system and we would see him if he were only ten feet off the deck."

"I will notify our Mexican buddies; we don't have anything in the area to stop him. Our drone is on the west end of its track; change the track and bring her in," his supervisor stated and then picked up his phone, the one that was a direct link to the Nogales Drug Enforcement Division. They had several helicopters and a fast single engine P-51 Mustang that was not as heavily armed as the UH-1 Huey helicopters but could easily catch most piston engine aircraft. The P-51 was not one that was built in the 1940s but a new one built to the specs of the original, but equipped with a turbine engine instead of the twelve cylinder Rolls Royce. She could fly at over four hundred fifty miles per hour and was armed with six fifty caliber machine guns. The Hueys were equipped with missile launchers and two M-60 machine guns, but were slower than the P-51.

"Hey boss, we have another low flyer coming up from the south on a direct intercept heading on the south bound bird," the drone operator yelled to his supervisor.

"Hell, what the hell is going on?" his boss commented as he turned back to the phone and spoke to his counterpart in Mexico. "We have two low flyers, one heading south and the other heading north, neither crossed the border yet, but we suspect they will in a couple of minutes."

"They are turning boss; looks like they are going to fly parallel to the border, heading east, not crossing."

"Keep an eye on them. If they cross the border I will tell Miguel to launch his bird to intercept." After pausing for a moment, he turned and picked up the phone and immediately connected with Miguel. "Miguel, we have two aircraft, one on each side of the border, flying parallel at nine hundred feet AGL, heading east toward you. Don't know what they are doing, but you may want to launch."

"Thanks for the tip; we have one of our helos preparing to take off in a couple of minutes for a routine run along the border. I will tell them to look for our two intruders. Do you have eyes on them from your drone? We will see what they are up to, my friend," Miguel acknowledged as the line went dead. This caused both men to stare at the phone and wonder; they heard no tone or static on the line. The line was dead.

"What's wrong, boss?" the drone operator asked seeing the worried look on his face.

"The phone is dead."

"Dead! Try your cell."

"No service. How is yours? Where is our drone?"

"Lost the link. No service, that's strange. Our drone is at 10K and fifty miles behind the south bound bird."

"Yeah, what are our bogey's doing?"

"They have disappeared," the drone operator said looking at his screen. "I just turned up the gain but still nothing. They could not have landed; I haven't taken my eyes off this screen and they just vanished. Try your radio."

"This is Murphy, anyone copy," he said into his radio and then waited for a response.

"Murphy, this is Gomez; read you loud and clear, what's up?" came the muffled response.

"Do you have contact with our drone?"

"No, we lost visual a few seconds ago. We were just trying to call on the land line but it is dead. What's up?"

"Not sure, let us know if your system comes up again. We are trying to get ours out now... Wait, one," Murphy said and then turned back to his drone operator. "What?"

"I have control again and the system is showing that our two birds have turned again, the one on the Mexico side is heading south and the one on our side is heading north again. All seems back to normal."

"Keep tracking the north bound bird. I will have Miguel launch and follow the one on his side."

****

"Mr. Sanford is there any word from the Cyber Command?" President Mitchell asked as Sanford walked into the Oval Office.

"Nothing this morning, sir. But I did get a report from Peterson over at CIA. Her team is in San Francisco and investigating the missing disk and death of the Army officer."

"Good, any progress, no guess not, too early. What about locating my daughter?"

"That is progressing and I should have updates later today," Tony reported, reaching for a cup of coffee.

"Anything on our terrorist in Iran?"

"Nothing new, but you know all this. It was in your morning report. And nothing has changed in the past hour since you read it. What's up? I know you are concerned about your daughter and I am too. But we are doing everything we can to get her back without compromising any secrets and get her back safely."

"I understand the need to keep our secrets a secret; but damn it, she is my only daughter and I can't afford to lose her. I lost my wife and losing her almost killed me. I still can't sleep at night and my mind wanders at times. You may have noticed," Mitchell paused and looked off into the distance before he spoke again. "I am not sure I can continue to do this, Tony."

"Yes sir, I have noticed and I am here to assist you. You will get through this. Is there anything I can get you to help? Do you want the doctor to prescribe something to help you sleep?"

"No, ah, maybe, let me think about it. I don't want the public to think I can't handle the job, but I need to get some sleep." He paused again and then said, "Yes have the doctor stop by and I will talk to him."

"I will have him stop by after lunch," Tony said and then sipped his coffee.

"Tony, are we doing the right thing? What with all the attacks, are we targeting the right people? The Koreans, Chinese, Iranians, who's next? The French, Italians, who? We are being attacked and someone is controlling them, but who? Your report indicated that a Nazi Swastika was found on the body of the man you killed, the Major from the Presidio. Are they German Nazis, rising from the dead or a new breed of Nazi? Are they controlling the Koreans, Chinese and Iranians?"

"We are not sure, but working on it and hopefully will have more information soon. We just don't know, sir."

"We will not lose this war, Tony. We will not lose. Now I need to rest. Please go, leave me alone for an hour," Mitchell said walking back to the sofa and sat down. "Tony, thank you," he said as Tony left the Oval Office.

****

"Caleb, why are we working with that German infidel, he is scum?" one of his men asked as they studied the next step of their plan.

"I have plans for our good benefactor; right now he is giving us a lot of money to finance our plans," Caleb responded and then looked at the map of the United States he had on the table.

"How much longer do we have to endure his insults? He does not trust us, he is not a believer and…"

"That is enough!" Caleb yelled, "We need his money and when the time comes he will be eliminated, along with his entire family. And if you keep questioning my plans I will have you eliminated too."

"Yes sir, I will hold my tongue."

"Now, we have kidnapped the President's daughter and she is being transported to Mexico. Once there she will be put on a jet and flown to Bagdad where we will take her and bring her here. Any questions? Not you," Caleb said pointing to his young freedom fighter. "Okay, now for the next phase of our quest. I need six volunteers to go to America and…"

He continued to outline his plan on bombing several of the busiest airports around the country. The targets he had picked were Chicago, Los Angeles, and Boston to be completed in the next two weeks.

Chapter 15 Dark Night in California

After picking up his cell phone, Chief of Police in Los Angeles Mark Harrington punched in his speed dial for his wife, Heather. It rang three times before she picked up, "Hi honey, it looks like it is going to be a late night."

"What's up Mark?"

"I can't talk about it right now, but stay close to home and I will be there soon. But you may want to get some extra firewood in the house and our camp lanterns," Mark answered without really saying what the problems were. "I will call you later."

" Okay, be careful," Heather said and ended the call. They had been married for thirty-five years and she had watched him start as a rookie police officer pounding the streets and slowly working his way up the ladder to Police Chief of one of the largest cities on the west coast. Los Angeles was a city that was divided in culture and humanity that could not be matched in any city across the planet. Over two hundred different gangs, every nationality was represented within the city, people that were dirt poor to the mega rich all lived within or around the city. Harrington had his hands full every day with the city, but would not trade it for any other on the continent or planet for that matter. Heather knew by the tone of his voice that something was wrong and she would obey his warning.

"Chief, we just got some more information. Looks like we are having a blackout, most of southern California is in the dark and with each minute more of the state is going dark. If this keeps going; by eight tonight, the entire state will be dark. And we have no idea why."

"Damn, the electric companies don't know?" Mark questioned.

"Their techies think they have been hacked and someone outside has taken over the grid."

"How?" Chief Harrington asked to no one in particular.

"Sir, the infrastructure is going down, the phones just quit, and we are now running on back-up generator. Since the state started controlling almost everything through the Internet, it was only a matter of time before someone figured out how to bring us down. I am surprised that the rest of the country is still operating. But maybe they aren't, come to think of it. We cannot communicate because ours is down, maybe they are down too. We are back in the stone age," the stations senior Information Technician stated to the chief.

"No power means the generator will only operate for a few days. The gas pumps will not work without power, refrigeration is off and well, you get the picture, sir," Chief Harrington agreed. He then stormed back into his dimly lit office, only to come out a few seconds later. "Conner's, get everyone into the conference room, NOW!"

****

White House Cabinet Room

"Sir, we have just received a report from the Governor of California, he has just declared a state of disaster and he has already called out the National Guard. The entire state has lost its electrical grid; it has been down for over an hour, and they have determined their system was hacked by some unknown person or persons; and, well they are not completely sure what was done, but the system is no longer under control of California. They are tracing back where the attack came from but so far have had little luck," National Security Advisor Tony Sanford reported.

"Hacked! How could that happen? Didn't the California Electrical Company secure their network as I heavily suggested when I took office," Darrell Mitchell asked.

"Sir, remember you asked all private companies to look into securing their systems if they had anything to do with the infrastructure. But because we as a government did not want to set policy, we only made it a suggestion," Tony reminded him. "And they said, if we want it done, we should fund it."

"Yes, I know, but I thought they really thought they understood the vulnerabilities we have with the network and being connected to the Internet."

"Maybe they understood but did not or could not spend the money. Or maybe they did not want to take the time to secure their network properly."

"If they could hack California electric, what else can be hacked? Can we protect the infrastructure of the country?" Mitchell asked.

"That is a good question. NSA and some of the best ethical hackers we could get went through the network and identified the vulnerabilities and a nine hundred page report was submitted to Homeland Security. You know each company was advised and suggestions made. What they did with it, we are not sure," Tony Sanford commented.

"Okay, what next?"

"FEMA has been alerted and is standing by to assist, if they can. Beyond that, the techies need to figure out how to get the system back online. California has some of the best hackers in the world and are onsite working the problem. Time frame, well it could happen pretty quick or not at all," Tony replied.

"Let's hope they can fix it soon; it gets pretty cold in northern Cal this time of year," Mitchell quietly stated.

"Sir, we just got informed that the power outage is moving across the country. Oregon and Washington were able to report their infrastructure is going down, wait," Homeland Security Director John Ramsay paused in his report. "The outages are moving faster, reports are Arizona, Utah, Colorado and Montana are going down. It looks like they have found the hole in our cake and are using it to bring us down."

"Okay, they have us by the short hair; what are we going to do about it?" Darrell Mitchell asked.

"I think you need to redirect our cyber warriors to target a more western target," Tony Sanford, National Security Advisor commented.

"I do believe you are correct," Mitchell said then paused, drifted off for a moment, as if thinking and then turned to Eric Fredericks, Director of NSA and said, "Eric, you heard Tony, redirect and locate that hacker and take him, her or it down; if you are unable to narrow it down to a specific person or server, then take down their Internet, server or if you have to, take down the whole damn country."

"Yes sir, I will be right back; I need to use the secure line in Mr. Sanford's office," Fredericks said and then stood and headed for the door followed by Tony Sanford.

"Tony, while you are in your office, grab that report on that terrorist group you have been working on with NSA. I think we need to concentrate on them too. I have a sick feeling that they are somehow involved in this," Darrell Mitchell ordered and then returned to his desk to start reviewing the stack of reports on his desk. Since he returned from Iran, he was having a hard time getting his thoughts together. And, as President of the United States, he needed to get his thoughts in line to be able to make solid confident decisions. He was wondering if he could still do that after his kidnapping and subsequent rescue. His mind drifted at times, but he was able to hide that fact from his staff. But he didn't know how much longer he could do that before someone would notice he was not functioning at full capacity.

About eight minutes later, Tony and Fredericks returned with the report. "Sir, there are actually two reports but they are linked somehow."

" Okay, brief everyone here on what you have," Mitchell ordered.

"One is on a German group and the other just popped up on the scope. At least we believe it's new, located in Iran. We have tracked the money from the German group; looks like they are financing the ISIS group in Iran. The Iranian group, member of the Islamic State Group seems to have unlimited funds and lots of firepower. Presently we have estimated the group as having between five and fifteen hundred active members, scattered all over the world. There are indications that they have sleeper teams all over America. We have not been able to narrow who or where they are, but are working on it."

"What else do we know about this German group?" Mitchell asked.

"We have not been able to narrow down who is in charge, only that he, or they, are buried under multiple layers of dummy corporations scattered around the world. We do know they are based in Germany, but exactly where, and who, we don't know. The last transfer to the ISIS group was a cool half million. We also found that this group moves a lot of money off shore. There were two transfers to the Cayman Islands for a half million each, two different accounts."

"Transferring money is not illegal," James Ramsey commented.

"No, but transferring money for illegal activities or financing terrorist groups is illegal, at least by our laws," Mitchell responded looking at his staff. He paused for a moment, as if thinking, but he drifted off to another time and place for a moment. Snapping back, he looked back at his staff and started to speak, but then thought better of it and just smiled.

"Eric, what is the latest on ISIS, the new group in Iran?" Ramsey asked.

"As far as we can tell they are doing a lot of training, running between fifty and one hundred combatants through the camp every few weeks. We have tasked several satellites to monitor them and are keeping close tabs on them," Eric Fredericks, Director of NSA, answered and then paused for a second sipping his coffee. "The photos show that they have some heavy firepower, combined with your typical AK-47s; they have been training on RPGs and vehicle mounted heavy machine guns, possibly M-60s or 50 calibers. Hard to tell on the photos, but they are vehicle heavy guns."

"Looks like we may be going to get some visitors, how can we prepare for that?" Mitchell asked.

"Not sure, keep our eyes on the ports for any illegals coming in, but you know as well as I do that no matter what we do, our borders are too open. They can get almost anything into the country, people, small arms, heavy artillery, you name it. If they don't bring it, then they can just buy it on the black market. I know you have been working with Border Patrol and the military to control our borders, but the only way we can ensure that our borders are secure is to close them down. Block all access which is damn near impossible. We have too many ways to get in, the border guards are there to keep the honest people honest, but walking or driving across where there are no gates is very easy. We can't check every container on every container ship coming in our ports. As for the airports..." Ramsey continued to outline the problems with the borders until he was interrupted by Mitchell.

"Yes, we all know it is an impossible task, but we need to do something to protect our people and way of life. I am open to suggestions, no matter how crazy they are."

Chapter 16 South of the Border

"Davin, are you sure we should have left Josh and Stephanie back in San Francisco?" Connie asked as she and Davin walked down the air stairs from the Gulfstream Five in Mexico City. She was smiling because she loved Mexico City; she especially thought the people and culture down here was awesome.

"Yes, they are there to coordinate with Army CID and Washington. Our job is to locate the German connection down here, and we know the computer drive was transported down here," he said and then stopped to look for the rental car desk.

"Mr. and Mrs. Pierce?" a voice behind them asked.

"Yes, may we help you?" Davin answered as he turned to see a man in a dark suit standing behind them.

"Sir, actually, I am here to help you," the man stated flashing a badge and identification. "I am Hector Rodriguez, Director of Policía Federal Ministerial, commonly known as the Federales. Would you please come with me?"

"How did you know we were coming?" Connie questioned.

"That was easy, if you think about it. Your pilot files a flight plan. We monitor all flights coming and going into the country. Once we knew your arrival time, I came down to meet with you and offer any assistance you might need. I know who you work for and why you are here. I have a car waiting. I will have one of my men retrieve your bags and bring them to your hotel," Hector said quietly.

"Okay, let's go," Davin said quietly and glanced quickly at Connie and winked as she squeezed his arm slightly to ensure his shoulder holster still had his trusted Colt in it. Their visit here was supposed to be undercover and now they had a Federale impeding their investigation. Or would he?

"I need to stop at the ladies room for a second. Do you mind waiting a couple of minutes?" Connie replied catching the wink and understanding that they may have trouble. After reaching the ladies room, she quickly checked to see if she was alone; and after finding that she was, she reached into her purse and removed her cell phone. She pressed the speed dial and waited a few seconds until she heard Josh pick up.

"Got a problem?" Josh asked immediately knowing that if she was calling they may be in trouble or suspected trouble.

"Yes, we were greeted by a Hector Rodriguez, a Federale. How did he know we were coming?" Connie asked.

"There has to be a leak somewhere, only the four of us, the pilots and a few people back at HQ knew our plans. I will find out, stay cool and call back in two hours," Josh said and then took a deep breath.

"Anything new there?" asked Connie.

"Nothing, we have two bodies and no leads. We are heading down to meet with the local police that found the two bodies. Hopefully, they can give us some help. The only problem we are having here is that the heat is off and so is the electricity. The entire state is in the dark, the power grid is down and nobody knows why or when it will be back up. Luckily we are using a SAT phone and they are still functioning, at least for now," Josh replied.

"Damn, stay warm. Got to go," Connie said, disconnected the call, and headed for the door. She stepped out to find Davin and the Federale sitting quietly in the lounge across from the restroom. They were both sipping on bottled water and chatting like old friends. Nothing seemed out of place; then she spied another man enter the lounge and walk over to Davin and Hector. She stood and watched for a moment and then started to walk over. The hair on the back of her neck was standing up; something was not right, but she could not put her finger on what, so she continued walking toward the three men. Maybe she was worried for no reason; there could be a number of ways that they knew they were coming down and probably knew why too, and, yes, normal protocol was to notify the local authorities that there was an investigation going on by American CIA and FBI. They did this for many reasons: one, to ensure they were not arrested for bringing in weapons to the country; two, so they could get help if needed from the locals; and three, it was just common courtesy for this to be done.

"Mr. Pierce, this is my Lieutenant, Jose Martinez. He will get your luggage and bring it to your hotel; by the way, at what hotel are you staying?" Hector introduced and asked.

"The Hyatt Regency just off the airport," Connie replied as she walked up to the three men.

"Jose, get their bags from their plane and meet us in the lounge at the Hyatt," Hector ordered.

"Si," Jose replied and walked off and out the door heading toward the Gulfstream. On the way, he grabbed a luggage cart and pushed it ahead of him.

"Okay, let's go; we have a lot to talk about," Hector said as he dropped a stack of pesos on the table to pay for the drinks and stood and started toward the door. Davin and Connie followed close behind. Sitting outside the general aviation terminal was a new black Chrysler 300C. Hector opened the back door for Connie and pointed to the front door for Davin; he then walked around to the driver's door and climbed in.

"Oh, before I forget Ms. Peterson asked me to ask you to call her when you landed. She has some information that may be of help," Hector said as they drove.

The drive to the hotel only took fifteen minutes; and after checking in, they headed up to their room.

"Hello Ms. Peterson, this is Connie Pierce," she said into the cell phone when Ashley Peterson answered and then listened for a moment. "Yes, we met Hector; he just dropped us at our hotel …" Connie paused to listen, "Yes, I understand, yeah, we did meet, she seems to be very competent. Hopefully she will be alright…" she paused again, "Okay, understand, we will be careful and I will tell Davin as soon as we are alone…" Connie paused once more before replying, "Thanks for the information, bye."

"What did Ashley have to say?" Davin asked looking back over his shoulder.

"Will fill you in later, it is kind of private," Connie answered.

"Hector, since you have been able to track all aircraft coming and going into the state, have you had any recent activity that may have brought in a German national?"

"We did have a German tourist group come in two days ago, but they headed out to the Yucatan within a day after arriving. Another German came in, travelling with a woman and one other man. They flew in yesterday, were picked up by a limo and headed north out of the city. We had no need to track them beyond the airport. Those were the only German nationals that we know of. Of course the cruise ships that dock at our ports on the coast could have hundreds of Germans. Do you think they are the ones you are looking for?"

"Quite possible, anyway we can find out more about them, but travelling with a woman, well, that may not be the ones we are looking for, he should be travelling with another couple of men not with a woman that we know of. But can we see if we can locate where the limo took them?"

"No problem, Davin. I will get my team working on it right away," Hector replied and then picked up the telephone and called his station; speaking in Spanish, he ordered his team to locate the limo and find out where the German was taken. After replacing the handset on the hook, he looked back at Davin and said, "They will get started on locating the limo and the driver right away, should have information by dinner. Why not get settled in your hotel and I will pick you up at six for dinner," he said and then headed for the door.

"Sounds good to me. Some good Mexican food and a few Margaritas would really help me sleep tonight," Davin agreed.

"Sleep, hell Davin, we are in Mexico City, I am not going to let you sleep for a while," Connie teased.

"Looks like you may get lucky tonight my new friend," Hector teased quietly.

"I heard that, Hector; and yes, I may get lucky, depending on how many margaritas I drink."

"Whoa, dinner at six. Sex at eleven," he said and left the room. "We will be in the lobby at 5:45. See you then," Davin said as Hector closed the door.

Chapter 17 Dinner at Six, Sex at Eleven

Davin and Connie sat quietly at a table overlooking the city in the lobby bar in their hotel sipping a couple of cold Coronas. Hector got there at 5:45.

Davin sat quietly talking on his phone while across the table Hector Rodriguez was talking on his cell phone. After a couple of minutes, they both hung up and then looked over at each other and smiled.

"That was Director of CIA, Ms. Ashley Peterson. She has asked me to tell you that they have located one of the scientists that went missing several days ago. He was found dead in his car outside of St Louis. All indications are that it was an accident, but they are investigating along with the local authorities," Davin reported.

"Did she say anything else that might help us?" Connie asked.

"No, that's it for now. Still looking for our two missing agents," Davin replied and then looked over at Hector and started to say something but stopped.

"Look, you probably don't want me to interfere with your investigation, but keep in mind I am here to help you locate whatever you are looking for. But I need to know what that is," Hector explained.

"Hector, we wish we knew ourselves," Davin stated, "We got a tip that a possible suspect in a murder of an Army Major in San Francisco may have flown down here and we are trying to track him down. We were called in because the FBI does not have jurisdiction outside the states; and well, we really don't either, but at least our company charter says we can operate outside CONUS, continental United States."

"I know what CONUS means; I served four and half years in your Army before returning to my home country, attached to the 101st Airborne Division out of Ft. Bragg. Loved it but on a jump into Ft. Benning I broke my right leg, compound fracture and they said I would not be able to run or jump again, so I ended up getting a Medical discharge and now collect some good disability checks from your government. I still can't run but as a cop I don't have to run as long as my trigger finger still works," Hector said chuckling.

"I did not realize you were one of ours. Thank you," Davin replied. "Okay, did you get anything on that German and his girl friend?"

"I had my team check on the German for you, and we have some information; not perfect, but it may help," Hector commented and then dialed his office. Five minutes later, he hung up and said, "Finish your drinks, my wife loves to entertain and we can pick this up in the morning. It is time for dinner and she hates for me to be late."

"Yeah, it is six fifteen, what time is she expecting us?" Connie asked.

"Dinner is at seven and it is a thirty minute drive; we need to go or she will have my butt," Hector commented and placed a stack of pesos on the table to pay for the drinks.

As they exited the elevator into the lobby, Davin noticed three couples, two were at registration, checking in, and one couple was sitting on the sofa in the middle of the lobby. There were four other singles, two reading the newspaper, one talking on her cell phone and the forth window shopping at the hotel store located on the north side of the lobby. None looked suspicious.

As they climbed into Hector's car located just outside the lobby door, they did not notice the female that was on her cell phone following them out and behind her the window shopper followed her. Since Hector was a police officer, he was able to park his car in the special reserved parking spot just outside the lobby.

The drive to Hector's home in traffic took less than twenty-five minutes, during which they exchanged small talk such as the weather, life in Mexico, and illegal activities in both countries just to pass the time.

"Davin and Connie please let me introduce you to my wife, Sandra," Hector said as they entered the house.

"Pleasure to meet you Sandra," Davin replied as he stuck out his hand to take hers.

"The pleasure is all mine, Mr. Pierce. Please come in, dinner is ready; would you care for a drink," Sandra replied.

"A couple of margaritas would be great; Hector says you make a mean one," Connie answered quickly.

"Four margaritas coming right up. Please have a seat," Sandra said and then turned and headed for the bar located across the room.

****

    Joanne Morgan caught an early flight to Seoul, South Korea. Before getting on the flight, she was able to exchange her CIA credentials for Korean national credentials she had in a locker located in the employee area of the San Francisco airport. Many agents that were required to travel to various countries would keep secure lockers scattered around the world. In Joanne's case, since she was Korean by birth and worked at the CIA on Korean matters, she kept secure lockers in the major international airports around the country. In this case San Francisco was her departure point and she had weapons, passports, money and clothes in the secure locker. Joanne packed a small bag and did not take any weapons; she left the locker room and headed directly to her assigned gate. The flight would be long so she picked up a book at the book store on the concourse. In the book were additional instructions from her handler who was always within easy reach; he was also going to be on the plane to Korea. Although he did not meet with her nose to nose and never would, he was always close enough to provide support if she needed it.

    When she arrived in Seoul, she would go to her secure locker located in the employee section of the airport and retrieve a weapon and ammunition, along with any additional equipment she felt she needed.

    Her handler would check into the same hotel and rent a car; he was here as a tourist and nothing more, until he was needed. He also had a secure locker which was located at the American Embassy; and as a tourist to South Korea, he was required to check in with the embassy upon arrival. This was standard procedure for all tourists; and when he did, he would retrieve his weapon and additional equipment.

Chapter 18 Back to the Stone Age

"Spooky, we have a problem!" Dusty exclaimed as she witnessed a hacker located over eight thousand miles away go in and change the commands she had just implemented.

"What is it?" Spooky asked.

"Our hacker is better than I gave him credit for. The grid has gone back down west of the Mississippi," Dusty replied as she continued to type rapidly, attempting to redirect the commands that had just been entered by the unknown hacker. "Damn he is good. He has control again. Sir, this is going to be a game of who can outlast the other. We will win, but it will take some time."

"Do you need more help?" Wiggins asked.

"Yes, get Savage back in here! It's going to take both of us to nail this dude down." Over the next three hours Dusty and Data played cat and mouse with the elusive hacker; they had narrowed it to the hacker being in a province outside of Beijing, China. They knew what kind of operating system he used and the programs he was running, but beyond that they were at a loss. West of the Mississippi, the grid would come on in isolated areas; it would come back on and then within minutes go back down. This was driving the local police and fire departments crazy. It would be silent and dark for hours and then the phones would start to ring, the lights would come on and all would seem back to normal; but then within minutes, it would go dead quiet again. This would happen in a different area of the country every few minutes. It started with New Orleans in the French Quarter then it would go down and South Dallas would come back on line and go down in a few minutes; Denver up, then down; Los Angeles up, then down; this continued around the country. With the power grid fluctuating as it was, it was only a matter of time until something would break; and when it did, they would not be able to bring it back up before major repairs were done to the hardware.

It started outside of Seattle when the electrical power plant that controlled the airport and south Seattle overloaded and exploded. The explosion wasn't large, but large enough to kill eleven employees and shut down all power to the area for the foreseeable future.

In Las Vegas, Nevada, the power shut down for ninety minutes and then came back online for forty-five minutes. The casinos started to come back online and bring all their systems up drawing more power than the weakened system could handle. The drain on electrical power was already near its limit in Las Vegas and the constant hard shutdowns and drain on the system when it started up again was too much for the older equipment.

Hoover Dam was one of the main electric generation facilities providing power to Vegas, Boulder and the suburbs surrounding the city. With its massive generators, it could handle most of the spikes that occurred, but not all. Because the system crashed and then came back up within minutes of crashing, the draw for electrical power overloaded the system. Transformers around the city exploded, sub-stations caught fire and exploded and two of the four generators located within Hoover Dam shorted and melted many of their components. Las Vegas and the surrounding cities went dark again; this time it would not come back until major repair work would be done on the generators and surrounding systems.

Since most of the infrastructure in the United States and many other countries was controlled remotely by using the Internet to issue commands, they were vulnerable to attack from anywhere in the world and that is exactly what was happening. Hackers had succeeded in breaking into the systems and took control which had now put most of the United States back in the Stone Age, no power, no phones, no fuel, factories shut down, the list went on and on. It didn't matter that most systems operated over the Internet using a VPN (Virtual Private Network) which would normally be a very secure connection. Somehow they were compromised.

Mexico City, same evening

Just south of the border in Mexico City all seemed well; the lights were on and they had no idea that the country just north of them had just been sent back to the Stone Age. With the exception of several border towns that purchased electricity from the United States, all seemed well in Mexico.

Along the border, things were different; the United States Border Patrol was working overtime trying to keep illegal aliens from crossing the border. It was thought by the coyotes and drug runners that because the United States was dark, the Border Patrol was blind. They were not; with the use of generators, backup battery systems and the use of many other classified systems, they were able to stop most of the border crossings, but not all. It was business as usual for the Border Patrol. With the power outages, the President ordered the National Guard called up to support the Border Patrol in Arizona, Texas, California and New Mexico.

****

"Hector, I have to agree, this was the best Mexican food I've had in years. We will have to come back here, soon. Your wife is a great cook," Connie commented and then took a sip of her margarita. "Where did she go?"

"Anytime you wish to come back, I will be happy to bring you back to my home," Hector commented. "She is putting the kids to bed."

"You make a mean margarita, Hector," Davin said and then continued, "We need to get some sleep, and tomorrow is going to be a long day."

"Sure, it is getting late; I will have my driver take you back to your hotel," Hector said and then got up and walked over to the phone on the wall beside the door to the kitchen. He spoke rapidly and then hung up. "The car will be out front in a couple of minutes. I will come by in the morning to pick you up and we can review the manifests and videos. And possibly have the location of that German and his girl friend."

"Sounds good. Thanks again for an excellent meal and company," Connie said and then stood and reached for her jacket. Minutes later, they were sitting in the car and heading back across town to their hotel.

"This is a beautiful city, Davin. Why don't we come down sometime on vacation and explore the history and enjoy the culture," Connie said looking out the side window as they headed down the avenue. She was obviously not paying attention to the direction they were heading. Davin, on the other hand, was closely watching the direction and the outside scenery. "Is something wrong, Davin?"

"Not sure. This is not the way back to the hotel," Davin stated.

"You're right," then she reached up and tapped the driver on the shoulder. "Where are we going?"

"Your hotel, señor."

"This is not the way," Davin said.

"Short cut, señor, we will be there in a few minutes," the driver said without turning his head.

"Okay," Davin answered and then slowly reached under his jacket and thumbed the holster's thumb release and looked over at Connie and whispered, 'Get your gun.'
The driver turned at the next street and accelerated, turned left at the next street and then into a parking garage. As he slammed on the brakes, he screeched to a stop in front of two black vans. Before the car stopped, two heavily armed men wearing masks jumped out of the vans and ran over the car and pointed their weapons at Davin and Connie.

"Lay your weapons and cell phones on the floor and get out of the car, NOW!" one of the men ordered. Davin could see that there was a driver in the van and another in the sedan that was parked in front of the van.

"Holy crap, what the hell is going on?" Davin asked.

"What is going on, Mr. Pierce is you are being kidnapped," a tall blonde haired man said as he walked up to the car, speaking with a heavy German accent. "I believe you are looking for me."

"Who are you?" Davin asked as he climbed out of the back seat with Connie closely behind him, leaving their weapons and cell phones on the floor as directed. Looking around, he could see that there were only five kidnappers, the three in the van most likely hired killers, the other two, unknown, maybe a body guard for the blonde haired man.

"I am Hans Bormann and you are Davin Pierce and his lovely wife Connie. It is my pleasure to meet both of you, but we need to be going now. Please get into the van with these gentlemen," Hans Bormann commented, pointing toward the van. "We need to go before we attract too much attention, please get in the van."

"And if we refuse?" Davin asked, standing firm and looking seriously directly into the eyes of Hans Bormann. "Are you going to kill us right here?"

"No, I don't plan on killing you, at least not yet. You don't want my men to force you. You don't really want them to do that; they are not very gentle. And I would prefer for you to cooperate and not get hurt. Now please get in the van," Bormann insisted and abruptly turned and walked over to his car. After climbing into the front seat, he quietly told his driver to go.

"Okay, you only have to tell us once," Davin said to Bormann as he retreated to his car. He and Connie climbed into the back of the first van and watched as the black sedan they were riding in drove away. One of the masked men pulled dark cloth bags over Davin and Connie's heads. Minutes later, Davin and Connie were being driven out of Mexico City to an unknown destination.

"I know you will not say, but I have to ask. Where are we going?" Davin asked knowing full well that these were hired thugs and probably did not speak English. All he got was silence for an answer.

"Honey, I don't believe they understand English," Connie stated quietly.

"Be quiet, no talking," barked one of the guards

Chapter 19 Do You Really Want to Do That?

"What's the status, Dusty?" Wiggins asked as he entered the secure room carrying three cups of coffee, passing one to Dusty and another to Savage.

"What's up? Chief, what's up is that those pigs are damn good; it must have taken them months to embed this code into all those systems."

"What exactly do you mean?"

"Okay, in layman's terms, they have embedded a virus that is acting really strange and is replicating itself every time it cycles, which is about every thirty minutes. Let's look at it this way; Los Angeles has twelve separate electrical substations that handle a particular zone in and around the city. Each substation has its own computer system that reports back to the main hub which is located in zone one. When substation two shuts down, their computer controller is still functioning, not off, but running on a backup generator or battery system. It will stay off for roughly fifteen minutes then come back online and turn all the power back on. Then one of the other substations will shut off and be down for a while and then return online. The problem is that it is all done randomly; we don't know which one is going down or for how long or when or if it is going to come back up. One good thing so far is that we **have control of several of the main hubs in four states and are working on getting control of more.** The problem starts to arise when the systems shut down and come back on immediately, which overrides the built in safety systems. At this point the system could overload, causing a melt down or total failure. This means the hardware has failed and will not come back on line without hardware repair," Dusty said taking a breather before continuing.

"Okay, I understand that, but what can we do to get the substations back up and to remain up?" Wiggins asked just as Major "Spooky" Sorenson walked into the room.

"That, chief is the six million dollar question. Our hopes are once we have control of the main hubs, then we can replicate what we did and hit each substation with a virus of our own that will remove or shut down theirs. We are not sure how it will work, but that is the plan."

"How many main hubs do we have control over right now?" Spooky asked.

"Sixteen," Dusty replied. "We had more, but Hoover dam just had a major overload failure and fried two of the generators; it will not be back up for a long time. Las Vegas and surrounding cities are now in the dark for the unforeseeable future. It may take months to repair those generators; the other two were back-ups and under maintenance when this started, they are due to be operational in about a week, if they are lucky."

"Out of how many?" Spooky asked.

"In California alone, there are forty-two. Each state has at least twenty with Nevada and California having the most. Nevada, because of the high demand in Vegas, has two main hubs and at least six to ten substations. All of which are down now. "

"Damn, what is your estimate as to how long it will take to get the states back online?" Wiggins asked.

"If we are lucky, it will take at least a week working around the clock; but we haven't been lucky so far. This person or persons are intent on keeping us in the dark, even to the point of causing major melt downs and hardware failures. And if they are able to, they could cause a catastrophic overload in a nuclear facility which, as you know, would be another Chernobyl. We are trying to prevent that but it could happen; they do have control of the system right now."

"Can you bring in the day shift assist? We can make this go faster, and maybe stop any more catastrophic failures," Dusty asked Spooky.

"Sure, I will bring in six more ops and let's pray this works," Spooky agreed and then turned to Wiggins and said, "I need to report to the President. I will be right back," she said and then headed to her office.

"That isn't going to be a fun call," Dusty said quietly, but did get a look from Savage and Wiggins. "Top, we are doing the best we can, but these guys have been planning this and embedding the code for months, possibly years. It goes pretty deep. They may have actually designed and built the code originally; it is hard to tell. But we are working to fix it as fast as we can."

Dusty stopped to take a breath and waited for Spooky to walk up. "Now that Major Sorenson is here, I need to tell you the worst part of what we have found." He paused for a second and then continued, "We have copied the code that California is using to run their electrical grid and it isn't pretty. Not completely sure yet, but it almost looks like the code that is being used was written by our hacker. And over the past couple of years, he has added patches, fixes that is, that enhanced his code and made it replicating. We may have to delete the entire program and start all over again. In other words delete, reformat the system and write a whole new program."

"How did that happen?" Wiggins asked.

"Simple really, if can happen when a company such as an electrical company puts out for a bid to build a system to control their infrastructure. Of course, a system like that is classified, but the company that wins will dole out the unclassified code to various companies so they can get it done on time and under budget. It costs a lot to employ engineers, cheaper to subcontract. Some of those subcontractors may not be United States citizens and are actually in India, China, and Korea or, well anywhere in the world. That code written by the subcontractor is usually massive and is rarely completely checked except for compatibility with the rest of the classified code. They are merged together and now you have a built in virus that is just waiting for the trigger. They have triggered it and now we are in deep."

"Damn, we possibly did this to ourselves," Spooky commented. "I need to notify the President," she said and charged out of the room.

****

President Mitchell, along with his senior staff, was sitting in the White House Situation Room, waiting for Mitchell to finish his phone call from Cyber Command.

"I understand, thank you. Keep your people working! I have to discuss this with my staff," President Mitchell said. He hung up the phone, turned to his staff and paused as if he was thinking, but his mind drifted again; he was having a hard time controlling it.

"The situation is not good. Cyber Command is working as fast as they can, but the hacker, or hackers, that is doing this to our country has created a nightmare for our people. It almost looks like they built the code originally and we just bought it and installed it on our systems. They are looking into who actually built the code." He paused again and let his mind drift for a moment. "They have estimated that it may take a minimum of a week, possibly more, to get everything back online and as long as never. I need solutions; we already are having rapid crime in the areas where the power is down. The police are not able to control it; the governor of each state has already called out the National Guard. Can we also provide some active military support?"

"I agree. I will see what is available and send them out. We still have to protect the bases," Tony Sanford commented. "And with many of our troops deployed we are getting low on troops on the home front."

"We have to be careful; we don't know where this is going," Mitchell said. He then turned back to Tony and said. "I want the entire country on full alert. Full combat gear, lock and load, as they used to say. By the way, where is the Vice President, I haven't seen him for days?"

"Sir, do you really want to go there?" John Ramsey, Director of Homeland Security said looking concerned. "It may cause nationwide panic seeing the military in full combat gear roaming the streets."

"Yes I do. And effective immediately, inform the governors of each state that we are sending in the military to assist in keeping order until this crisis is over and to invoke Martial Law and a curfew until further notice."

"You can't do that, Mr. President," Harvey Stewart, the Assistant Director of Homeland Security commented, not understanding the full impact of the situation.

"Mr. President, the VP is in Florida; I will brief you later on what he is doing," Sanford commented quickly. He needed to slip in this statement to answer the President's earlier question.

"We are at war. I can do it, and you are excused, Mr. Stewart, for your lack of knowledge on the situation. Mr. Sanford will put the order in writing and I will sign it." He stopped for a moment and his mind drifted a little, but he was able to stop the drift and continued, "I want it enacted within the hour," Mitchell said trying not to raise his voice in anger but found it hard to do.

"Yes, sir, it will be on your desk in the next twenty minutes; may I be excused to write it?" Tony Sanford stated and stood to leave.

"Make it so, Mr. Sanford," Mitchell said, using words that became very familiar to the public from the TV series *Star Trek, The Next Generation* by Captain Picard of the Enterprise. It was a show that Mitchell loved to watch over and over, but his first love was *NCIS*, crime and mystery with a cast of regulars that were passionate about their work.

"Yes, sir; consider it done," Sanford replied and then stood to leave the room.

"No, wait a second. We need to do…" Mitchell started then went quiet as if in thought and then repeated himself, "Don't go yet, Tony, I need to talk to you in private. We need to ensure our nuclear plants are protected. Do we have air coverage over them and other infrastructure sites, museums, government buildings and, well, you know what I am looking for?"

"Sir, we have had air coverage for two days now, since you ordered it. If there is a potential air attack, we are covered," Tony Sanford said and then sat down again.

"Oh, okay, good," Mitchell replied and turned his attention back to the document in front of him. He ignored the room full of his staff and advisors.

"Okay, that will be all for now, I need some quiet time to think, everyone except Tony is dismissed." Mitchell finally looked up and spoke to the room.

"Sir, are you okay?" Tony asked after the room had cleared and the door closed.

"Tony, I don't know. I have been under a lot of stress and, well, I keep sliding back into, I am not sure what I slide back into, but my mind just goes blank for a time. I need you to back me up and if I start to do something completely out of context or wrong, please stop me and get me back on track. Try not to do it in front of everyone, maybe I should just stay in my office and have you give the briefings," Mitchell stated. "I think they did something to me that may have affected my abilities to lead."

"Did the doctor give you anything to help you sleep?" Tony asked.

"Yes, and that is helping, but not completely," Mitchell replied.

"I can believe that, you are under a lot of stress and are still recovering from a horrible situation and it will take time to recover. I will be here to help you get though this and anything else that comes down the pike," Tony replied.

Chapter 20 Missing in Mexico

At six thirty in the morning, Hector Rodriguez was sipping his second cup of coffee at his home on the edge of Mexico City when his cell phone rang. He was a cop and this was nothing unusual for him, but what he heard was unexpected.

"Chief, we just found Officer Carlos Ramirez dead in his car in a parking lot beside a vacant market. Shot in the head at close range. Sorry, sir. I know he was a friend of yours," the Desk Sergeant reported.

"He picked up my guests last night. Check at the Hilton Airport to see if my guests are there and have them wait for me. I should be there in twenty minutes," Hector ordered. He grabbed his weapon and coat as he headed out the door of his home.

"Yes sir," the Desk Sergeant said to a dead line.

Hector left his home and ran to his car. He quickly drove to the hotel, screeched to a halt in front of it, ran into the lobby and up to the front desk. He picked up the handset of the phone and asked the operator to connect him to Mr. Pierce's room. He let the phone ring several times; and when he did not get an answer, he hung up, turned to the desk clerk and asked, "Have you seen or heard from Mr. or Mrs. Pierce this morning?"

"No sir, they did not return last night; the computer does not show they entered their room at all last night."

"Hell!" Hector exclaimed. As he turned and started to walk away from the desk, he pulled out his cell phone and punched several numbers on his speed dial and waited for someone to answer. "Sergeant, I believe Mr. and Mrs. Pierce have been kidnapped. Put out an A.P.B. (All Points Bulletin) and get me all the evidence you have on the Ramirez murder. I will be at the station in thirty minutes." After exiting the hotel, he jumped in his car and sped out of the hotel parking area; he stopped briefly at a Starbucks drive through window. He needed coffee, strong coffee; this was going to be a very long day.

"Good morning, Hector," the Desk Sergeant said as Hector burst into the station.

"What the hell is good about it, Sergeant?" Hector commented as he passed by the desk and walked into his office. After picking up his desk phone, he called down to the evidence room and asked for the evidence to be brought up to his office. He sat back in his chair and waited, thinking of his next phone call, one that he really did not want to make but had to.

After pulling his cell phone out of his jacket pocket, he stared at it for a moment, and then dialed a number that he knew by heart, the private cell phone of Ashley Peterson, Director of CIA. The phone rang three times before he heard Ashley on the other end.

"Hello Hector, how is everything down there? How are Davin and Connie doing?"

"Ashley, we have a problem. We have reason to believe Davin and Connie have been kidnapped. They left my home at eleven last night with one of my trusted men; they never made it back to the hotel and my man was found dead just outside the city at a vacant market area."

"Crap, I will get their partners down there to assist. I will let you know when they will arrive," Ashley said, "Call you back shortly. I need to get in touch with Josh and Stephanie and get them heading your way."

"I will get the evidence ready and send you copies," Hector stated.

"Keep me posted. I will have my forensics assist. I will call you as soon as I have an E.T.A. on Josh and Stephanie." She pushed the disconnect button on her phone. After waiting for a second, she dialed Josh Randal. After four rings, Josh answered his phone.

"Josh, we have a problem," Ashley stated, paused and took a breath.

"What is it, did Davin get a speeding ticket and get thrown in a Mexican jail?" Josh joked.

"Maybe, they have dropped off the grid. Go secure." After a couple of seconds, they both got the tone indicating the line was secure.

"He is still active isn't he?" Josh asked, referring to the chip that had been planted in him for the Presidential rescue. The chip would be able to narrow down his location to within ten yards, if it were still active.

"Yes and no; I had my tech check his location and it shows he is off grid. I need you and Stephanie to get down to Mexico City ASAP," Ashley ordered. "Hector Rodriguez will pick you up at the airport and assist you in anything you need. Their last known location was dinner with Hector at his home."

"Who is this Rodriguez?" Josh asked as he signaled to Stephanie to listen in. He pressed the speaker button on his cell phone.

"He is a good friend of mine who happens to be the Director of Policia Federal Ministerial. He is one of the good guys. You can trust him."

"Wow, if we can get through the riots and road blocks, we will get to the airport as fast as possible," Josh commented. "Do you know what is going on out here? Riots, robberies, National Guard running around with loaded weapons and they have a curfew in effect. I haven't seen one of them since before leaving high school."

"Sorry, you have your badges, use them; get to the airport as quickly as possible. I will have a chartered jet waiting to fly you to Mexico City. Wait; is there a large parking lot close to you, one that can handle a helicopter? Do you have the chip detector with you?

"There is a hospital two blocks away with a helo pad. Send the chopper. We will get there as fast as we can. I will call when we are on board," Josh reported.

"Go to the hospital, if there is a chopper there, I will have arranged for them to run you to the airport; if not, I will have one there in fifteen minutes," Ashley stated, promising something that she might not be able to deliver.

"Heading to the hospital now, will be there in a few minutes." Josh hung up, turned to Stephanie and said, "Step on it."

Minutes later, they walked into the Emergency Room entrance and were met by two police officers, one with his hand up stopped Josh and Stephanie before they got very far in the room. "Are you Josh Randal?" the big officer asked.

"Yes," Josh replied.

"Come with me," the officer ordered and then they turned and walked at a fast pace towards another door leading outside on the north side of the building. "Your ride is waiting."

As they exited the hospital, the officer stopped and pointed toward a police helo sitting on the pad with its engine running and rotor turning. Josh and Stephanie ran towards the helo and climbed aboard. As soon as the door closed, the pilot twisted the cyclic lifting the helo off the pad and immediately turned east toward the airport.

"Welcome aboard, should be at the airport in fifteen minutes. Ms. Peterson is a good friend and when she called I could not refuse her request. When you see her, tell her she owes me dinner," the pilot said over the noise of the rotor.

"You got it, what is your name?" Josh agreed and asked.

"Max" he replied.

"You got it Max, thanks for the ride," Stephanie said with a small smile.

"I will be landing right beside your next ride; the air traffic controller has already cleared us for a fast approach and landing. Hang on; I will be making some rapid turns and descents to stay away from the active runway."

"Got ya!" Josh said and then looked out the window and saw the airport about five miles away. He reached over and took Stephanie's hand in his and quietly said, "They will be fine; we will find them."

"SF approach, Police helo 697 on fast approach at one thousand feet, heading two seven zero," the pilot reported to approach control.

"Police 697, continue approach, descend to five hundred feet, turn left to two four zero, cleared for landing at Robinson FBO. Report landing and when ready to depart on frequency 119.5."

"Roger, police 697, descending, turning to two four zero. Thanks," Max said over the radio to airport approach control. After several quick turns and descents to ground level, Max set the helo down gently about fifty feet from a black Bombardier Challenger 350. She looked brand new, able to carry eight passengers non-stop three thousand two hundred nautical miles at 0.80 mach. And do it in style and comfort.

"Thanks Max," Josh yelled as he and Stephanie exited the helo and ran to the Bombardier stairs, which started to close as soon as Josh and Stephanie were on board.

"Please take a seat and belt yourself in. We are rolling to the active runway for immediate departure. After we level off, please relax; sorry we don't have an attendant on board. My copilot, Mary will be back as soon as we level off to provide you drinks and a snack. Our flight time is about two and half hours. We are not fully stocked; did not have time to restock after our last trip. Ms. Peterson only called us a half hour ago," the pilot said over the cabin intercom.

"No problem," Josh said to Stephanie.

"We also have a stop in Nogales to pick up a few passengers. Ms. Peterson said to call her and she will explain. Please use the air phone located in the sideboard next to your seat."

Chapter 21 Executive Dilemma

"The capture of six Mexican drug runners east of Nogales, Arizona as they were attempting to move two hundred pounds of raw cocaine into the United States turned up some interesting intelligence. One of the runners was a lieutenant with the Guzman Drug Cartel and, with a little encouragement, divulged some information about the President's daughter. An Islamic terrorist by the name of Laden, no relation to Bin Laden that we know of, recently flew down to Mexico in a private plane with a hostage. He landed at a private airfield to transfer to a jet for a trip to Germany. But, once he landed, things went bad for him. The Guzman Cartel knew his hostage was the United States President's daughter and decided to change the agreement. Laden died with a single shot to the head; his body was hastily buried just off the airport. Guzman then took Tara Mitchell to his home where she was placed under guard in a private suite," reported Tony Sanford as he sat across from President Mitchell briefing him and the rest of the executive staff, pausing for a moment to let what he said sink in and then continued.

"The lieutenant disclosed that she was being held by the Guzman Drug Cartel, and they had threatened to kill her if the President sent more troops to the border and attempted to stop his drug and illegal alien movements. The information was disclosed by the lieutenant after only an hour of interrogation, which left doubt in the minds of the interrogators. But they had to report what they knew to their superiors which they did within minutes of learning the fact. They also were able to find out her location and other details about the capture. The border patrol was also told to release him and his men and return the cocaine they had seized, or she was to die a horrible death," Sanford concluded leaving out a few facts that concerned only the President.

"Mr. President, Ms. Peterson is here to see you, she says it's urgent," Darrell Mitchell's personal secretary said as she poked her head in the door to the Oval office.

"Send her in."

"Mr. President, we have a problem in Mexico. Well, actually, we have several problems. Our source down there has established a link between the Guzman Drug Cartel and a group in

Germany that is led by a guy named Gregory Dietrich, aka, 'Sepp', a name he adopted from his grandfather, a Colonel General Josef 'Sepp' Dietrich. They are the German Mafia and are into all kinds of illegal stuff. We believe this Sepp dude is connected to the killing in San Francisco and now has the missing computer drive. We just got some updated information about Guzman. The German we have been looking for, Hans Bormann, arrived at the Guzman estate only to discover Tara Mitchell being held captive. Guzman seemed to be proud of himself for his prize. Our contact is not sure how, but somehow Bormann was able to leave the home with Tara Mitchell in tow. He also reported that Roberto Guzman is really pissed and vowed to kill Bormann, his boss and family and get his prize back. Guzman is a ruthless killer and will not spare expense or men to get what he wants," Ashley Peterson reported.

"Are you sure? I am not going to ask how you know, but are your sources pretty sure?" Mitchell asked.

"Very sure, but it gets worse."

"Worse?" Mitchell asked.

"Yes, worse," she replied.

"What is it?" Mitchell asked.

"There is one other thing, we are not sure if it is related, but have a sneaky feeling that this is related. Two of our agents are missing; Davin and Connie Pierce were last seen at my contact's home last night. When they left, they did not make it back to their hotel. My contact is a highly placed police officer and is digging deep into their disappearance. He is reporting to me directly. I have ordered Josh and Stephanie Randal to Mexico City to assist," Ashley reported and then paused when there was a knock on the door. "Do you want to see who that is?"

"Yes, I am expecting Director John Ramsey from Homeland. Stick around; he may add some light to the west coast problem," Mitchell said. He walked over to the door and as he opened it, said "Come in John."

"Good afternoon, Mr. President," John said as he entered the Oval Office.

"What have you got for me?"

"May I get a cup of coffee; this is going to take a while," John asked and walked over to the coffee carafe and poured himself a cup and added three sugars. "Sir, every state west of the

Mississippi is still in the dark, but Cyber Command has made some progress. My last report came in a couple of hours ago. They report that they have discovered the pattern and are able to stop the attacks, but only for one grid at a time. This is going to take a while to reset, one grid at a time."

"Is there any way of speeding that up?"

"No sir, they are working around the clock now and have every possible person working on it. I understand that CIA has also been working on this problem with Cyber Command. Is that true, Ms. Peterson?"

"Yes, we have been coordinating some of their efforts," Peterson responded with a concerned look.

"How bad is it out there?" Mitchell asked to both of them.

"Los Angeles, San Francisco, and various other large cities are experiencing mass rioting and the police along with the National Guard and as much of the military that we can spare are doing their best to keep the peace. We are not sure how long we are going to maintain control but for now we have control," John responded.

"And who is causing us all these problems? Ashley, is it possible your kidnappings and Mexican Drug Cartel are somehow related to the electrical problems in the west?"

"I don't see how, sir." She paused, turned to John, and asked, "Where are the attacks coming from?"

"Best we can tell is they originated in the orient, most likely North Korea or China. The Chinese do not benefit from this so our assumption is North Korea. But we have not ruled out China completely. They have the ability, and if there is a group that is not government backed, well, Cyber Command is doing what it can to bring the systems back online and also to back trace to the originating source. As of this morning, they were close and doing what they could to confirm their discovery. Until then, they are keeping it under wraps. Not even telling me; they don't want to cause a problem if they are wrong. They promised they would have the source by this afternoon and pass it on to me and I will tell you. At that point we, no, you need to make a decision. And let's make this perfectly clear, please don't kill the messenger."

"No worries there, John. But get me a target and I will make the decision as to what to do. But yesterday I ordered Cyber Command to shut down several servers in Iran, North Korea and China. Did they do that, yet?"

"Iran has been shut down. Their communications are in the dark ages; they have no Internet, no phones, neither land nor cell; and their television stations are also off-line. They have the ability to communicate with radio, VHF or HF only. But we can jam them off anytime we want. We have effectively turned off their country. We did not turn off their electrical grid, yet. But they are now operating in Stone Age."

"What about their military?" Ashley asked.

"They cannot talk to their aircraft, or military, unless they use smoke signals or radio," John confirmed.

"Good. Keep it that way. I don't want them to get a message out to their sleeper crews. Now back to the west, what is the estimate on getting everything back to normal?"

"Three days to a week, possibly longer, they have done a number on our systems. We may have to dump the entire system and build a new one from the ground up. The software that is, not the hardware."

"Damn. Put them in the dark," President Mitchell ordered the Director of Homeland Security, then turned to Ashley Peterson and asked. "Ashley do you need any assistance in your problems?"

"No sir. As soon as we have a location, we will send in our rescue team," Ashley commented, pausing "We will do it as covertly as possible. No promises, but we will try to limit collateral damage as best we can."

"Since you have the local policia on your side, you may want them to take the lead."

"No sir, Hector has already agreed to allow us to take the lead; but if they are still alive when we get in, then he asked to take the prisoners."

"Your call, Ashley; anything else you wish to pass on to make my day?"

"No sir, I think that will do it. I need to get out of here and back to work," John commented.

"Go, John, do you have anything else?" Mitchell asked as Ashley started for the door.

"Yes sir, we are getting some bad vibes from North Korea. You know they have recently tested their nuclear missile successfully and now they are making some threatening saber rattling about the outages they are experiencing with their Internet. They are blaming us for the outages and saying if we don't stop they will retaliate" Ashley reported.

"Tell them it isn't us and we are being attacked ourselves."

"We tried that already and they don't believe us," Tony commented as if it were just another day in the life of a political figure.

"World War III is about to start and it will appear to the world that we started it," Darrell Mitchell stated.

Chapter 22 Mexican Jail, Well, Sort Of

Forty miles southwest of Mexico City is the little town of Toluca. In a dirty warehouse on the outskirts of town, Davin and Connie sat and waited. They did not know what was going to happen to them. The room was dark and hot; they had three small metal frame beds with a wool blanket, a table, three chairs, and nothing else. Only a single bare light bulb hung from the ceiling; it was dirty and barely glowed, casting a dim light across the room. There was a window, but it was up too high to see outside. They had been given a light dinner over an hour ago, which sat cold on the table. They had no idea what time it was or for that matter if it really mattered.

"Davin, what are they going to do with us? That German Bormann dude acted pretty cocky. Do you think he really has the drive and can he decrypt it?" Connie asked, worried.

"He is pretty cocky, but shortly he will be dead; and we will be out of here," Davin replied confidently.

"How do you figure that, my dear husband?"

"Well, as soon as I get the opportunity, I will take care of him," Davin stated confidently. "I will need you two to do exactly what I say, no questions and do it immediately."

"This I have to see," Connie agreed, "Okay, I will follow your orders, this time; but you had better be right. I am not ready to die, especially down here in this dirty hell hole."

"Mr. Pierce, I hope you know what you are doing; I am scared and want to go home," Tara commented, trembling.

"I will let you know when, just wait."

Down the hall, Hans Bormann sat with two of his men, slowly reaching up to touch his wounded shoulder making sure the dressing was still in place. And then quietly and slowly began to speak, "Gentlemen, we now have three prisoners and a computer drive that can bring us millions of dollars. I have been in contact with Sepp and he is not very happy at the moment. But he is the least of our problems; this Guzman fellow has threatened to kill all of us for taking his prize and take the prisoners and drive for himself. He thinks he can do that without a fight, but a fight is what he will get. Our plane does not land for another two hours, so we have to wait." He paused for a moment to glance at the monitor on the table in front of him, and then continued, "Lock and load as they say in the Army. We are about to have company."

"Hans, we should move from here to a safer place, get some more men and weapons," one of his men stated, not seeing the grin on Hans Bormann's face.

"Move, yes, get the prisoners ready and we move soon," Hans ordered; but before they were able to move, there was a loud explosion outside. "Holy crap, our guests have just arrived," Hans said and reached down beside the table and picked up an M-4 with a M203 Grenade launcher mounted under the barrel, his cell phone and electronic tablet. His two men picked up their weapons, an AK-47 and UZI respectively. "Let's get to work boys."

The warehouse was built like a fortress which made it easy to secure and Hans had added several IED's (Improvised Explosive Devices) around the building just in case they had intruders. As he walked toward the door, he looked at the tablet display and grinned again.

"Jose, take the right flank; Ramon you are on the left. Don't fire until I do; I have a few surprises for them," Hans commented as they exited the office.

Seconds later, they heard another explosion, this time on the north side of the building.

"They are coming in from the north, but watch your rears; they may be smarter than I give them credit for and come in both sides," Hans said as he took a position behind several large crates and looked at his tablet again. He saw four men enter the north door which had just been blown open. He tapped the display to change the view, waited, and saw six more men enter from the east high bay door, which they were able to open without blowing it up. He waited and watched as the men from both sides slowly moved into the building, weapons at the ready and flashlights blazing the trail. Waiting until the men passed a mark on the floor that showed Hans the attackers were within range of the IED he had placed just for this occasion, Hans tapped a code into the tablet, waited two more seconds, and then pressed <ENTER>.

The explosion in the warehouse was not massive, but instead it was directed inward toward the attackers, just like a Claymore mine would do. All four attackers were killed instantly, never knowing what hit them. On the east side of the warehouse, the six armed men immediately took cover expecting another explosion which did not come. Instead each man dove into a blind dark corner expecting to be safe only to find they were entangled in what felt like a massive spider web; they experienced a death like none other. As they entered the safety behind a large crate or corner, they broke a light beam releasing a sticky fish net which entangled each of them and then a toxic aerosol was released into the area. Breathing caused a painful death within a minute. They had no idea they had walked into a trap. Within seconds, they were dead and the toxic became non lethal once again within minutes.

'So ends their attack' Hans Bormann said to himself, keeping his eyes on the tablet in case more attempted to come in. Seeing more armed men enter from the south, he waited. "Gentlemen, I guess they did not learn from their dead friends," he yelled out to his two men. Bullets started to strike the wall behind Hans; he was secure behind the crates he had placed there earlier in the day. "Here they come! Get ready."

As Hans looked at his tablet, he saw ten to twelve armed men coming in the building from all sides; he only had a couple more surprises set up for this, hoping that was all he needed. He might have under-estimated his enemy; Guzman had an Army of men, and he did not care if he lost most of them to get the prize, the disk, Mr. and Mrs. Pierce, and of course, the President of the United States' one and only daughter.

Hans entered another code and pressed <ENTER> without waiting, then entered another code and pressed <ENTER>. Two explosions rocked the building. The first collapsed the north wall and roof onto several of the attackers, killing at least six but leaving another five moving closer to him. The second explosion brought down the east wall and more roof, taking out five more attackers, but they were still outnumbered and time and IEDs were running out. Hans knew they were in the best position being on the high ground, so he stood and fired his M203 grenade launcher at the closest group, killing and wounding another three attackers. Then he opened up with his M4 5.56mm; his men took his lead and opened up with their weapons. More of the attackers fell, but the rest dove for cover and the firefight started. Hans knew that he had to get his prisoners out of there before he lost them to Guzman.

"Use your grenades, and get ready to move," Hans ordered, "Ramon, get Misses Pierce and the kid, leave Mister Pierce in his cell. Meet as planned. Jose and I will be right behind you, I have one more surprise for these killers and Mr. Pierce."

Within minutes Bormann, his two assistants and two female captives were racing away from the warehouse in a black windowless van. Watching in the rear view mirror, Ramon could see the warehouse exploding and collapsing into a large pile of rubble.

"That my friend is the end of Guzman's henchmen and Mr. Pierce just happened to get in the way." He glanced back over his shoulder and smiled at Connie Pierce and Tara Mitchell. He noted the serious look on Connie's face who could not believe that Bormann just killed Davin. "I am sorry to say, Ms. Pierce but I do believe your divorce is final."

"I know he is not dead and he will be coming after you. When he catches up with you, the only one dead will be you. He doesn't rely on bombs to kill; he will put a bullet between your eyes and be smiling while he does it."

"I just don't believe that will happen Ms. Pierce, even if he is still alive, which I doubt. Well, at least you will never see it; where you two are going nobody will ever find you. No more talking, be quiet back there," Bormann said growing tired of their conversation.

"Mr. Bormann, I hope you know my father will not rest until he finds me and…" Tara yelled.

"I said quiet!" Bormann yelled and then pointed his Glock 9 mm pistol at her. "Maybe I should just kill both of you now so I can have some quiet. Now shut up!"

Chapter 23 You Can't Do That

When Josh and Stephanie landed in Nogales, Arizona they were met by two Secret Service Agents. Polson and Miller were accompanied by the head of the Nogales Border Patrol. After linking up and gathering more information about the Guzman Cartel and suspected location of the captives, Josh, Stephanie, Polson and Miller decided to head into Mexico to search for the three missing people. This time they did not inform the Mexican government that they were coming in, heavily armed and with support from four members of a U.S. Army Special Operations Team. Ashley Peterson had authorized the mission with heavy weapons and had notified Hector Rodriguez that they were heading his way and when they expected to arrive.

The Bombardier landed at Mexico City International Airport and taxied to the General Aviation ramp and shut down the engines. Immediately the air-stair door opened and the ten passengers exited and assembled on the ramp beside the cargo door. Once opened, each person grabbed their case and walked over to the waiting black SUVs. Within minutes of landing, the aircraft had rolled back out to the runway for immediate departure and the SUVs were headed out the gate to their assigned safe house.

No one met them, and no one except the air traffic controllers knew they had landed or where they were from. Of course, Hector Rodriguez knew they were coming, but he was busy with recent explosions south of the city. He was headed there with his team to investigate. The team was made up of Josh and Stephanie Randal, two Secret Service agents, and four members of a U.S. Army Special Operations Team. Stephanie wanted Seal Team Six, but they were busy on another mission in Iran, working with the British Commando Team. So they took what she thought was second best, but she was not military and did not understand that this Alpha team was Seal Team Six's equal in almost every aspect, except one, and that was undersea operations. And that was not in their mission parameters like it was with the Seals.

Twenty minutes later, the SUVs pulled into the driveway of the U.S. Embassy to Mexico; the gate automatically closed behind them. Without saying a word, everyone exited the vehicles, grabbed their cases and walked quietly in the front door. They were greeted by a tall black gentleman, "We have been expecting you. Please follow me. The Ambassador is waiting in the library. Please bring your luggage with you. We don't have much time."

After following the gentlemen to the library, they were offered drinks as they entered and sat around a stately looking man sporting a beard, and wearing dark slacks which were stained with dirt as if he had been working in the garden, a torn tee shirt, and rubber boots. "Sorry for my appearance, been working in the garden. Please sit; we have much to discuss and not much time. Some recent events have escalated your time schedule. You must be Mr. Randal?"

"Yes, this is Connie my wife and ... well, no need for introductions; we won't be here long. Thank you for providing your home as an operations center," Josh Randal stated.

"Okay, here is what we know. Southwest of Mexico City in a little town called Toluca, there was a firefight after which the police found twenty-six dead and five seriously wounded members of the Guzman Cartel. If you don't know who he is, well, he is the largest drug cartel in Mexico, with hundreds of members that are loyal to a fault. He lost thirty-one of his henchmen today and the warehouse was almost completely destroyed. Our sources believe he was holding your missing agents and somehow escaped. There is no indication that his hostages were injured, and we assume they were taken with them when he left the building. What we don't know is if either of the Pierces are still alive."

"I don't want to hear that. They are alive and we are going to find them," Connie yelled. She was tired and did not want to admit her best friends were possibly dead.

"Now, be calm; I did not mean to upset you. I have a team of my best agents out there, right now, looking. They will locate them and then you can go in and get them out," the ambassador said.

Josh sat quietly across from the ambassador looking at his tablet, smiling.

"Do you find this funny Mr. Randal?" the ambassador asked.

"No sir, but I just received some information that will help us complete this mission without delay," Josh commented, as he glanced down at the mini receiver he had in his hand. The receiver had just picked up a weak signal from the chip that had been implanted in Davin and Josh before going to Iran to rescue the President. They had not been removed, just deactivated, and were reactivated prior to starting this mission.

"How so?"

"I am not at liberty to disclose my sources, but rest assured, I just got a call to let me know it is time to leave. We will be leaving here as soon as we can unpack our gear. Gentlemen and lady, time to change. We leave in ten minutes," Josh ordered, reaching up to his ear to simulate clicking his Bluetooth. "Is there a place we can unpack and get prepped?"

"Yes. Do you need the address of the warehouse?" the ambassador said as he picked up his phone and called his assistant, who entered the room almost immediately. "George, show these gentlemen and lady to the game room."

"No sir, we have it, but that is just our first stop. We should be back here in four hours; if not, then something happened and we may not be back. Don't wait up for us," Josh commented, half joking, half not.

"Yes sir," George said to the group, "Follow me, please."

Ten minutes later, the team boarded the SUVs and headed out of the property. Each member dressed as a Mexican Federal Police Swat Team member carrying Mexican issued weapons, including M-4s, MP-5s, Barrett 50 caliber sniper rifle, and assorted hand guns including Glocks, Colt 45 autoloaders, and Berretta M-9s. All members spoke Spanish and English so they had no problem bluffing their way into most areas. Not many people would question the Federal Swat team when they arrived on a site.

"Josh, have you still got a signal?" Stephanie asked as she eyed Josh who had his eye glued on the small receiver on his lap.

"Yes, but weak; it just came online about an hour ago and has been getting weaker by the minute," Josh commented quietly. He and Stephanie were sitting in the back seat of the first SUV and were talking quietly.

"How far?" the driver asked without turning around.

"About two miles, step on it!" Josh yelled.

"Yes, sir," the driver said, pressed down on the accelerator and ran the SUV up to seventy-five miles per hour with sirens blaring and lights flashing, forcing the traffic to the side of the road. He glanced in the mirror to make sure the other SUV was still behind. Two minutes later, they screeched to a stop beside several Mexican Police cars, several fire engines and four ambulances. "It looks like we are late for the party."

"I'll do the talking; you get the men unloaded and wait at their vehicles," Josh ordered the driver.

"Roger that, El Capitan," the driver responded as he bailed out of the SUV and headed over to the other vehicles.

Josh walked over to the first officer and asked in Spanish, "Who is in charge?" He received a nod and a finger pointing toward a tall man wearing dark slacks, a tan short sleeve shirt not tucked in and what looked like Army style boots. "Gracias," Josh replied and walked over to the man in charge. "We got a call to report here, something about unexploded ordinance, but it looks like we missed the party," Josh said as he walked up, speaking Spanish.

"Si, Commandant Hector Rodriguez, I don't believe I have had the pleasure, Mr. Randal," Hector responded and extended his hand after immediately recognizing Josh from photos that he had received from Ashley Peterson. Josh shook his hand.

"Damn, I am going to have to get my picture off Facebook," Josh said smiling. "Can we talk privately, Commandant?"

"Sure, walk with me," Hector said as he turned and started to walk away from his men, far enough so they could not hear. "Call me Hector. What is on your mind, my friend?"

"We have reason to believe one of our men is somewhere in that building; well, what is left of the building and we need to do a search. Call it a clearing operation and only my men should go in. You can tell your men that you have reports that there are still unexploded ordinance in there and possibly some bad guys still alive."

"That works for me, go ahead and search. We did a perimeter search, and did not find anything except a blown up car and a lot of bullet cases. Looks like they had a small war here; if you find anyone alive, bring them out. If they are dead, then just let me know where the bodies are and if it is safe to enter. We will keep the civilians at bay."

"You got it," Josh said and then turned to his team and signaled for them to follow.

"How accurate is that thing?" Stephanie asked as she caught up to him and was far enough away from the team so they could not hear.

"Down to about ten feet. He is getting weaker. We've got to move," Josh said and started toward the one remaining door that would put them within sixty feet of the signal. As he reached the door, he signaled to his team to spread out and said, "Possible unexploded ordinance and maybe one or two bad guys still alive; don't know how, but be on your toes." The team spread out and slowly headed into the remains of the building, weapons out and in the ready position.

Chapter 24 The Basement

"Major, we have a problem!" Dusty yelled across the bay at her shift commander when she saw what was happening on her computer.

"What's happening now, Lieutenant?" Major Sorenson asked as she hurried across the bay.

"Well, you need to see this," Dusty responded pointing to the computer screen. On the screen were the words:

'Be advised that we know who and where you are and if you do not return control of our infra-structure within the hour, we will launch the most devastating attack on your country; it will make the downing of the World Trade Center look like a picnic. Islamic Jihad'

"When did that pop up?"

"A couple of seconds ago," Dusty replied.

"How long to get their infrastructure back up?" Sorenson asked.

"At least four hours; if we start right now."

"If their Internet is down, how did they get this message to us?" Spooky asked.

"Must have sent it through a server located in a country that is not being blocked," Dusty replied

Okay, I can see that. I need to notify the President," Sorenson (Spooky) said turning and headed for the door, only to stop and turn back to Dusty and her team. "Start turning Iran back on, but keep China and Korea in the dark. And the President's going to ask, how is getting the west coast back on line going?"

"We have restored electrical power to New Mexico, Arizona and Washington; but for some reason, we are having trouble with California and Oregon. The rest should have power in a couple of hours."

"Were you able to remove or kill the embedded software that started this?"

"Only partly, we are still working on that part," Dusty answered, looking very tired.

"I'll be right back, keep at it," she said and left the room.

"I should have told her that Iran did not send that message," Dusty said to the technician sitting next to her. She jumped up and ran after Spooky. "Major, there is something you need to know."

"What is it?"

"Iran did not send that message; the hackers just wanted us to think they did."

"If Iran didn't send it, who did?" he asked, not knowing if he really wanted to know.

"North Korea!"

"Why would Korea send that?" The major stopped to think and then continued, "They want us to believe that the Iranian Terrorists are going to attack when it is really going to be the Koreans. Damn!" Pausing, "World War III is about to start."

"Yes I know."

Major Sorenson reached her office and picked up the secure phone, punched in a few numbers and waited. After a few seconds, she heard a few tones and then entered her access code and inserted her identification card in the slot provided. The phone rang twice before being answered.

"Hello," a male voice answered.

"Major Amanda Sorenson, U.S. Air Force Cyber Command, I need to speak to the President immediately; critical information," she stated.

"One moment, Major," he said and then put her on hold.

"Hello Major, this is Darrell Mitchell, what is so important that you had to call, again? You know, we are going to meet someday; I know the voice but would love to meet you and, ah, well, what have you got for me?"

"Sir, we just received information that there is going to be an attack within the hour on a major location. We do not have the location as yet. but the information stated that it will make 9-11 look like a picnic," Sorenson reported.

"Sounds serious and your source is reliable?"

"Yes, sir! Extremely."

"Thank you, Major. We will take precautions here; you do the same down there. Anything else you need to pass on?" Mitchell asked.

"No sir, not at this time. If we learn more, I will call. Thank you, be safe."

"You too; good bye," Mitchell said as he hung up the secure phone and turned to his National Security Advisor and Secret Service Director and said, "I think it is time we went to the basement, gentlemen. Pass the word, evacuate all federal buildings, critical staff to the basement, and the rest, let them go home and be with their families. Only critical White House staff goes down, the rest release to go home to protect their families. Alert the National Guard and all reserve units; mission orders will follow. We will not push Martial Law yet, but I am not ruling it out. Leave the guards in place. We still need to protect the building," Mitchell ordered knowing full well that he was about to put military forces on high alert on American soil, something that had not been done since the Civil War. Doing so violated several laws unless approved by Congress, both in the House of Representatives and the Senate.

"Yes sir," Douglas Williams, Director Secret Service, replied and then turned and headed out of the Oval Office to start the evacuation. It would take forty minutes to get everyone out of the White House and down the elevator to the basement which had a Maglev train that would carry all of the White House staff to Mount Weather. Williams along with a small security force would remain at the White House to protect it, if necessary.

National Security Advisor Tony Sanford immediately called over to each Federal building and alerted them to evacuate immediately, critical staff to the basement and non-critical staff released to go home to their families. He informed them to leave a security team at each building consisting of at least ten trained security officers. Each federal building was also equipped with an elevator that could hold up to twenty-five people at a time to transport them to a bomb shelter located below the basement. In an emergency, there was a set of stairs and they were put to use also. Each stair case was sealed to prevent inadvertent access to the shelter. Once the alarm was sent, the doors unlocked for access to the shelter.

The President headed for the hall and the elevator that was located behind a false wall panel just across the hall from the Oval Office. The basement under the White House was the new underground entrance to the new Mount Weather, located in the Shenandoah Mountains. From there, they could go anywhere in the country via the high speed train located one hundred feet below the surface. The train connected the main station at the basement with similar underground facilities located around the country. Some connected to super secret missile silos housing intercontinental ballistic missiles armed with nuclear warheads. The use of Air Force One as a combat command center was out-dated, since the basement was completed several administrations earlier.

The police of Washington D.C. had their hands full once the alarm went out. Many people that heard of the impending attack started to leave the city, clogging the highways heading out of town. Thousands of people loaded everything they could in their cars and trucks and headed for the perceived safety out of town. Scared and unsure of their future everyone was quite literally heading for the hills.

****

"What is wrong with the Internet?" Calib asked the computer, expecting it to respond with an answer. He reached up and slapped the side of the monitor, but not too hard.

"Sir, our messenger just drove into camp. Do you want to see him now?" a member of his ISIS asked as he stepped into the tent.

"Yes, my emails are not going anywhere; send him in," Calib responded looking very annoyed at his computer.

"He is a she, sir. I will bring her right in," he said before he reached behind him, pulled the door flap open, and let her in. She entered and stood waiting to be asked to speak.

"What can you tell me?" Calib asked not looking at her.

"Sir, I have just returned from Tehran and the entire city is without electricity. Nothing is working. And I have heard that the country has had an Internet virus attack which has shut down the infrastructure and they are unable to bring it back up. The government is working on it, but is not getting very far," she reported.

"It is the damn Americans. They have done this to us," he almost yelled at her and then stopped to think before continuing. "Go to Bagdad and see if they are experiencing the same problems. If not, get online and send this message to all our operatives. If Iran is down also, then head on to Kuwait to send it. Fly if you must, but make it happen as quickly as you can," he ordered and typed a message on his computer and printed it. "Do so immediately; we will not stand for this. Now go."

"As you command, sir," she said and then turned and left the tent. After getting into her Jeep, she sped out of camp and headed west across the desert.

Chapter 25 Just Kidding, Really

At precisely one hour after the message flashed on Dusty's computer screen, there was an old Douglas DC-6 passenger airliner which had been out of service for forty years flying low over Lake Mead just north-east of Las Vegas in what seemed like a tourist sightseeing flight. The plane had been over the lake for about two hours when it turned back toward Las Vegas and flew over Hoover Dam at about four thousand feet. That was a little high for good photography, but due to flight restrictions around the dam, it was the minimum altitude the plane could operate at. After passing over the dam, the plane banked abruptly, turned back toward the dam, dropped in altitude from four thousand feet to fly into the canyon and headed directly toward the face of the dam. There was nothing to stop the plane from flying under the bridge but seconds before it would slam into the face of the dam, at about one hundred and fifty miles per hour, the plane erupted into a massive explosion.

High above Hoover dam, a Predator drone armed with four Sidewinder missiles was orbiting. It was being controlled by Captain Jay H. Church as he sat smiling. He had just stopped the destruction of the Hoover dam by tracking and launching a sidewinder missile at the DC-6 that was heading up the canyon directly at the dam with intentions of destroying the dam. Using a new Air Force communications system that would broadcast on all aircraft frequencies at once, he had attempted numerous radio calls to the aircraft without getting a response. He knew the pilot heard him, but had refused to respond until the plane was about fifteen hundred feet from passing under the bridge; which was about two thousand yards from the dam. The pilot made one comment just before Captain Church launched his missile.

"Too late Captain, the damn is mine!" the pilot yelled over the radio with an oriental accent as he piloted his aircraft toward the bridge and the dam.

The explosion was at least five times larger than a sidewinder would have caused. The DC-6 was loaded with high explosives. The explosion and resulting aircraft crash caused no damage to the bridge or dam, but left a lot of wreckage scattered up the canyon. The country had been put on alert earlier in the day when there were reports of a pending attack from terrorists. The DC-6 had been identified as stolen the day before from an airfield outside of Tucson, Arizona.

There was some damage from the explosion as far away as Las Vegas. Windows broke and the earth shook as if they were having an earthquake. Most visitors to Vegas never noticed anything and those that did thought it was a just another movie being made somewhere in town. Las Vegas still operated even with the blackouts; most of the casinos had reverted to their emergency generators which could operate most of the electronics within them. There were some inconveniences to their guests, but most did not know the country was under attack as they sat and gambled.

****

"Mr. President," Tony Sanford stated as he entered the basement office of the President. After getting a nod from President Mitchell to go ahead, Tony reported "One of our drones just shot down a DC-6 attempting to crash into the Hoover Dam. No casualties, but a lot of aircraft parts scattered all over the bottom of the canyon. We have a team heading to the site to investigate. The plane must have been loaded with explosives; well, watch this." Tony pressed a couple of buttons and a video of the explosion popped up on the flat screen TV in the office.

"Wow, that thing was loaded; do you think it was enough to bust that dam?"

"Yes, more than enough to take the dam down and cause a flood of mega proportion. That would have killed thousands. We got lucky, sir."

"Seems so, Tony," Mitchell commented as he viewed the video shot by the drone after firing a Stinger missile at the DC-6. "Has a press release been issued?"

"No sir, but a press conference is scheduled in fifteen minutes; we have a speech for you being written as we speak. It should be ready in a couple of minutes for your review."

"Good, we are not bringing the news crew down here are we?"

"No sir, you will be on a video conference from the media room, down the hall. The news people will be in a location that has been cleared and deemed safe."

"Where is that?"

"It is a little out of the way for some of them, but they will get over it. We have them meeting at the Hyatt Regency Hotel, main conference room. They will be okay with it," Tony commented. "Remember the Hyatt was built with a shelter and they are setting up there."

"Okay, let's get this over with, two explosions and maybe more, I think the people need to know what the hell is going on," Mitchell stated getting madder at every passing second. A knock on the door interrupted Tony and Mitchell said, "Come in."

"What the hell are you doing here?" Mitchell said as he saw Director Ashley Peterson enter the office.

"I got a call saying you were headed down here and to assist in your acclimation to the area. We have made some major upgrades recently. Only three other team members know of them, and they are tied up making sure all the systems are up and running properly," Ashley said. She then looked over at the coffee cart and pointed; after getting a nod from Mitchell, she walked over and poured herself a cup of coffee, added a splash of cream and a little sugar. "Thanks, been a long day."

"I know, and it is only ten a.m. Okay, so what are these updates you are talking about?" Mitchell asked.

"Well, let me finish this cup and I will be happy to show you and Mister Sanford all the new gadgets and what they can do for you. But while I sip this, I can tell you that we have upgraded the security, communications, the kitchen, and now have the fastest train on the earth."

"Security, I thought we had everything possible down here to protect us from intrusion."

"Well, almost; some of the earlier systems were Beta versions, now they are all upgraded to Version 1.0 and have all the functions activated. They have been in use for just over three months and have worked perfectly."

"So what does it do now?"

"Glad you asked. You had a chip placed in you when you took office; well, that chip also acts as a monitor not only for your location and health, but it now can be used to alert security officers that you are in danger. This is almost like Star Trek; all you have to do is tap right here," she said pointing to the base of her neck touching her collar bone. "There is a little sensor located there that will immediately send out an alarm which will be received by our monitoring station and they will dispatch the security force. All senior staff have them now, mine is here," Ashley continued as she touched her right collar bone.

"Isn't that kind of awkward? What if I am in the shower and run my hand across it; am I going to have a bunch of wild heavily armed commandos burst into the bathroom?" Mitchell commented.

"I'm kidding. Really, I was just kidding Darrel; your chip only sends your location and health. There is no instant alarm that is touch sensitive. But I had you going for a minute there," Ashley said laughing.

"Sure did, but all kidding aside. What are the upgrades I need to know about?"

"Have a seat and I will explain," Ashley said and then described all the upgrades to their underground fortress, explaining how each one worked and why they were installed. She took extra time on the entrances and exits to the fortress. She put special emphasis on the security, monitoring of each individual in the facility, knowing exactly where they were, when they entered, when they left, and most important, the ability to sterilize any magnetic or digital data entering or leaving the facility. The only way a person could get a disc, digital camera or any recording device out of the facility was to have it approved by either the Director of Security or the Deputy Director of Security for the facility. Then, and only then, the item would be placed in a special compartment to get it past the system.

The red phone on the President's desk started to ring. "I think I need to answer that, been expecting a call from the Prime Minister over in England," Mitchell commented and walked over to his desk. He picked up the hot line and quietly said. "President Mitchell."

He listened for several seconds. "Okay, we will head over to our Situation Room to watch. Ten minutes, sure we are already set up and will monitor. Thank you," he said. He started to hang up, but held the handset in his hand just looking at it, as if thinking; finally, he hung up the handset. The President then said, "Ladies and gentlemen, we need to move to the Sit Room, our friends in England along with Seal Team Six are about to take down Calib Mohammed and his ISIS State Group. If you wish to view it, we need to move now."

Three minutes later, Mitchell, Sanford and Peterson were sitting in front of a large screen monitor waiting for the show to begin. They did not have to wait long.

"Switching to satellite image now, sir," the video technician stated.

"The plan is for several of our drones to launch the attack by firing a spread of air-to-ground missiles into the compound. The British Commando team will then move in to mop up. Seal Team Six is only there as back-up for this operation, if anything should go wrong or any of the terrorist attempting to escape. There is an estimated one hundred fifty ISIS members in the camp. They are tasked to stop them."

As they watched the screen, the scenario played out just as planned. Two drones with cameras shot a total of eight missiles into the compound, destroying every building, almost all the vehicles and hopefully sending each member of the group to hell. The British Commandos moved in, and only fired their weapons sporadically. A vehicle suddenly raced out of the compound and headed south at a high rate of speed. It destroyed by the Seal team before it got two hundred yards from the compound.

****

"Alpha Base, Wolf Ten, body count at one forty eight, weapons cache and vehicles destroyed. Request extraction and clean up."

"Roger Wolf Ten, Extraction approved; helos on the way. Regroup with Wolf Four at point Charlie," Base ordered. "Clean up team is inbound."

The communication between the Commando Group and their base confirmed a mission success. A special team had been sent in to make the compound disappear completely, which would take about twelve hours.

Chapter 26 Out of the Frying Pan, Into the Fire

"Good afternoon, this is Colonel Blair over at Army CID; is the agent running the Hanson murder case available?" Blair asked the desk clerk, as she walked into the San Francisco FBI office.

"Let me see, I believe he is," the clerk responded. A minute later, the clerk looked up at Blair and said, "Agent Miles will be right down; would you like to wait in the conference room?"

"Sure, that would be fine."

"This way," the clerk said and pointed to a door on the right hand wall. Blair and Ricky Donald walked over and entered the open door. They sat down and waited for Agent Miles in the plush room.

A few minutes later, a person who had just entered the room said, "Hello, I am Agent David Miles, I must apologize; I am not fully up to speed on the case, just assigned it this morning. Sorry to say the agent that was handling it was killed in one of the recent terrorist attacks."

"Sorry to hear that; we won't take long. We also need to report to the CIA about their missing agents. But for you, here is our report," Blair said handing Miles a small folder containing the written report. "Not much to report, Hanson was killed by a 32 caliber, shot twice in the back and bled out on the rocks. We have a fingerprint on one of the shell casings, pointing to a low life, Eric Shubert, aka Weasel. But he will not be talking anytime soon; he was found dead floating in the bay, washed up on a beach, well, most of him washed up. The fish feasted on him a bit. That is about all we have at the moment; still working it, but mostly dead ends, literally."

"Thanks for the information; if you find out anything else, please let us know. The killing of an American soldier on home soil is not to be taken lightly. If there is anything we can do to assist, don't hesitate to ask," replied Agent Miles.

"Thanks." Blair and Donald stood to leave. "There is one thing; the FBI may have information which we have not been able to access on a couple of Germans, Hans Bormann and Gregory Dietrich. If you could get us everything you have on those two, it would be greatly appreciated."

"Bormann and Dietrich, I have heard of them, let me see what I can do. Why do you need that?" Miles replied smiling.

"A case we are working on, that's all. Thanks, send it over to the Presidio when you get it," Blair said. They left the conference room and headed back to the office.

Meanwhile, Lieutenant Todd Sandlewood was on the secure phone calling Ms. Ashley Peterson, Director of the CIA.

"This is Ashley Peterson, how can I help you?"

"Ms. Peterson, this is Lieutenant Todd Sandlewood with Army CID, San Francisco. We understand you have been looking for a couple of missing agents."

"Yes, have you had any luck locating them?"

"We have, and yes, they are alive. They are at San Francisco General right now getting minor cuts and abrasions cared for. They were beaten up, but nothing broken." Todd commented being a bit hesitant to continue.

"Is there something you are not telling me?"

"They will make a full report, but we found them in a rundown hotel in a bad section of town. They were handcuffed together to a bed, and well, they were both naked."

"Handcuffed! Naked!" Ashley almost yelled. "How did you find them?"

"Some of the guests reported yelling from one of the rooms and complained to management who checked the room and found them. They called the police, who called us and we called you. We got them dressed and to the hospital for dehydration and their minor injuries. They will be on a flight back to DC in the morning."

"Thanks! Have Agent Sikes or Jones call me when they get released from the hospital. I need the whole story."

****

"Over here, Stephanie. Help me move this," Josh called to her as he pushed a large timber to the side, "He is over here."

"Conrad, bring a couple of the guys over to the east side of the building; we found him," Stephanie called over her hand held radio. "Bring a medic and some tools; we have some downed walls to move."

"Be right there," Conrad replied.

Minutes later, four men showed up with shovels and pick axes. "What have we got?"

"Davin is trapped under this; he is still alive, but barely. Let's move this stuff, carefully," Josh said as he continued throwing smaller pieces of wall and metal away from Davin's location.

Twenty minutes later, they reached the foot of a metal bed partially collapsed with a foot sticking out. Josh reached down and pulled on the foot. After hearing a moan as a response, Josh said, "He is alive." As he paused to scan the bed and the concrete that was piled on top of it, he continued, "Damn, that bed saved his life."

"Grab the other end of this beam," one of the men said to anyone who would listen. After moving the beam to the side and watching as Josh dropped to the floor, he started to pull debris from under a large slab of concrete wall. "Davin, can you move?"

"No," a weak response came out from under the bed.

Minutes later, Josh was able to reach under the bed and with the help of a flashlight he could see that Davin had two of the bed rods embedded in his side and his leg was bent at an unnatural angle. "We will have you out of there in a few minutes, hold on buddy," Josh said, unsure of how they were going to get him out from under the bed without causing the wall to crush him.

The medic showed up a few minutes later carrying a Jaws of Life, a Come-A-Long (which is a portable block and tackle), and his med kit.

"Señor, use this to raise the bed and we will pull him out," the medic said while looking at the leg sticking out from under the end of the bed. He handed Josh the Come-A-Long. "Maybe hook one end to that pipe and the other to the rebar in the wall."

The Come-A-Long was attached as directed and slowly they were able to pull the wall up high enough to slide Davin out from under the wall. They pulled the bed with him since two of the rods were embedded in his side. It worked perfectly, but left a lot of blood on the concrete floor as they did it. It took fifteen minutes to move the crumbled wall off the metal bed which trapped Davin. Using the Jaws of Life, they finally were able to cut the metal rods from the bed leaving the rods in Davin until they were able to get him to the hospital. Unsure of the damage they had done, they did not want to remove them and cause more injuries without proper medical assistance and the ability to exam him more closely before removal.

"Let me take over, señor" the medic said as he knelt down beside Davin. "Someone get a stretcher and my assistant; we need to get him to the hospital immediately. Those rods may have cause internal damage, leave them in for now."

"How bad is it?" Stephanie asked.

"Bad, he has lost a lot of blood and has a broken leg for sure and possible internal injuries," he reported in Spanish, after a quick but thorough examination.

Almost a half hour later, Stephanie and Josh stood outside the operating room at the local hospital, waiting for the doctors to put Davin back together. The rest of the team went back to the Embassy to wait.

****

The residential section of Mount Weather started to fill up quickly as the federal employees started arriving. The President would set up his underground White House in an identical copy of the one on the surface. President Mitchell was walking from the underground train to the temporary White House deep in thought. His mind wandered a bit; he was worried about Tara and the state of the nation. When Tara returned, she had a room designated for her in the underground White House.

"What's going on topside, Tony?" Mitchell asked as they walked along the long hallway.

"Pretty quiet," Sanford replied, but before he got a chance to say anything else, Eric White, shift lead for the White House Secret Service came running down the hall toward them.

"Bad news, sir," White said and continued before anyone had a chance to say anything, "There has been an explosion at the U.S. Supreme Court Building. Fire and police are on site; so far there are eight confirmed dead and many injured."

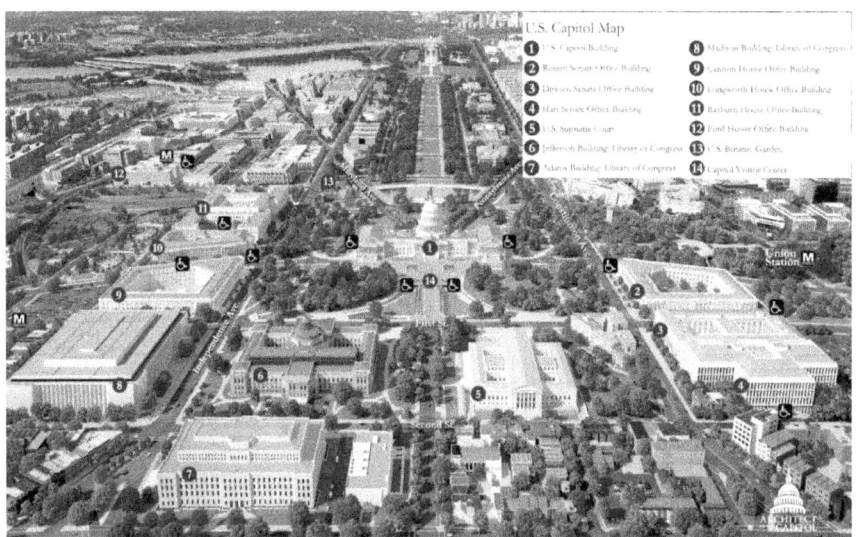
U.S. Federal Buildings located in Washington D.C.

"How many were still in the building after I ordered everyone to go home?" Mitchell asked growing a bit angrier. "Have you talked to the V.P. today?"

"There was reported to be about one hundred still in the building, just shutting down systems and securing the building. Most of the dead are security personnel. And, yes, the V.P. is down in Florida at NASA working out some details on an upcoming classified launch. And before you say anything, this is his special program; it is one he was working on before he became V.P. and he wants to ensure it goes off without a hitch."

"Damn, keep me posted as to survivors and damage. Did you get any more information about these terrorists? What the hell is going on up there?" Mitchell said, stopped and thought to himself about the V.P. and then continued, "That's right he was an Astrophysics Professor at M.I.T. and did have a special project going with some of his grad students. When is the proposed launch?"

"One week from tomorrow, at one in the afternoon. And if his experiment works, it will open a whole new area of study for his students and many more around the world," Sanford commented about the VP's proposed launch.

"At least something good may come of it," Mitchell acknowledged.

"Sir, we are in an undeclared war; one that is being fought on our own soil," Sanford reminded the President. "We need to concentrate on saving the nation and stopping these terrorist attacks."

"Yes, yes, we just took care of one ISIS group which I believe will only cause others to come out of the closet, as they say, and start to attack in earnest." After pausing for a second, he slipped back to the VP and said, "Okay, he is there and we are here with our own problems; when you get a chance, call him and ask when he will return to D.C. Now back to work."

Chapter 27 Hospital Blues

The waiting was the worst part. Davin was in the largest hospital in Mexico City with Josh and Stephanie waiting for the doctors to finish working on him. He had been in the operating room for over two hours. The paramedic had worked feverously keeping Davin Pierce alive as he was transported to the hospital. Davin died during the transport, but the paramedic was trained well and was able to revive him.

Two hours after Davin arrived at the hospital, Josh and Stephanie Randal were still sitting in the waiting room. Finally Josh stood and walked over to the nurses' station and asked about Davin, only to be told that Mr. Pierce was still in surgery and the doctor would be out to see them soon.

"Mr. Randal, I am Doctor Sandoval," he said as the doctor walked into the waiting room, two hours later. "I have some good news and some not so good. Your friend is in pretty bad shape. We lost him twice in there, but he is stable for the moment. He needs some specialized help which we cannot provide here; we do not have the expertise needed. You need to get him to a hospital in the states as soon as possible. We are not equipped to treat all his wounds. We can keep him alive, and as I said, he is stable for the moment and will be able to be moved in a day or two. As soon as he is able to travel, you need to get him back to the states. He had massive internal injuries which if left untended would surely have killed him. I have done what I could to stop the bleeding and to keep him alive. We removed the two bed rods in his side; luckily they did not do too much damage, although the damage was severe. The worst part is that he received a head injury which has put severe pressure on his brain. We are not equipped or have a brain surgeon on staff that can help him. We will keep him in the ICU for now. There is one other option; is it possible that, with your connections, you could get him to Doctor Eugene H. Holms from Walter Reed. He is the best neurosurgeon on the planet and your friend needs his help. Either get Doctor Holms here or Mr. Pierce has to go to him. He can save your friend. He also has some damage to his back, but that will heal over time; we were able to repair that. His left leg had a compound fracture along with several broken bones in his arm and hand. He will be able to function completely in time; he needs rest and Doctor Holms right now."

"Can we see him?" Stephanie asked quickly and then stopped and asked, "A neurosurgeon, what exactly is wrong with Davin?"

"Soon, he is still in recovery, I will have a nurse let you know when he is awake. As for his other injuries, he has two puncture wounds, which broke several ribs which punctured his right lung; those we were able to repair. His left leg is broken in two places; we were able to set those, thanks to the paramedic's fine work. His left wrist is broken in two places and two fingers and his thumb are broken. All have been set and will heal in time. The problem we cannot fix is his head; there is water forming on his brain; if not stopped, he will suffer from permanent brain damage and possible death."

"Thank you doctor," Stephanie said as the doctor turned and headed down the hall toward the doctors' break room.

"Stephanie, I need to make a call to Ashley; maybe we can get Doctor Holms down here, instead of transporting Davin to him," Josh said and then pulled his cell phone out of his pocket and pressed several buttons to activate the speed dial.

"What about Connie?" she asked, but he did not hear her as he walked away.

"Ashley, Josh, we have Davin; he is in the ICU, pretty banged up," Josh reported. After pausing to listen, he continued, "He will survive. At least the doctors here believe he will, but he needs some specialized help." After pausing to listen again, he continued, "He has a severe head injury and needs a specialist. Can we get Doctor Eugene H. Holms out of Walter Reed? The doctor suggested we fly Davin to Walter Reed, but he can't be moved for several days, which may be too late. Can you get Holms to fly down here immediately?"

"Josh, I will see what I can do. Is he the only doctor that can do the job?" Ashley Peterson asked.

"I really don't know, but he is the one that was requested by the doctor here," Josh replied.

"Okay, anything else?"

"Yeah, Connie is still missing. Do we have permission to find her; she is not chipped so finding her may be difficult?" Josh asked.

"Pull out all the stops. Find her," Ashley said, then stopped and took a deep breath. "The country is on high alert, the U.S. Supreme Court Building has been attacked and the President has called up the rest of the military and is about to declare Martial Law. I am surprised he hasn't already done so. Are Polson and Miller working with you two? They are trying to locate the President's daughter; she is missing and possibly in Mexico. We recently got a weak signal from her chip and are tracking it. It shows she is at the international airport."

"Yes, they are, thank you. They are running down some leads right now and will be back to meet with us in an hour or two. Has the President's daughter been kidnapped? Damn, what the hell is going on?" Josh asked, thinking Polson and Miller were tracking leads to the President's daughter.

"Yes and it is possible that she and Connie are being held by the same people. So stay close to Polson and Miller; she has a chip in her and we are… wait," Ashley replied and then listened to the person that just entered her office before continuing, "Okay, I just got word that Tara Mitchell has boarded a jet at Mexico City's International airport. We are trying to get the flight plan and should have that within the hour. I need you, Polson, and Miller to track that plane and intercept it when it lands."

"How are we going to do that? They have a head start," Josh asked confused and worried.

"Just get to the airport as quickly as you can. I will arrange transportation and also learn their heading by the time you get there."

"Thank you, Ashley. We will find her. I will get Polson and Miller to the airport as quickly as possible. Please call Stephanie as soon as you confirm Doctor Holms." He then hung up his cell phone and slid it into his pocket as he walked back to the waiting room.

When he arrived at the waiting room, he found Stephanie pacing the floor.

"What did you find out with Ashley?" Stephanie queried.

"She is going to get the doctor down here as quickly as possible and President Mitchell has gone underground. His daughter has been kidnapped and I need to get Polson and Miller to the airport as quickly as possible. Do you know where they are? The country has been attacked again; the U.S. Supreme Court Building has been bombed," Josh replied summarizing his conversation with Ashley.

"I don't…" she started to say but stopped when she saw Polson and Miller in the hallway headed towards the waiting room. "Holy shit, first the west coast goes dark, now bombings. What is Mitchell going to do?"

"Martial Law!" Josh said quietly. He turned as he heard footsteps coming down the hall. "Great, you two are back, what did you find out?" he asked as Polson and Miller walked into the waiting room.

"Not much, Hector Martinez has been a great help. But he is just as lost as we are in locating this German. We do have a name, Hans Bormann; we contacted Interpol to see if they have any information on him, but no word yet. Martinez has called up his best that are running down a few clues that were found at the warehouse. Military grade explosives were used, German manufacturer. That's about it for now," Polson reported. "What do you know?"

"First, the three of us have to get to the airport as quickly as possible. Ashley told me they tracked Tara to the airport where she boarded a plane. Destination unknown at the moment, but she will get that info to us by the time we get there. She is arranging transportation to wherever that plane is going. We need to go now," Josh said. He then leaned over and kissed Stephanie, just as Hector walked into the waiting room.

"Great, perfect timing, we need to get to the airport as quickly as possible, can you help?" Josh asked.

"I have a helicopter parked on the roof of this hospital in case of emergencies; let's go wake up the pilots," Hector said and headed for the elevator. Ten minutes later, the rotor was turning and they took off, headed toward the airport in a Bell Jet Ranger Police helicopter.

****

"What are you doing here, Ms. Peterson? Twice in one day, that must be a record," President Mitchell asked when she entered the office.

"Sir, we need to talk," Ashley said as she walked across the plush carpet and took the offered hand and shook. "We have a situation that needs your help."

"How can the Office of the President assist the CIA today?" Mitchell asked half jokingly.

"One of our operatives, Davin Pierce, has been severely injured in Mexico City and requires the immediate assistance from a specialist, to be specific, a Doctor Holms from Walter Reed. He needs to fly to Mexico City to save his life, immediately."

"Why don't you call him directly, he may be a reasonable guy and do as you ask," Mitchell said quietly.

"Well, that would work except I have asked and he refused. No questions, just refused. He is a Colonel in the Army Reserves and could be called up," Ashley stated becoming a little frustrated.

"Not sure if that will be necessary. Call him again, use this phone. Just tell him who you are and why you need him and then if that doesn't work, I will activate him and send him down there. But that will take some time. Not sure if we have time to spare. How is Davin doing?" Mitchell said pointing to the phone on his desk.

"Not well, he is pretty banged up and has a crack in his skull which is why we need the doctor on a plane today; otherwise, Davin may die."

"Call the hospital," Mitchell said again pointing to the phone on the corner of his desk, as she was reaching for her cell phone. "Remember, you left your cell on the train.

"Okay, yeah, I forgot about that part of this secure facility; it is on the train," Ashley said as she reached over and picked up the handset, dialed a number she had committed to memory, and waited. After four rings, the phone was answered.

"Walter Reed Emergency, how may I direct your call?" the female voice said.

"Doctor Holms, please, this is an emergency," Ashley said quickly and then waited.

"One moment, please, I will see if I can locate him," she said and the wait began. Three minutes became four, four became five and then a voice came on the line.

"Doctor Holms, you said this is an emergency. How can I help you?" Holms asked.

"This is Ashley Peterson, again; we talked earlier, but I could not give you all the information you needed to help me."

"Ms. Peterson, I told you earlier I cannot go to Mexico City. I have patients here and just cannot get away."

"Let me explain, sir. I am Ashley Peterson, the Director of CIA, newly appointed by President Darrell Mitchell, and I am asking you to help one of my top field operatives who has been severely injured in Mexico. Without your help, he will probably die. The doctor taking care of him asked for you personally; said you are the best and that you have the experience and expertise to save my operative."

"Who asked for me by name? Never mind, that really doesn't matter. I assume he can't travel. How do I know you are the real Director of the CIA?"

"Well, would you recognize President Mitchell's voice; he can verify who I am. Or you can hang up and call the White House; ask to speak to the President, and we will tell the operator to let your call go through."

"Yes, I have heard him speak often and trust he can verify that this is real. Sorry for being deceptive, but I have had calls like this before and had to go off on a wild goose chase. You understand, don't you? I will call in a couple of minutes."

"Yes I do, we will be waiting for your call," Ashley said and hung up the phone; Mitchell called the operator and informed them to expect a call from Doctor Holms and to pass it through.

A couple of minutes passed before the phone rang. "This is Doctor Holms over at Walter Reed, can you verify..." the doctor was cut short when Mitchell spoke.

"Doctor Holms, sorry to cut you short, but this is an emergency. This is President Darrell Mitchell and Ms. Peterson is the Director of the CIA and is asking nicely for you to save our man in Mexico."

"Okay, when do I leave? It is a pleasure to speak with your sir; I will get my go bag and be ready to leave in twenty minutes," Doctor Holms replied to the President.

"I will let Ashley set that up for you," he said handing the phone back to her.

"Doctor, how fast can you get to Dulles; we will have a Gulfstream VI sitting at the general aviation terminal in one hour, fueled and waiting for you," Ashley stated and waited for his reply.

"I will be there in an hour. I just have to pass off my patients to my assistant, shouldn't take long."

"Good, I will see you there," Ashley commented and then hung up the phone.

"Are you going?" Mitchell asked.

"No, just wanted to meet the good doctor," replied Ashley. "And thank him." She then turned and left the underground office.

Chapter 28 Down in the Bayou

That same day, down in the French Quarter of New Orleans, six young Korean men and three women were eating lunch of Blackened Sea Bass and Cajun Shrimp. And while sipping their wine between bites of fish and shrimp, they were discussing their next move.

"I am going to miss this food; the combination of French and spices of the south really brings out the flavor of this Sea Bass. Awesome, just awesome," one of the women said in subdued Korean breaking the ice that was floating around the table.

"I have to agree, but we were sent here to do a job. We have been living quietly among our enemies for years, but now it is our time to act. Our orders are clear and destiny is in our grasp. And we have a job that needs to be completed soon, or our country will make sure we and our families will not survive," a response came back at him also in Korean from across the table.

"Look, we all have lived in this country for the past ten years, working and playing with these people; they are good people, not as honorable as we are, but good people none the less. Why must we do this? Why not just fade away into the woodwork, as my neighbor always said. It is true they won the war and left our country divided, but our parents started that war long before we were born; they just finished the job. I have no beef with these people," the third man in the group said.

"I know we have all made our home here, but we were sent here to do a job; and we will do that job or die trying," the leader of the group stated and then looked over at his second in command and smiled.

"We have everything in place. The Supreme Court Building was easy, but we need to make a bigger statement. The Hoover Dam was a bust; they shot down the plane before it made contact. Somehow they knew what Kim was going to do, but, well, his plane exploded short of the target. He may have detonated the bomb too soon," the man on the right of his commander sitting at the head of the table said to the rest of his team. They were speaking quietly in their native language of Korean so they would not be overheard, or at least not likely to be understood by anyone within earshot.

"I told you that was a bad idea; the United States would have something in place to protect their dam or any major infrastructure facility, nuclear power plants and anything like that. We need to go in on ground targets, an attack we can get to without trying to fly in. They will shoot us down like they did Kim. True, the World Trade Center was brought down by airplanes, but that was before the country was on high alert to such tactics; now they are, and we cannot sacrifice another team member with the airplane attack. And with the country on higher alert, I am not sure anything that we attempt to do will be successful. The President has called out the military and from what I have heard is about to enforce martial law, which will restrict our travels. We are only on work permits; I am surprised they haven't attempted to arrest us already, like they did to the Japanese at the beginning of World War II. They must know by now that our country planned and executed the attack on the Supreme Court Building and the Hoover Dam," the youngest female member of the team commented. After pausing for a moment, she then added, "I have a boyfriend and want to marry him and can't if I am dead or in prison."

"You can back out now if you like; I will not stop you. Go home to your boy friend and live long, if you can. We will proceed without you," the leader stated getting a bit angry with her, but understanding what she was saying. He too had become very comfortable in Dallas, Texas, met a woman and wanted to be with her right now; but his sense of duty and honor would not let him. He did not mention the attack that had been planned for Washington D.C.; that one would not fail, it was fool proof.

Tasha stood, bowed and left without saying another word. The Koreans made sure she left before they discussed the target to be sure she could not leak the information; they watched as she faded into the crowd outside the restaurant.

"What is our target?" the lady on his right asked.

"The United States Cyber Command located at McDill Air Force Base outside of Tampa, Florida," he stated without blinking an eye. "That is why we have been asked to meet here in New Orleans. The drive from here to McDill is not long and I have people already there assembling the equipment; it should be ready by the time we arrive."

"Wow, an Air Force Base, why take the chance?" his second in command asked.

"Because they are causing our country a lot of problems; from what I have been told, they have been attacking our Internet usage and have shut down much of our country's infrastructure," he answered as he looked around at his remaining team.

"The base is heavily guarded, but you know how easy it is to get on base. They do have what they call an *'Active Barrier'* at all the gates. But we can bypass that by taking out the gate sentries first and then drive right in as fast as we can. We will get on and destroy their cyber command facility. Doing so will prevent them from attacking our infrastructure and allow our people to cause more damage to theirs."

"Sounds like a suicide mission," the second woman on his left stated.

"It is," the leader said. "We probably will not survive. If you want out, now is your only chance. Join Tasha and just go."

"I have to agree with Tasha and would like to bow out of this mission; I have a family now and wish to be with them. I am sorry; I will not speak of this and wish you luck." Another lady stood, bowed and left the table, disappearing in the crowd. The planning continued with one less member.

"What is the plan?" the only remaining female in the team asked.

"The plan is simple; Kim Lee will position himself in one of the stolen Humvees within view of the gate closest to the Cyber Command building. It is about a mile and a half from the building. He will, on my command, shoot the two guards at the gate preventing them from activating the *'Active Barrier'* or close the gate. I will drive the first Humvee through the gate followed by the dump truck loaded with high explosives. I need a volunteer for the dump truck. And then Kim Lee will follow with his Humvee, and we will shoot any and all resistance as we speed toward the building. I will pull off to the side to allow the dump truck to pass and run into the building, and detonate his explosives as close as he or she can to the building. The amount of explosives should completely destroy the building and all that are in it."

"There is no way we will survive this; but if that is what our leader wants, then that is what he will get. We will die in honor. When do we do this?"

"Two days, I already have our people working on the dump truck."

"What people?"

"We have been teamed with another team from, well, another team that is versed in high explosives. They will join in the attack. There are three of them that are experts in their field. You will meet them later today. They are not Korean, but from the Middle East."

****

At McDill Air Force Base, in the building behind several layers of fence and barbed wire, was the Joint Forces Cyber Command. The building was located just off the flight line. It was guarded by six armed guards, two dogs, and two companies of U.S. Army 82nd Airborne Infantry on patrol around the air base, rotating with two more 82nd Airborne companies. Of course, any attackers had to get on base which was at a higher threat level.

The teams in the Cyber Command had been working hard to get the country's electrical grid back online since the attack yesterday. They were only partially successful in their efforts. After getting one grid up and before they could get the next one up, the first one would crash again. They received an ultimatum from Korea to turn their infrastructure back on or have devastation brought down on the United States. To show they meant what they said, they had attacked the Supreme Court Building, killing six and injuring many others, and had made an attempt to destroy the Hoover Dam, ending in failure.

"Dusty, status report?" Wiggins asked as he entered the main Cyber Commander Computer room.

"Wow, Master Sergeant, we have succeeded in getting Korea back online, but ..." She paused to take a breath.

"There is always a 'but'... continue, Dusty," Wiggins said taking an opportunity to interject a comment while she caught a breath.

"Well, our efforts continue to be slammed; every time we think we are getting ahead of that hacker, he slips around us and sends out another Denial of Service, using a variety of methods, from Buffer Overloads to just going into the Root and taking over the system completely. We are right behind him, but can't seem to get ahead. The code they had embedded in the system is still active although we removed a lot of it; it is riddled with viruses. Again, but ... we will beat this S.O.B. I have Savage working pinning down exactly where he is located; and once we have that, we will shut down his grid and get the local military or police to take him down. We are getting closer; we know he is in China. But he is only up for a few minutes at a time, which is making it more difficult, but we will get him. And we are not completely sure it is actually him coming online; the code they put in is very advanced and acts like it knows exactly what we are doing and anticipating our next move. It is almost like he embedded AI, Artificial Intelligence, within the system."

"Can you estimate how much longer before we take him down?"

"No, I can't; but if I were to guess, I would say in the next twelve hours," Dusty replied and then said. "I need to get back to work, let the commander know we are doing our best."

"I will and thank you," Wiggins said. He then turned away from Dusty and left the computer room.

Meanwhile, down the hall, Major Amanda Sorenson was on the phone with President Mitchell again, keeping him up-to-date as to what was happening.

"Yes sir, we are doing everything we can to get the country back up and online again. Yes sir, I have our best people on it and they are working twenty-four, seven." After pausing to listen, Sorenson said, "Okay sir, will do; goodbye." She hung up the phone and said to herself, *'Holy crap, we need to get this shit fixed now.'* A knock at her door brought her out of her thought process. "Come in," she yelled.

"Sorry to bother you, Major; I have a status update for you," Master Sergeant Wiggins said as he entered the office.

"What have you got, Todd?" she asked.

Wiggins gave a short brief of what he had learned from Dusty just a few minutes ago.

"Let me bring you up to date. All hell has broken loose in Washington. The President is about to declare Martial Law; the Koreans have already started their attacks. The Supreme Court Building has been damaged, six dead and several injured in an explosion. There was an attempted attack on the Hoover Dam, which failed; and he has all the military on high alert, called up the Reserves and National Guard to protect the country. The FBI got wind of several targets, and they were able to stop them before any damage was done. Mitchell told me that one of the captured terrorists, all Korean of course, let slip that one of the targets is located on the west coast of Florida, possibly us!" Spooky stated. She then leaned over, and with her elbows on her desk, she covered her face. She was almost in tears, but held them back as best as she could.

"Okay, we can handle this; the 82nd Airborne is patrolling the base; four Swat teams are on rotation along with the normal guards and their dogs at the gates. We will be fine, Amanda. We will be fine," Wiggins commented, paused for a few seconds and then continued, "I will alert the team and our protectors. Would you like me to issue weapons?"

"No weapons yet, but don't get too far from the arms room. You have your key I presume," Amanda ordered and Wiggins shook his head in agreement. "Good, I have mine; so if we are under attack, one of us needs to get to the Arms Room as quickly as possible. Now you probably need to get back to work; I have a few things to discuss with the base commander. Get out of here, Todd," she said affectionately. They had known each other for almost eighteen years, having served together as young enlisted troops on various assignments. Sorenson decided to apply for Office Candidate School and was approved. After a few years, she moved up in rank and soon got her own command with Wiggins as a platoon Sergeant of a Military Intelligence company. They had been together on every assignment since. When the assignment to join the newly formed Cyber Command came up, she was asked to join and work as a shift supervisor with a direct line to taking command of the unit when Lieutenant Colonel Franks retired in two years. She was the senior shift supervisor within the group and would get the command job when it became available. Her only stipulation was for Sergeant First Class Todd Wiggins to be transferred in as her NCOIC. He came on board and received his promotion to Master Sergeant shortly after his arrival to McDill Air Force Base, eight months earlier. As a career soldier with sixteen months twelve days and a few hours to go before he could retire, this duty station with the Major was the ideal place to end his career. He recently purchased a used forty-five foot fishing boat and was in the process of rebuilding the engines and getting her sea ready. Another month and the 'Running Wild' would be ready for him to get some fish.

Chapter 29 White House Blues

"This is ridiculous! I am the President of the United States, the most powerful nation on the planet, and we are down here in the basement hiding like rats. I am NOT going to let a bunch of threats from Korea or any other country run me out of the White House. Let's go back upstairs. I will run this country from the Oval Office, not down here. If there is an imminent threat on the White House, then I will come back down here. I don't give a damn who is threatening our country; I need to be up there," President Mitchell said to his Director of Secret Service White House Division.

"Okay, sir, if you insist. I don't believe it is wise to put yourself in harm's way, but you are the President. I will notify security that we are moving back upstairs. Give me ten minutes," Doug Williams agreed and asked for a few minutes to get things in motion. "What about your support, do you want them to return to the surface?" Williams asked.

"You have five," Mitchell said with a smile. "Give them the option, but I am going up." Within minutes, President Mitchell and his security team were moving toward the train to take them back to the elevator that would bring them up under the White House. Twenty-five minutes later, President Mitchell was moving behind his desk in the Oval Office.

"Feels much better up here; I am sure you have increased security around here. I like looking out the windows at the snow, isn't it beautiful, Tony. Where is Tony?" Mitchell suddenly asked as he looked around and did not see his National Security Advisor anywhere.

"Yes, sir, I have doubled security. We also brought in a special team to assist," Doug Williams commented.

"Special Team, do I really want to know what they are specialized in?"

"No sir, you don't," Williams said with a smile.

"Understand; get CIA, FBI, NSA and Sanford in here as soon as possible. I want a meeting with them, and yeah, Homeland Security too, in forty-five minutes, in the Situation room."

"You got it sir," Williams agreed.

Exactly forty-three minutes later, President Mitchell stood up and started for the Situation room. He was concerned about the attack on the Supreme Court Building and Hoover

Dam, but he was confident that his people would prevail and beat the threat back into the Stone Age.

At forty-five minutes from when he requested the meeting, he walked into the Situation room. "Lady and gentlemen, thank you for coming on such short notice. We have a lot to talk about and little time and some serious decisions to make before we leave this room. Before we start, does anyone need to use the rest room, get a drink or have a question or two?"

"Yes sir, I have a question," John Ramsey, Director of Homeland Security said, waiting for an acknowledgement to continue. After getting a nod from the President, he began, "Before I ask my question I would like to make a statement, in defense of Homeland."

"Not required John. We are all working under extreme pressure and sometimes we miss things, but in this case, you did not miss anything," Mitchell commented.

"Thank you sir, I appreciate your vote of confidence."

"That was not a vote for confidence, John," Mitchell retorted.

"Thanks anyway, sir. My question, yes. Okay, my question is, have you any idea who is behind these threats and attacks; we don't over at Homeland."

"Yes I do. Well, we do. That is why you three are here. Ms. Peterson and Mr. Sanford have been tracking these terrorists, yes, terrorists. The Koreans are leading the attacks along with a small terrorist group located in the desert in Iran. Ms. Peterson's group located them. And we eliminated them!"

"You did what?" Ramsey yelled across the room.

"Who eliminated them?" Harvey Stewart, Assistant Director of Homeland Security asked.

"We launched two fully armed drones from the carrier George H.W. Bush sitting in the Med. Along with a British commando team and Seal Team Six, we destroyed the camp and everyone in it. We have a confirmed kill of one hundred forty-eight ISIS terrorists and no friendly injured. We also have four FA/18s on deck fully loaded and ready to launch at a moment's notice to push back any retaliation from the Iranian government. There are also four in the air, fully loaded, and depending on the go time will determine which team goes in," Ashley confirmed.

"We eliminated the entire camp, and then sent in ground forces to ensure total destruction. We kept SecDef (Secretary of Defense) in the loop. The British were fully agreeable to the plan, and volunteered to lead, which we allowed them to do," Mitchell commented and then paused for a minute to collect his thoughts.

"Yes, he did," the Secretary of Defense said from the back of the room.

"That could mean war with Iran and possibly the entire middle east," Ramsey commented.

"We will deal with that when and if it comes," Mitchell said and then continued, "Moving on to the Korean problem. I have been in contact with Cyber Command at McDill and they assure me they are almost finished with getting the country back up and running. It should be done within the next twelve hours, plus or minus. They are also working on locating the individual or team that has created the outages on the west coast."

"What are we going to do about the Koreans?" Harvey asked, knowing full well it was out of his authority to do anything overseas.

"That is where Ms. Peterson comes into play again. But we are going to try to handle this diplomatically first; if that doesn't work, we go in and take them out," Mitchell stated, pausing for a breath before he continued, thinking of the outcome and then added, "Or have local forces handle it."

"How are we going to do that without causing another war?" Eric Fredericks, Director of NSA asked.

"We are in essence at war with Korea and Iran right now; we haven't sent in troops or launched any missiles, but we are at war. They have attacked us, and it is time we stopped this madness. If we don't stop it now, we will have every country in the world who hates us coming over here and declaring war on us. With all this and the trouble with illegal aliens coming across the borders by the thousands, we need to stop it NOW!"

The room went completely silent with the President's statement. After a couple of strained seconds, Mitchell calmed down and spoke again. "What I am about to order goes against an earlier administration that wanted to give amnesty to all the illegal aliens in our country. I am extremely happy that did not happen; and he was defeated because of his insanely crazy vote getting attitude, and attitude toward the destruction of our country. Effective immediately, I am signing an Executive Order to initiate *Martial Law*. I want records checked on all suspected aliens, no matter what country they are from; if they are in this country illegally, they are to be arrested and shipped back to their country immediately. Yes, it will cost millions; but it is already costing millions in welfare, hospitalization of illegal's and everything we are paying out to house them. Close the borders, anyone crossing illegally will be arrested and returned. If they resist, they go to jail, tents if we have to. Re-instate internment camps like they did in World War II."

"The cost will be outrageous; where will the money come from?" Homeland Security John Ramsey asked, looking around the room at the other key members of the counsel.

"Effective immediately, we provide foreign aid to only the countries that are stricken with a disaster. That alone will provide us with several billion dollars to do this; it is about time we cleaned up our country. Tony and John, you two will make this happen; handle your respective areas and I will take the flack. Tony, I also need you to set up a press conference to be held at six tonight, so I can tell the nation what is going on. By then Cyber Command should have the west coast back up online, so they will know what is going on."

"Don't you need Congressional approval for this?" Fredericks said and then added, "That will most likely kill any chance you will have for a second term," Fredericks commented off-handedly.

"I don't give a damn about re-election; and as for Congress, they will approve. I have already had several discussions with leading members and they are in full agreement. I, we, need to save this country or there will be no need for any elections," Mitchell said with no passion but a lot of conviction. The seriousness of his statements hit home on all that were present. They all knew the country was in trouble and needed a fix and quickly. The United States of America was on fire and burning, and now Darrell Mitchell was the man that was going to fix it or die trying.

Chapter 30 Is There a Doctor in the House?

Six hours after Doctor Holms took off from Dulles International Airport, he was scrubbing up in the City Hospital of Mexico City. He had read the diagnostic for Davin and it didn't look good. But he was considered the best in his line of business, and he had hopes he would be able to save this man.

"Doctor Holms, I am Nurse Margarita Sanchez; I will be assisting you during the operation. Is there anything special you need for me to do during the operation?"

"No, just make sure I have clean instruments and hand them to me without question; this is a very tricky operation and if we are to save this man I have to be quick and clean. I should be in his head for no more than twenty minutes, at which time he will either be repaired or dead. I won't know how much damage he has until I open him up. Now let's get in there, we have a man to save," Doctor Holms said and then headed into the operating room.

The operation started off well, but instead of taking less than an hour, the doctor finally completed four and half hours later; he and his nurse were wet with sweat. They walked out of the operating room on weak legs and Holm turned to Margarita and said. "Ms. Sanchez, if you ever want a job at Walter Reed Hospital just say the word; I will hire you in a second. You are an excellent nurse." "Thank you, I will consider that," Margarita said and then walked off to the ladies room to freshen up.

Doctor Holms walked into the waiting room to meet Stephanie. As he entered, she stood and he greeted them with, "Mr. and Mrs. Randal, I presume." "Actually, no, I am Stephanie Randal and this is Police Commander Hector Rodriguez," Stephanie replied.

"Sorry it took so long Mrs. Randal, but it was more complicated than I thought before I went in. Mr. Pierce is in recovery, and with luck, he will fully recover. We will not know completely, until he wakes up. He is one very lucky man, would have killed a normal man. We will let you know when he is awake; until then get some dinner and a drink or two. He will be out for at least three hours. I am going to change and have some dinner," Doctor Holms said and then turned to leave, but stopped.

"What is it doc?" Stephanie asked.

"I noticed he had sustained a head wound some time ago. Can you tell me about it?"

"You know who he works for; well, things happen at times. That time, he and Josh, my husband, were in Viet Nam on a flight together; they took fire, small arms only, but still deadly. The bird took about fifty hits. The co-pilot took a round in the hip that grounded him for a while, but he was back in the air inside a month. But Davin wasn't so lucky; a bullet ricocheted off some of their electronic gear and entered the left side of his helmet. It did not enter his head, but it blew a small hole as it entered the helmet and blew off the back of the helmet, took off part of his ear, and scraped his head. They did a fast exit from the area and made it back to base without crashing. The ground crew said they were very lucky; the fuel cell had been punctured and was spilling fuel all the way home. They had the right engine out and the other was about to starve for lack of fuel."

"Wow, lucky, what were they flying?"

"Army classification is RU-21A, modified Beechcraft Queen Air, used as an Airborne Radio Direction Finding bird, ARDF for short."

"Yeah, I have seen those; they have one over at Ft. Meade on display. Interesting birds, no weapons, just fly into harm's way and pray. You know a lot about what happened, they must have told you the story many times."

"Yes, they did. Back then they were young, gutsy and very stupid at times. They had a job to do and did it; lost some good friends over there, but they were lucky I guess," Stephanie said. As she reached out and shook the doctor's outstretched hand she said, "Thank you."

"No, thank them for their service; I will make sure Mr. Pierce gets through this and makes a full recovery. Now get some dinner. They have a meal being prepared for me in the doctors' lounge and a cot on which to take a nap; now go, I will see you in a couple of hours."

"Let's go, Mrs. Randal, there is a nice little cafe just across the street and there is a beer with my name on it in there, maybe two," Hector said

"Right behind you, Hector," she said smiling for the first time today, knowing her friend would recover.

They left the hospital and walked down the street to the café. Being tired and with the streets crowded, they did not notice the young couple keeping an eye on them. The man and woman also entered the café, and took a table across the room from Hector and Stephanie, both acting like young lovers but keeping a close eye on them. After two beers, Hector noticed the two were eyeing them and quietly mentioned to Stephanie that they were being watched. He did not know if they were good guys or bad, so he told her that he was going to the restroom to get a closer look, since the couple sat near the hall to the restrooms.

Minutes later, Hector returned and sat, ordered a third beer, and quietly spoke to Stephanie.

"Ms. Randal, the young gentlemen is armed, could not tell if he was policia or not; he is not one of mine. She, well, she could be armed but not sure where she would have it, since she is only wearing a mini skirt and that light blouse; it is baggy so she may have something small on her back, I could not tell for sure. But, in any case, we need to finish our dinner and just keep an eye on them too; hopefully they are good guys just covering our back."

"Thank you for letting me escort you to dinner. With Josh gone, you really looked like you needed a friend. If they leave when we do, I will confront them and see what they are up to," Hector said between bites.

"That could be dangerous, Hector."

"I have back-up."

"Where?"

"You; I understand you are a trained agent, and I do hope you have your side arm," Hector stated then took another bite of his steak.

"Yes, I have it," she stated. "Nine millimeter Berretta PX4 Storm Compact."

"Good weapon," Hector commented. "Let's see if they follow us when we are done."

Twenty minutes later, they finished their dinners. Hector paid the bill, stood, walked out the door, and started down the sidewalk heading to the hospital. Without being too obvious, Hector glanced over his shoulder when they stopped at the corner as if looking for traffic. What he saw was the young couple walking out of the restaurant holding hands.

"We have a problem, they are following us," Hector commented.

"No, we don't," Stephanie said as she turned and started walking toward the young couple. When she was within ten feet of them with her hand on her gun, she called to them and asked, "Excuse me, you look familiar, do I know you? My name is Stephanie Randal and you are?"

"I'm John Hough and this is my partner Cindy Andrews. I guess you are wondering why we have been following you."

"Well, yeah."

"We work for Ashley Peterson and have been tasked to back you up," John said as he pulled out his credentials and handed them to Stephanie. Sorry for not introducing ourselves to you earlier, but we were asked to be covert. Guess we blew that part."

"Just a bit, John. Come on, I want you to meet Hector, the chief of police here in Mexico City."

Chapter 31 Out in the Cold

In 1776, a group of men sat around a table and signed a document that formed the United States of America. Now the country was on the verge of being torn apart by terrorists. Terrorists had learned that technology came in many forms, from weapons of mass destruction to the use of the computer to cause havoc and destruction with and without killing a single soul. The use of the computer and the Internet had allowed the smallest underfunded country to become a mini super power that could reach any nation on the planet to cause destruction of their infrastructure without firing a shot or putting troops on the ground.

"Wiggins, we have another problem," Dusty yelled across the room to her NCOIC of Cyber Command.

"What is it now, Lieutenant?" Wiggins asked as he rushed over to Dusty from his desk.

"Hell just froze over."

"What do you mean?" Wiggins asked as he looked over her shoulder at the screen of her computer.

"The entire west coast from the Mississippi has gone cold and we can't get it back. All indications are that several power plants have gone cold."

"Nuclear or coal burning?"

"Two nuclear and three coal burning. There are indications that more are about to crash; it could take weeks to get them back online. One nuclear plant had a meltdown, the area has been evacuated, but reported eighty-six dead and at least six hundred injured."

"Hell, I need to inform the commander," Wiggins said and rushed out of the bull pen.

"Savage, I do believe the country is in deep shit," Dusty commented as she turned back to her computer.

Ten minutes later, Master Sergeant Wiggins was standing in front of Major Amanda 'Spooky' Sorenson. He was explaining what had just happened. She held up a finger for him to stop talking and picked up her phone and dialed the direct line to the White House. She waited for a couple of seconds before the line was answered.

"Sir, this is Major Sorenson, U.S. Air Force Cyber Command Shift Supervisor, again. I have some news for the President."

"This is Tony Sanford, National Security Advisor, you can tell me; President Mitchell is tied up at the moment," Tony commented. "I will pass it on."

After briefing the NSA, she waited for Tony to ask questions which he did not, and only said, "Major, let me know if anything else comes up. I will get back to you as soon as the President is briefed. Thank you," he said and then hung up the phone.

"Todd, keep me posted, also arm all the troops. I believe we are at war. And as you say 'Hell has frozen over' and we are in deep."

As he walked back to the bull pen, Tony stopped at the men's room and splashed cold water on his face. This day was not going well, and he felt it was not going to get any better.

****

Hector Rodriguez, Director of Policia Federal Ministerial sat quietly at his desk at Policia Headquarters. He had heard that a specialist had arrived in Mexico City to operate on Davin Pierce and see if he could save the man. Hector was concerned, he loved America as much as he loved his own country, and he did not tolerate crime, death or destruction of either country. His job was to protect his people and all visitors to his country; he felt he had failed in light of the current situation. Mr. Pierce was severely injured on his watch, and he had a terrorist running around his country causing more death and destruction.

"Director, the United States is under attack, and our President has asked for us to increase security around all the government buildings and hospitals. Do you want me to call in the off duty officers?" Hector's chief of detectives announced and asked as he entered his office.

"Yes and send in Jose, I need to talk to him."

"Yes sir," he said and then left the office to get Jose. He knew exactly which Jose to get, as Jose was the most common name in Mexico and there were at least eight in the station house at any given time. The Jose that was requested was the station's most qualified SWAT team sniper with eight years experience in SWAT. He had trained at the U.S. Marine sniper school and graduated with the second highest score in the school. He was a cool calm sniper that knew how to get the job done quickly. Between graduation and returning to his home country, he had over seventy confirmed kills. Since returning to Mexico, he was adding to that number all members of the drug cartels that plagued his country.

Minutes later, Jose stepped into the office. "You wanted to see me sir?"

"I do, please sit down; I will be right with you," Hector said and then continued typing on his computer; moments later he finished, hit send and then looked up at Jose. "Okay, we have a terrorist on our soil and it is our job to find him and, well, we need to remove him from the earth if we can. I need you to work with me to do this. Are you up to the task?"

"Director, I am up for it, where do we start?"

"Back at the warehouse, we leave in ten minutes, bring your best rifle," Hector said referring to Jose's sniper rifle, one of the newer automatic Barrett fifty caliber rifles with a high powered infrared scope and ten round magazines. Jose was the best sniper under Hector's command. Hector used Jose as often as possible when the opportunity presented itself to be able to remove a known drug lord or at least one or two of their lieutenants.

"Do you think we will need it?"

"Yes, Jose I do believe given the opportunity we will need it. Now go and prepare; we leave in eight minutes. Bring plenty of ammunition," Hector said and returned to writing his daily report on his computer. He paused and looked carefully at the phone on his desk; he needed to find out. Slowly he reached over and picked up the handset. He dialed the number for the hospital and then waited for someone to answer. After a moment, he heard a voice. "Yes this is Hector Rodriguez Chief of Policia, and may I speak to someone about Mr. Davin Pierce... yes I will hold, thank you."

A minute or two later, a voice came online and asked if she could help.

"Yes, as I told the young lady that answered, I am Hector Rodriguez, Chief of Policia and I just wanted to find out the status of Mr. Davin Pierce." He listened to the nurse and said, "Thank you," before hanging up the hand set. He stood, and picked up his weapon. As he started to walk out of his office, he said, "Come Jose, we need to go."

Chapter 32 Cyber War Turns Hot

At four fifteen in the afternoon, the skies were cloudy and it looked like it would rain any second. The temperature tipped the mercury at sixty-eight degrees Fahrenheit; the humidity was fifty percent and the skies were clear at McDill Air Force Base, on the west coast of Florida. The guards, sweating under the weight of their full combat gear, were on high alert.

Picking up the phone at the main gate guard shack, the young Corporal said, "Front Gate, Corporal Sher..." He collapsed on the table as the bullet penetrated his head just below his helmet. The guard standing outside the shack fell a second later as a bullet hit him in his chest; he fell backward into the door of the guard shack. Three patrolling guards saw their buddies fall and immediately took cover and trained their weapons at the front gate, expecting more fire or something to penetrate the gate. One got up and started to run toward the guard shack, but was shot and fell well short of the gate. They did not have to wait long. An RPG was fired and slammed into the parked Humvees which the guards used for motorized patrol; seconds later, a large dump truck barreled through the gate led by a Humvee and the guards opened fire on it. Two more vehicles raced behind the dump truck using it as cover; the passengers of the vehicles were firing automatic weapons at the soldiers inside the base. The soldiers guarding McDill Air Force Base opened fire on the charging vehicles with deadly accuracy, but were unable to stop them from entering the base.

"This is Sergeant Morris, one hundred feet from the main gate; we are under attack," he yelled into his hand held radio to his commander.

Reinforcements started racing toward the gate; some never made it because a passenger of the attacking force fired an RPG into the leading Humvees, killed four soldiers and blocked the road. Seconds later, the dump truck slammed into the Humvee, and pushed it out of the way so the remaining terrorist vehicles could race past.

"We have a breach at the main gate. We have men down, need medics," Sergeant of the Guard reported to his commander as he returned fire on the invaders. "They are driving armored vehicles and a dump truck; looks like they are headed for the flight line. We were not able to stop them."

It was about a mile and a half to the flight line from the main gate. This route passed the Base Exchange, commissary, gym and barracks of the airmen. As they raced past these areas, the gunners in the two armored vehicles opened fire on anyone they saw using AK-47s and machine guns, killing or wounding several more airman and soldiers as they raced past. As they approached the flight line, they turned abruptly to the right and raced toward the building that housed Cyber Command, their target. The dump truck was full of high explosives; this was a suicide mission for the driver and possibly for the invaders in the armored vehicles. Four hundred yards from the building, the rear armored vehicle exploded when it was hit by a M203 grenade fired by a base defender as the vehicle passed by his position. He reloaded and fired again, but the grenade fell short of its target. Three invaders were in the vehicle; two died instantly and the third was severely injured and trapped inside the burning vehicle. Four soldiers ran to the vehicle with weapons ready to fire if need be, while two soldiers kept their weapons trained on the sole survivor while the other two pulled her out. She was dressed in black combat gear, flak vest, and a side arm, looking very much like the same uniform worn by the base SWAT team. The terrorists in the lead Humvee continued toward Cyber Command firing at anyone with or without a weapon.

"They are heading for Building 16A, we can't let them get there; stop at all costs," Major John Maxwell yelled into his radio. He switched channels, called the guard in building 16A, and yelled "Evacuate the building!"

Building 16A received the evacuate order and immediately sounded the alarm. The two hundred and twenty occupants of the building heard the alarm, quickly got up, and ran for the exits. It would take less than a minute to get everyone out and clear of the building, but they did not have a minute.

About two hundred and fifty yards from Building 16A, the dump truck started to accelerate. It raced at over seventy miles per hour directly at Building 16A. One hundred and seventy five yards from the building, a Humvee that was racing on a diagonal road slammed into the lead armored vehicle at sixty miles per hour, pushed it into the curb and broke its front axle, almost flipping it over. Seconds later, eight soldiers surrounded the vehicle and ordered the occupants to get out. As the driver's door opened, instead of a person climbing out, a hand grenade was thrown out.

"Grenade!" yelled three of the soldiers at the same time, and everyone dove to the ground as the grenade exploded. In the confusion, the occupants of the vehicle jumped out and started shooting at the soldiers. The firefight did not last long. The return fire covered the attackers, killing two of them instantly, and the third a few seconds later, but not before he pulled the pin to another grenade and tossed it into the vehicle. The resulting explosion killed four of the soldiers and wounded two more.

The dump truck broke through the first ten foot high security fence which was fifteen yards from the building, and then went through the secondary fence at ten yards without stopping. The dump truck was almost to Building 16A, closing within five yards, and then down to five feet. The driver was slumped over the wheel bleeding from multiple wounds, but determined to get to his final destination. Smiling, the driver pushed the button to detonate his cargo which exploded about five feet from the side of the building. The resulting fire ball and concussion engulfed the front of the building. It reached over two hundred feet into the air and outward over seventy-five feet in all directions; the destruction of the building was complete. Even though the building was constructed of reinforced concrete, the walls fell like dominos crushing those inside that did not get out in time.

The invaders' mission was a success in destroying Cyber Command. The total killed exceeded one hundred fifty and more than two hundred injured in the attack. It was only by sheer luck that most of the Cyber Warriors were able to escape serious injury by evacuating the building just seconds before the explosion.

All of the attackers were killed except one injured female who was now in the custody of the Military Police and being treated for her injuries. She was not talking, but it was very obvious she was of Korean nationality and well trained in her mission. Medical teams were treating the injured all along the route the attackers had taken.

"Are you okay, Major?" Sergeant Wiggins asked as he walked over to the Major kneeling beside 2nd Lieutenant Jessica 'Dusty' Moore lying on the grass. She was bleeding in more places than could be counted, but alive. Her hair, which was normally blonde and curly, was covered in black and burned. The medics were working as quickly as they could to stop the bleeding.

"I'm fine Todd; Dusty is not doing well. She was pretty close to the blast zone, and the medics say she will live, but they need to get her to the hospital, " Major Spooky Sorenson stated. "Did everyone make it out?"

"No, we lost four technicians, several administration are not accounted for and three guards are confirmed dead, not sure on a couple of others. I have not located them yet," Wiggins reported.

"Todd you are bleeding, get that arm looked at."

"I will be fine; right after I account for everyone, I will find a medic to look at it," Wiggins agreed, as he dabbed some blood off of her forehead and handed her the cloth he had gotten from a medic moments before. He then turned and started to walk away; pausing for a second, he turned, looked at his commander, and asked, "What the hell is going on?"

"I think we pissed off someone, and they are turning up the heat on us. But this is America, and we will not be beaten down like this. We are now in a war, and they, whoever they are, have just kicked the sleeping lion."

"I think Admiral Yamamoto said something like that on December 7th, 1941."

"Yes he did," she agreed, turned her attention back to Dusty and watched as the medic prepared her for transport in the ambulance that had just arrived.

Chapter 33 Retaliation

"Mr. President, Cyber Command has been attacked and the building destroyed," National Security Advisor Tony Sanford said as he rushed into the Oval office.

"When, how?" exclaimed the President.

"We got a call from Major Sorenson as it was happening; she could not say much because they were evacuating the building. The base commander just got off the phone with me and informed me that over one hundred fifty were killed and they have more than two hundred injured. One of the invaders was captured alive; all attackers were Korean except for three who were Middle Eastern. He will get back to us as soon as they have more information. Cyber Command is down; several of the team were killed and others injured, but for now Cyber Command is out of business."

"Has the terrorist talked, where are they from, who is backing their team?" President Mitchell asked and then paused for a second with a blank stare on his face. He finally shook his head and continued, "Call an emergency meeting of Congress, but first get all the usual suspects in the Situation Room, in thirty minutes. Congress needs to be in session in two hours; we are looking at a continuation of hostilities, and I need support from the country. We meet in the basement Situation Room for security."

Twenty-five minutes later, President Mitchell walked into the Situation Room, not looking very happy about what was about to be discussed. "Gentlemen and Ladies, we have a situation that has escalated this war. I have called an emergency session for Congress to meet in just over an hour. McDill Air Force Base has been attacked; we have many dead and wounded. Mr. Sanford, have you talked with the base commander again?"

"Yes, the female captive is North Korean and part of a sleeper cell that was activated; she is willing to tell all for a deal. Not sure what kind of deal, but a deal none the less; and as I said earlier, there were three Middle easterners in the group also," Sanford said, "We are going to talk again in a half hour."

"Okay, if the North Koreans are behind this, they need to pay. Mr. Sanford get the North Korean Prime Minister on the line; I want to speak with him now. I am giving them one option, stop the attacks or we will."

"Yes, sir," Sanford said and reached for the phone. He dialed the international number for the Prime Minister of North Korea.

"Mr. President, what is your plan, the country is already in a shambles and with martial law in place we should be able to control movement of foreign nationals around the country?" General 'Hard Nose' Johnson asked.

"My plan is as it has always been; defend the Constitution, the Country and protect the citizens to the best of my ability. As I ordered several hours ago, arrest and confine all illegal aliens and suspected terrorists, deport them as quickly as possible or confine in internment camps. We have been attacked by various factions that hate us, have a grudge, or are following orders from their government. In any case, they are our enemies and have severely damaged our country. My plan is to talk to the Prime Minister of North Korea; and if he is behind some of these attacks, we will retaliate in kind. Rest assured, when we attack, the military commanders on the ground will have one order and one order only."

"Give the order, sir," General Johnson requested.

"In time, General; first I need to talk to the Prime Minister. Mr. Sanford, do you have him online yet?"

"Yes sir," Sanford acknowledged, and passed the hand set to Mitchell.

Mitchell turned and spoke on the phone, keeping his voice down on an even tone. After speaking for a few minutes and listening about ten minutes, he hung up the phone, shook his head and then turned back toward his advisors.

"Well, what did he say?" Sanford asked.

"You really don't want to know, but I guess I have to tell you. Listen up everyone," Mitchell said quietly. "Ladies and Gentlemen, I have just been informed by the new Prime Minister of North Korea that they have had a coup and the former Prime Minister, who has been missing for a month has been found and killed along with most of his cabinet and family. And, yes, the previous regime had declared war on us, and set multiple sleeper cells into motion to attack and destroy key elements of our country, starting with the total destruction of Cyber Command. She told me that they would continue to attack our country until we surrendered. Which we will NEVER do! We are at WAR! A war has been declared against us and now we need to retaliate immediately."

"Wholly crap," General Johnson said before anyone else said anything. Everyone started to talk with each other attempting to solve the problem but only making a lot of noise. "Did you say she?"

"Quiet, let me speak, remember I am the President, at least for now, and yes, I said she." After the room quieted down, President Mitchell spoke in his normally quiet yet strong voice, "Generals and Admirals, I want you to put together a comprehensive battle plan and have it on my desk in three hours. I am going to Congress to tell them what has transpired and that you are putting together the battle plan. Alert your troops and sailors that we are at DEFCON 3; we are at war and need to prepare for battle. Admirals, have the Pacific fleet move into striking range of North Korea. Generals alert South Korea Command of an imminent attack."

"Are we cleared for nuclear, if need be?" the General asked, knowing full well that DEFCON 3 did not mean nuclear.

"No, but be prepared," Mitchell said without any remorse.

Chapter 34 Aerial Cat Fight

At the Mexico International Airport, the skies were cloudy with rain over the mountains, and the wind blew hot at about four knots out of the southwest. It was a typical day at Mexico's busiest airport. At the general aviation terminal across from the main terminal sat a new Gulfstream VI with the engines spooling up and the air stair door still open. The pilots were preparing for an immediate departure, as soon as their passengers arrived; they were running late, but the call he just received informed him they should be there in the next five minutes. Glancing out the cockpit window, the copilot saw two SUVs come through the gate and stop just beyond the wing tip.

"They are here, Captain," the copilot said and then stood and turned toward the cabin to inform the cabin steward. "Prepare the cabin; we lift off in five minutes."

"Almost ready, just need to put away their luggage and secure the door once they board," the steward replied.

"Welcome aboard," the copilot said in greeting the three gentlemen and two women as they climbed the stairs. Neither woman said a word as they entered the cabin and neither looked very happy.

"We need to take off immediately," the first gentleman said in English and then turned to the man following him and in German said, "Strap them in mid-cabin and keep an eye on them."

"As soon as we close the door, we are ready to leave; please take a seat and fasten your seat belt," the copilot said and then turned back toward the cockpit.

"Would anyone care for a drink before we leave?" the cabin steward asked.

"Yes, beer, German, if you have one," the leader responded, the other two declined a drink, but the girl raised her hand.

"What would you like, ladies?"

"Water, please," the youngest one said in a very quiet voice and the other just raised her hand up and showed one finger to indicate she wanted one also.

"We will be departing momentarily. I will be right back, please take your seats," the cabin steward said as she turned, walked over and secured the door. She then headed into the galley to prepare the requested drinks. As the Gulfstream started its taxi to the runway, she passed out the drinks and then took her seat in the front of the cabin.

"Gulfstream 849er cleared as filed, hold at intersection. Landing traffic on intersecting runway...." After a moment's pause, the air traffic controller continued, "Gulfstream 849er cleared for takeoff; maintain runway heading until reaching five thousand, turn right to intersect airway, climb to cruising altitude. Contact departure on 119.55 after reaching five thousand. Have a good flight."

"Gulfstream 849 rolling, cleared as filed, turn right at five thousand to intersect airway, climb to cruising altitude of Flight Level 42. Thank you, have a good day."

The Gulfstream took off without any problems and started its flight to Berlin with a short stop in Nassau, Bahamas for fuel. Hans Bormann sat in the overstuffed chair sipping his cold beer, smiling at the fact that they had gotten away from Mexico City without being stopped. Looking over his shoulder at his two assistants and the young Tara Mitchell, President Mitchell's daughter, he smiled again. He knew that he had been able to kill a CIA agent that was following him and get clean away; well almost, he had to kill several Mexican police. His prizes were the two beautiful ladies in the back of the plane, Connie Pierce, FBI agent and Tara Mitchell, the President's only daughter. They would be great bargaining chips for his boss, Gregory Dietrich.

Just as the Gulfstream passed through one thousand feet, back at the airport four black SUVs screamed through the gate and braked beside the first two. Eight heavily armed men and one woman jumped out and raced over to the parked SUVs, weapons ready, "Out of the vehicles now!" yelled the SWAT commander in Spanish and then again in English. There was no response, nobody exited the SUVs. Cautiously, they approached the lead SUV, pulled open the door, and found it empty. He ordered another member to check the second vehicle, also finding it empty.

"Damn, we are too late," the commander stated the obvious and then looked down the runway and up into the sky to see the contrail of a departing jet fade into the overhanging clouds.

Fifteen minutes later, the commander saw four unfamiliar aircraft approach and land, immediately taxi to the General Aviation ramp, and shut down. Shaking his head in disbelief, he started to walk over to the aircraft. As he got closer, he recognized them as being FA/18 Fighters with United States markings. Confused he continued walking toward them; moments later, he heard the approach of a helicopter coming from the city.

"Good morning, sir. Sorry for the intrusion, but we are here to pick up some passengers. I am Lieutenant Commander Beckett. We will be leaving in a few minutes. I would appreciate it if your men would guard my aircraft until we leave."

"Hello Lieutenant Commander Beckett, I'm Commander Torres; strange we meet at the same time, is it possible we are here for the same reason?"

"I don't think so sir; we are here to pick up some passengers, why are you here?"

"We got a call to stop a business jet from departure that had a suspected terrorist on board; we got here too late, and they got away."

"No, but I believe that helo landing over there has our passengers. Would you please excuse me? We are pressed for time," Beckett said and then turned and walked toward the helo. Three passengers climbed out of the helo and ran over to the pilot.

"Mr. Randal, Polson and Ms. Miller, I am Lieutenant Commander Beckett; Ms. Ashley Peterson has asked us to get you in the air as quickly as possible and track the Gulfstream that departed this airport fifteen minutes ago. I will brief you as you get your flight suits on, come on let's move," Beckett stated as they started to walk toward the four waiting jets.

"Wow, Ms. Peterson has some pull with someone. I have never been in a fighter jet before," Miller commented as they walked over to the jets. Minutes later, they were handed flight suits and helmets and were being briefed on what to expect during the flight.

"They filed a flight plan for the Bahamas and then continuing on to Berlin. Ms. Peterson asked if we could divert them to GITMO, so that is the plan, but we need to get you three there before that can happen. Are you ready for the ride of your life?"

"Yes," all three said in unison. Within ten minutes, the four FA/18 fighter jets were climbing out of Mexican airspace and accelerating to one thousand one hundred miles per hour, nearly twice what the Gulfstream was able to attain, with a max speed of only six hundred ten miles per hour. Since the pilots of the Gulfstream would not fly at max speed to conserve fuel and extend the range, they would most likely average about five hundred miles per hour ground speed. That would allow the FA/18s to catch and pass them, arriving at GITMO well ahead of them.

****

In the National Security Agency war room, on a muggy wet afternoon, Warrant Officer Robert Kelsey sat at his desk reading reports and decrypted intercepts from the day. He suddenly stopped, picked up the previous intercept and re-read it. Then he put it down and read the new one he had just started reading. They were intercepts that gave the go ahead for an attack in the first intercept and the second gave a location, Washington D.C.

"Captain Hogan can you come over here? I need you to look at something," Kelsey yelled over to his section chief.

"Be right there, Kelsey."

Moments later Captain Hogan was reading both intercepts and could not believe what he read either. "This can't be; it's impossible."

"This can't be happening right now. It's not possible. Someone is yanking our chain real hard."

"We need more information on this, before I run it up the flag pole; we need conformation and need it now." Hogan stated, looking at the designators at the top of each page to see where they originated and quietly, in almost a whisper, he commented. "North Korea, McDill, and now the White House."

"If these are true, then we have to ... The base was just attacked a few hours ago and the date time stamp on these coincides with that attack," Kelsey stated. "All indications on those two confirm that there will be an attack on the White House within the hour, a nuclear attack. We have to warn the White House, now. There is no time to evacuate the entire city. Keep working, I am going upstairs to warn them."

Minutes later, Hogan was on the secure phone to the White House speaking with the Director of White House Security informing him of the intercept. What they did over there was up to them.

Chapter 35 Shoot the Messenger

Inbound, from the south, was a Delta 757 headed for Reagan International Airport. It was on schedule and had followed all the flight rules required to fly into an airport located very close to the no fly zone located around the Washington area. Air traffic around Washington D.C. was always crowded; but with traffic for Dulles International, Andrews Air Force Base, and Ronald Reagan airport, it kept Air Traffic Control (ATC) pretty busy. When there was bad weather such as rain, snow, or high winds, the controller's job intensified. Today was going to be one of those days with light snow, cold, and winds added to the complexity of their already busy jobs.

Between eighteen and twenty thousand feet over the city, there were four F-16 Fighting Falcons and two A-10 Warthogs fully armed for combat circling the city. They were providing added air cover, and ready to act on a moment's notice. They maintained radio silence with ATC, but continuously communicated with each other as each pair orbited in their assigned sector. It was twenty-seven degrees at ground level; but at altitudes above ground level, the temperature drops at a rate of two and one half to four degrees per one hundred feet, which made it pretty cold at twenty thousand feet. With all their heaters on max, each fighter pilot was attempting to stay warm and alert during what so far had turned out to be a very boring four hour mission. The light snow and cold caused some icing on the wings of their aircraft; but with the heated leading edge on the wings, they were able to handle that too. The cold was a bit harder to handle; with the heaters on maximum, it still was cold in the cockpit. They had about an hour to go before being relieved. All was quiet, each flight monitored ATC approach and tower frequencies, listening for anything that was out of normal parameters.

"Wildman, it is your turn to buy breakfast. I am in the mood for steak and eggs. How about you?" Captain Valerie 'Tinkerbell' Bell asked over their secure radio.

"Yeah, steak and eggs would be great. Just another fifty-five minutes until Bravo flight arrives; and damn, I am getting hungry," Wildman replied and then paused to listen to a new call from Reagan ATC.

"Delta 487, descend to eight thousand and turn right to zero two five degrees, airport is fifteen miles, weather is light snow, temp twenty-seven and light wind at four knots, two hundred seventy degrees, gusts to ten."

"Roger, Delta 487 descending to eight thousand and right to zero two five degrees, airport fifteen miles," replied the pilot.

Minutes after turning right, Delta 487 accelerated and continued to descend through eight thousand instead of leveling off at his assigned altitude. His new heading placed the airplane in a direct path to the White House.

"Delta 487 return eight thousand immediately, traffic at your one o'clock at six thousand," the air traffic controller ordered.

"Tinkerbell, I think we have a possible boogie. Stand by," Wildman said to his wingman as they listened to air traffic control.

"We will miss him," the pilot of Delta 487 commented to himself completely ignoring the air traffic controller. Delta 487 leveled off at four thousand five hundred feet and was still heading directly for the White House.

"Delta 487, climb immediately and return to course," he ordered again seeing the jumbo jet leveling off at four thousand five hundred feet with a direct heading toward downtown Washington and the White House. The controller did not wait to call again; he knew that the jet was not going to comply, and immediately placed a call for the already airborne fighter aircraft patrolling the Washington area to intercept and either shoot down or force the Delta 487 to leave restricted air space.

"Already on it ATC. Descending to intercept," Wildman replied to Reagan ATC. And then he switched over to the ATC frequency that the Delta flight was operating on. "Delta 487, this is U.S. Marine A-10 Major Simon ordering you to divert your flight out of restricted air space immediately or we will be forced to shoot you down," **Major 'Wildman' Simon ordered.**

"Air Force Fighter, Major Simon, go ahead and try," a snide remark came over the radio.

" Okay, if that is the way you wish to play it," Major Cory 'Wildman' Simon said to himself and then repositioned his A-10 to see inside the cockpit of the Jumbo jet and what he saw was not what he expected. There was nobody at the controls and sliding over closer he saw nobody in the windows of the passenger cabin.

"Tinkerbell, you're up," Major Simon ordered and immediately slid in behind the Delta aircraft. After keying his radio, he ordered his wingman to fire on the unmanned aircraft as he pulled up and away from the target.

"That thing crashing into the city could cause a lot of problems, sir. Do you wish me to fire, I have tone and lock," Tinkerbell acknowledged.

"Yes, fire."

"Firing!" Tinkerbell said as she pulled the trigger to launch her missiles.

Seconds later, two Sidewinder missiles were released from his wingman's A-10 and sped toward the target only to explode well short of their target. She fired two more just as Simon fired two from his aircraft. All four missiles homed in true, but exploded well before hitting their intended target.

"What the hell?" Simon yelled. "They have some kind of shield or something that is preventing our missiles from getting in, try guns Tinkerbell." Panic was obvious in his voice.

"Roger, Wildman," Captain Valerie 'Tinkerbell' Bell acknowledged, switching to her 30mm nose mounted mini gun and firing a short fifteen second burst which did penetrate the targets right wing causing the engine to flare but not to shut down. "Guns work. He is going down, looks like he is heading for the White House, only three miles out, Wildman. Firing again!" She fired another thirty second burst which ripped into the side of the target, but did not bring it down.

"Nice shooting, but not good enough. We are going in; say goodbye to your President," said a voice over the radio, just as Wildman opened up with his 30 mm mini gun and fired four more missiles at the same time. This time, the mini gun's rounds ripped into the cockpit and left engine; smoke started to pour out of the engine. One of the missiles hit the left wing and blew off twenty feet of wing, causing the target to pitch sharply to the left and go into a death dive. "No matter where we crash, our bomb will still destroy your city. Nice try flyboy. Have a nice day." With that, the radio went dead, and the target spun rapidly down to earth impacting on the mall in front of the Smithsonian Museum. Luckily, since there was Martial Law in effect, the mall was nearly empty; all the people that had been on the mall had run for cover upon seeing the aircraft spinning down. There was no nuclear explosion or an explosion of any size except for the total destruction of the airplane, plowing through the foot of snow that had accumulated on the ground.

"Reagan control, target is down, we need to RTB (Return to Base) to reload, our relief is inbound. The target was being flown remotely; there was nobody on board, at least nobody we could see. I think we just stopped an attack on the White House," Wildman reported to the Reagan Air Traffic Control (ATC).

"Thank you for your quick response. I have called emergency services and will notify the FAA for further instructions," ATC replied.

"We're outa here," Wildman commented.

Down on the mall, the excitement was just beginning. Emergency services were on the scene within minutes and what they found was scary.

"What the hell, no bodies, no luggage, seats or anything, nothing but a broken fuselage and several large crates," the first fireman on the scene reported to his Captain over the radio. "No need for medical services, you can send them home. This looks like one of those practice scenarios that we have to train on, nothing more."

"Is there a fire?" his Captain asked from the second truck to arrive but still several hundred feet away from the wreckage.

"A few patches, mostly fuel fires which we can handle quickly. We will have it under control in a few minutes. But nothing big…" After pausing for a moment, the fireman radioed back, "Whoa, sorry, something just exploded. Hang on a moment, I will be right back."

Five minutes later, the fireman called his chief again and reported, "Sir, the fire is out, the explosion was just some fuel that was trapped under the wing which ignited. We have also located several large crates in the fuselage and one of them has a timer on it and it is ticking, counting down. Looks like a bomb of some sort."

"Roger, I will call the bomb squad; you get everyone out of there," the Captain ordered.

"Roger that sir, we will be out in a minute."

Chapter 36 Made in Korea

The Washington D.C. Police Bomb Squad got to the crash site within minutes of being called, and stood looking at the large black box without really know what to do. The box was about the size of a coffin with hinges on one side and locks on the other three. There was a timer ticking away on the top; it showed forty-five minutes and seven seconds and was counting down. Three black SUVs pulled up to the curb and six heavily armed men jumped out and hurried over to the bomb squad.

"We will take it from here," Captain Jacob Gibson ordered the lead man as he flashed his credentials, showing he was assigned to the Nuclear Bomb Disposal team out of Fort Meade, to the lead bomb squad Sergeant.

"Normally I would argue the point, but I think this is bigger than our expertise. How did you get here so fast? We just got the call, and just got here."

"We are stationed close by just for things like this; thank you for responding quickly. Forty-three minutes and counting, let's open it up," the Captain ordered. His lead tech walked over, kneeled down beside the bomb, and inspected it closely.

"It's all yours, Captain," the Sergeant responded, and then said to his team, "Let's go boys, these guys can handle this better than us."

"Made in Korea, boss. This is not going to be an easy one, and time is running out," the tech responded.

"Can you disarm it?" Captain Gibson asked as he looked over his tech's shoulder.

"Honestly?" his tech replied shaking his head in disbelief. "What do you think, boss?"

"I think you need to disarm it and fast. That thing is still ticking and it is Korean which means they may not have gotten the clock to work accurately."

"Okay, hand me my bag, please," the tech said calmly, reaching back to take his tool from Gibson.

"Forty-one minutes, eighteen seconds and counting," Gibson stated in the radio he was holding up to his mouth. "Maybe you should evac the Eagle and his eaglets."

"All ready in the bunker," Doug Williams replied over the radio. "Keep me posted on progress; we are moving the rest of the staff now."

"Will do," Gibson responded.

****

"President Mitchell, the threat is real," announced Doug Williams as he burst into the underground Oval Office, seconds later.

"Has the staff been notified?" Mitchell asked as he stood behind his desk.

"Yes, and they are heading for the bunker; there is less than forty minutes on the clock," Sanford said as they headed for the door. President Mitchell stopped and turned. He looked back into the Oval Office, not knowing for sure if they would be able to disarm the nuclear bomb not more than a quarter mile from the White House.

"Sir, we are far enough away so you are safe here!" Sanford insisted. "Let's go to the Situation Room and monitor from there; we will be more comfortable."

The President entered the elevator along with four Secret Service agents and three staff members. Sanford pushed the B-9 button and watched as the door closed and the elevator started its rapid descent to B-9, one level below the underground Oval Office.

"Do you think they can disarm it before we lose half our city's population?" Mitchell asked to nobody in particular.

"I hope so," Williams replied.

Minutes later, they were exiting the elevator and started down the hall toward the Situation Room. Williams headed back up to the White House to coordinate with Gibson of the bomb squad.

If the bomb went off, the fall-out would spread all up and down the east coast for years. The yield of the device would determine the amount of physical destruction to the city and its population in the initial explosion; but the nuclear snow, also known as fall-out, would spread on the prevailing winds up and down the coast. They suspected the yield was more than three times that of the bombs that destroyed the Boston and Denver airports.

****

Down on the Mall, the bomb tech had just gotten the bomb case open and was checking to see if there was a possible trip switch on the hinge. The tension was so thick you could cut it with a knife, and a knife is all that the tech had in his hand as he ran it slowly around the hinge and opening of the bomb. Slowly he moved, not missing an inch on the case. After running completely around, he pulled the knife back, dropped it on the ground and reached over with both hands to lift the lid. "Boss a little hand please." They lifted the lid slowly in case of a trip wire, which there wasn't.

"Holy moly, Boss Man," the tech exclaimed. "This is some piece of junk."

"At least it doesn't look nuclear," Gibson sighed in relief.

"Yea, but there are enough explosives in here to level four, maybe six city blocks; this is the newest plastic explosive and not available except to the military, our military. How did they get their hands on this stuff?"

"We will figure that out after you disarm it," Gibson said.

"Right!"

The clock kept ticking down the minutes, twenty-five to go; when the tech finally said it was safe, the clock continued to tick, stopping at twenty minutes left.

"Boss, something's not right, this thing is putting off some serious rads!" one of the assistants stated as he was checking the area with the radiation detector. "Are you sure this thing is safe to move? I think we have a sleeper."

"What, Chad didn't you check the whole thing?" Gibson yelled at Chad as he was walking away with his tool kit.

"I didn't dig down in it, let me see," Chad said as he knelt down beside the case again and slowly lifted a few of the gray packets of plastic explosive. "Holy shit, Boss, you have to see this."

"We have a nuke. Damn," Gibson said, "Disarm it Chad, the clock is ticking, again."

"Forty-five seconds left on the timer, I don't have time to disarm. Boss, we are toast," the tech yelled as he stood up and backed away; he knew he could not out run a nuclear explosion. He turned and smiled at Gibson and said, "Looks like we go out with a bang, Boss."

"Three months before I can retire and I go out with a bang. Not the bang I wanted," Gibson replied as he stared at the nuclear bomb in front of him.

Chapter 37 Touch and Go

Room 356 in the Mexico City Trauma Hospital was quiet. The occupants were sitting quietly waiting for Davin Pierce to wake up from his long sleep; twelve hours had already passed and he had not moved. The doctor had been in and out at least six times during the night to check his vitals and had said nothing.

"Can somebody bring me a beer, is anybody here?" a weak voice sounded from the bed.

"No beer, buddy; here is some cold water." Stephanie replied as she handed Davin a cup with a straw. She was smiling now that her boss was finally awake.

"Who are you?" Davin asked as he looked up at a beautiful lady, "Are you my nurse? I hope so and can you get me a beer?"

"I am Stephanie Randal your best friend's wife and your ex-secretary, don't you remember?"

"How long was I out?"

"Three days plus," Stephanie replied.

"Three days? Have you been here the whole time?"

"Yes, don't you remember anything; do you know your name?" Stephanie asked quietly.

"No, where am I anyway? I take it, I am in a hospital somewhere; and by the looks of me, I was injured somehow. Can you tell me what happened? How did I get here?"

"Your name is Davin Pierce and you live with your wife in Palm Beach, Florida and you work for the CIA."

"The who? Who is the CIA?" he asked shaking his head a little, "Oh, shouldn't do that." He reached up and touched the bandage on his head.

"The CIA is the Central Intelligence Agency located outside of Washington, D.C. You work for the Director, Ms. Ashley Marie Peterson. Your best friend and partner is Josh Randal, my husband," Stephanie answered.

"Okay, I understand that; but how the hell did I end up in this hospital, and where are we?" queried Davin.

"We are in Mexico City and we were down here looking for a stolen computer drive from a classified location. There was an explosion and you were trapped; we pulled you out and here you are," Stephanie commented as she pushed the call button for the nurse or doctor.

"There is more, and I don't know how to say this Davin, but I guess straight out is best. Connie, your wife, is missing; we believe the guys that tried to kill you took her. Josh is running down leads, trying to locate her. He calls in every few hours to check on you and give me an update," Stephanie said and then, "No you stay in bed, mister. You were almost killed and the doctor said he wasn't sure you would recover."

Just then Doctor Holms walked in, "Ah, I see our patient has finally awakened," he said seeing Davin awake, "Let me take a look at my handy work," he said as he leaned over Davin, removed the bandage, and examined his head. "Looks good, how do you feel, Mr. Pierce?"

After the examination, he had the nurse redress Davin's head.

"Like I have been run over by a truck. When can I get out of here?"

"Not for a while my friend, you have had a major head injury; and I need to be sure you are not going to die on me twenty minutes after you leave. Besides, there is a large crack in your skull, and it needs to heal a bit more before you leave my care. Not to mention your broken leg and other injuries. We will talk about your other injuries later; my concern is your broken skull. Are you up to a few tests?"

"Fire away doc. Can I get something for this massive headache? Or do I have to live with it."

"I can't give you anything like an aspirin, because we need your blood to clot, not run wild. I do have you on a morphine drip, which I will increase a little to help ease the pain." After testing Davin for dexterity, arm strength and vision, the doctor declared that besides being a little weak Davin was healing well. "I will be back in the morning. I want to run a CAT scan, MRI and a few other tests; and if they come out good, you can probably leave in about a week."

"A week is not good. My wife is missing and I need to find her," Davin protested.

"You are not going anywhere for a while. It was touch and go for a while there on the operating table; you came very close to going downstairs for a permanent rest," the doctor said and then turned to Stephanie and said, "I trust you have a weapon and you will make sure he doesn't leave. It is imperative that he stays in the hospital; if he leaves, I cannot promise he will survive. He needs rest to mend properly. Besides his leg and hand is still healing," tapping the cast on Davin's left leg.

"Got it doc. I will make sure he stays here."

"Oh, by the way, there is a young couple in the waiting room that would like to come in," the doctor said as he was leaving.

"Who are they?" Stephanie asked.

"John Hough and Cindy Andrews, said they were friends of yours."

"Sure send them in," Stephanie replied as she looked over and smiled at Davin.

"Who are they?" Davin asked.

"They work for your boss and are here as back up, if we need it," Stephanie replied as John and Cindy walked in the room.

"Sorry to interrupt, but Ashley asked us to check in on you and Mr. Pierce. Is there anything we can do for you two?"

****

"Mr. President, we just were notified that they were not able to disarm it, and it is counting down, should detonate in about twenty-five seconds," Tony Sanford stated to the President as they sat quietly in the basement Situation Room located three hundred feet below Mount Weather approximately one hundred miles outside of Washington D.C.

"What is the expected casualty count?" Mitchell asked.

"Two hundred thousand," Sanford responded, "eighteen, seventeen, sixteen..."

"No need for the countdown. Mr. Sanford."

They sat and waited.

Chapter 38 KaBoom?

On the Mall, Captain Gibson and his crew worked as fast as they could to disarm the nuclear bomb, but they had to remove a thick plastic cover which was screwed into the case with over one hundred screws. Using several non-metallic battery operated screwdrivers, they were unscrewing as fast as they could knowing full well they had no chance in hell in succeeding in getting the cover off to reach the detonator before it reached zero and exploded, killing hundreds of thousands and destroying downtown Washington D.C. including most of the museums, the White House, capital building, monuments and a lot of history that could never be replaced. This disaster would be worse than the 9/11 attack on the World Trade Center and the two earlier nuclear explosions earlier in the year, one in Boston and the other outside of the Denver International Airport.

Fourteen, thirteen, twelve, eleven, ten, nine, eight, seven, six, five, four, three, two... "Oh, shit, Boss!" yelled his tech. One! Pop, fizz and smoke filled the case below the plastic cover, but there was no explosion.

"Made in Korea, it's a dud, Boss," Chad exclaimed and wiped his sweaty brow; they were working in twenty-seven degree weather, in the snow, yet both men were sweating like they were on the beach in Florida.

"Get that cover off now, it still may blow. We need to make sure it is disabled," Gibson yelled as he picked up his radio and called Tony Sanford. "Mr. Williams, it's a dud. We are working on making it permanently disarmed."

"Thank you, Captain Gibson. I will pass it on to the President," Williams commented with a smile and then to himself, "We just avoided a major tragedy."

****

Forty-one thousand feet south of Cuba, a Gulfstream cruised in relative peace; they had the whole sky to themselves, or so they thought. Flying at forty-two thousand feet and two hundred yards to the left of the Gulfstream were two Mig-35s, the Soviets latest fighter interceptor. The Migs were just within Cuban airspace. They had improved serviceability, were equipped with the latest glass cockpit base on Russian avionics, an optronic target tracker, and designed primarily for air-to-ground attack missions. The aircraft was equipped with a conformal electro-optical missile launch warning and laser warning sensors, as well as an integral active self-protection (jamming, chaff and flare), as part of the self defense system. It had four additional hard points and could haul an external payload in excess of six tons. Standard procedure for the Cuban military was to covertly escort any unscheduled aircraft approaching Cuba. This Gulfstream was purposely staying just outside Cuban airspace. They were watching the Gulfstream and also watching the two F-35 American fighters flying at thirty-six thousand feet south of Cuba just on the outside of the Cuban air space unsure of what their intentions were. As long as the F-35s stayed south of Cuba and the Gulfstream stayed south of Cuba, there would not be a problem. After receiving orders from their base, the lead Mig accelerated and closed the gap between them and the Gulfstream, pulled up beside the cockpit of the private jet, and keyed his microphone.

"Gulfstream aircraft, this is Commander Jose Martinez of the Cuban Air Guard, please identify yourself and your destination," the commander called over the radio to the Gulfstream, using the frequency for Cuba Center for aircraft control. The Gulfstream was required to monitor when close to Cuban airspace.

"Hello, Commander, this is Gulfstream 834, a charter flight from Mexico City, heading to Nassau, Grand Bahamas; my passengers chartered us for a little vacation. We are a crew of three with five passengers," the pilot of the Gulfstream replied, and then he clicked to the cabin intercom and said. "Look out your left window."

"We have been ordered to escort you to Cuba and for you to land at our base." Commander Martinez stated without putting his command voice into the order.

"Wow, that's one of their new Soviet Mig-35s, awesome," Hans Bormann said as he looked out his window. He stood and walked to the cockpit. Upon entering, he looked at his pilot and co-pilot and asked. "What is your plan, Captain?"

"Well, I will do as they ask for starters; we have been ordered to fly to Cuba and land. They have not said they will shoot us down if we don't comply, but that is next."

"Please respond Gulfstream!" Commander Martinez ordered, "You have penetrated Cuban airspace illegally and we have been ordered to escort you to Cuba, NOW! We do not want to shoot you down."

"See, I told you that would be next," his pilot commented to Hans, and then responded over the radio, "We are in International airspace, sir."

"No, Gulfstream you are presently in Cuban airspace and are ordered to land or be shot down. Do you wish to comply or not?" Martinez ordered, "We would hate to destroy such a beautiful aircraft."

"Not good, if we land and they find out we have the President's daughter and a kidnapped U.S. FBI Agent on board. Or maybe they already know who we have onboard," Hans said to himself, thinking of what to do next.

"Gulfstream my wingman has missile lock on your aircraft, please comply; we do not want to destroy you," Commander Martinez stated as he turned his fighter to the left to get more distance between him and the Gulfstream in case they had to destroy it.

"Turn toward Cuba and start to descend," Hans ordered, "We will handle the Cuban military on the ground, we can't do anything if we are dead." And then thought to himself, *'They don't know who is on board, yet. If they did, they would not threaten to shoot us down.'*

"Commander Martinez, we are turning to a new heading of three six zero and descending to twenty thousand. What frequency do we need to tune in for approach and what heading do we need to take upon reaching Flight Level two zero?"

"We will be right behind you; maintain speed and continue to descend; I will have a frequency for you in a moment," Martinez stated.

"Hans we will be on the ground in twenty-five minutes, what are we going to do?" Hans' assistant asked as he walked up behind Hans in the cockpit.

"Not sure, but we cannot let them have our captives or find out we even have them," Hans said. "And we cannot throw them out of the plane. What do you think we should do?"

"That is a good question and I don't have a good answer. One thing for sure, we need to hide the weapons."

"Yes we do, go back and collect them and put them in the floor compartment. Make sure you wipe our finger prints from them. Keep your pistols. We can say we didn't know the rifles were there," Hans ordered.

"Right!" his assistant said and went back to the cabin to collect the weapons.

"Where are we?" Connie asked.

"We are landing in Cuba, so behave yourselves and you may get out alive," Hans said as he returned to the cabin and sat down and buckled his seat belt.

"Cuba, why are we landing in Cuba?" she protested.

"Well, it is simple; we have two Cuban Mig-35s following us who ordered us to land here or they were going to shoot us down."

"We will be touching down in a couple of minutes; make sure your seat belts are fastened," Hans said politely. Twenty minutes later, the Gulfstream was on final approach into a small airfield on the south side of Cuba. Just as they touched down, the two Mig-35s flew past at low level, circled the field, and then pointed their fighters back out to sea as they started their climb out of the airport traffic area.

Looking out the window, Hans noticed some things that did not seem right to him. He saw four FA/18 Super Hornets sitting on the tarmac; that's not right; he did not believe Cuba had any FA/18 aircraft. He dismissed that because he was not sure if they were really FA/18s or Mig 29s, they looked similar from a distance, so he was not sure.

"Okay, we are on the ground in Cuba; stay cool, and we will be out of here shortly. You ladies give us any trouble or try to tell these guys who you are; I will put a bullet in your head. And yes I know killing you in front of Cuban officials will probably get me killed, but if I kill them first, you will die and these pilots can fly us out of here," Bormann ordered. "They may shoot us down, but you will be dead."

"Give it up Bormann, you will not win this one; the Cubans probably know who we are and asked you to land here so they can kill you and take us for ransom or worse," Connie stated, trying to panic Bormann.

"Not going to work, Mrs. Pierce; no matter what happens, you will be dead along with your husband. Whatever happens, you answer their questions."

"What if they ask for passports?"

"We will cross that bridge when we get to it," Bormann answered and then walked to the front of the airplane.

Chapter 39 GITMO

"Mr. Randal, that was pretty slick; how did you know they would cooperate?" Major Johnson U.S. Army Intelligence Command, Guantanamo Bay, Cuba stated as they watched the Gulfstream taxi to the terminal building in which they were standing. As the jet came to a stop, a squad of heavily armed Military Police rushed out and surrounded the jet.

"They did not have much of a choice, I would say," Josh commented, smiling at the outcome.

At that point, Josh Randal and Major Johnson walked out on the tarmac and approached the door of the jet as it started to open and the engines started to spool down, making the area very quiet. They were followed by Miller and Polson. There were no other aircraft within a hundred yards of the jet and all that could be heard were the barking of sea gulls and the light breeze blowing the trees in the distance. Sitting on the edge of the tarmac were four FA/18 Super Hornets with their pilots doing a cursory inspection and assisting with refueling.

"That was one hell of a ride, John. I loved it," Amber Miller was saying to Polson as they followed Josh. "I knew Ms. Peterson had some pull; just did not realize how much. Thank you for inviting me on this mission."

"No problem Amber; you need to learn, and sitting at your desk is not going to make you a great agent. Thanks for joining in," Polson agreed, "Okay, let's watch what happens; we are about to get to the end of this one," he said as they stopped about ten feet behind Josh and the Major, who were at the foot of the air stairs as they were extended out of the Gulfstream.

"What is the meaning of this?" Hans demanded as he stepped through the door and started down the steps. "We are a private charter aircraft heading to the Bahamas; you have no right to force us to land, and wait... you are not Cuban, where are we?"

"Mr. Bormann, I am Special Agent Josh Randal and this is Major Johnson, Army Military Intelligence. We asked you to land here, in Cuba, on the U.S. Military base known as Guantanamo, GITMO for short, because we have reason to believe you have two American citizens on board that aircraft being held against their will. Oh, and this young lady and gentleman coming up behind us are Secret Service Agents Amber Miller, and John Polson. U.S.

Marshal Matthew Davis is here to arrest you and anyone else on board that plane. Do you have a problem with that, Mr. Bormann?"

"Yes I do; I am a citizen of Germany and you do not have the right to arrest me or anyone on board my aircraft. Forcing us to land here against our will is a violation of our rights, and I demand you release my aircraft."

"We can't do that, sir," Josh stated and then to Amber. "Go ahead, board the plane and see if they are on board."

She hesitated and looked over at Polson to seek approval; he quietly said okay. Taking that as his approval, she started for the stairs.

"Mr. Bormann you also have in your possession a portable computer hard drive that was stolen from a classified installation four days ago; it ended up in San Francisco and somehow landed in your hands, from a fellow named Weasel. He, by the way, is dead and you are the prime suspect in his death; now, are you going to come quietly or cause a problem?"

A soldier walked up behind Bormann and searched him. He discovered a 9mm pistol in his waist band.

"Since I am standing at a military base owned by the United States and you have multiple armed soldiers around me, I guess I don't have a choice, now, do I?" Bormann stated the obvious. "That is my weapon, you have no right to it, we are on a private charter aircraft and I am a German citizen with a legal right to carry that, issued by my government."

"No you don't, please put your hands behind your back Mr. Bormann," Josh ordered. He put handcuffs on Bormann and turned him over to Major Johnson and U.S. Marshal Davis.

Amber Miller and two armed soldiers headed up the stairs pushing Hans Bormann aside as they did. Once in the cabin, she saw Connie Pierce and Tara Mitchell sitting about midway down the cabin and a man standing behind them with a gun pointed at Tara's head. One of the guards turned into the cockpit to make sure the pilot and copilot were still there, which they were, going over the shut down procedures for the aircraft.

"Sir, killing either of those ladies will only get you killed," Amber Miller said calmly as she pointed her own weapon at the gunman and her guard raised his M-16, pointing directly at the gunman. "We can do this peacefully or there will be a lot of bloodshed which is not necessary and very messy. So please hand your weapon to Mrs. Pierce and put your hands on the top of your head. Nobody gets hurt and we all can go home tonight; well, you will be going to jail and we will go home."

"We are German citizens; you have no right to hold us!" he protested.

"Well, if you must know, your plane has landed at a United States military base in Cuba and is being impounded for doing so. You are being arrested for being onboard said airplane and trespassing on United States government property," Amber stated.

"But you forced us to land."

"Not exactly, the Cuban Air Guard asked you to land and was directing you to their airbase; your pilot elected to land here by mistake. Small technicality! Now please hand the weapon to Mrs. Pierce," Miller insisted. Seconds passed, but then he handed the weapon as directed, and put both hands behind his head. Just then, another gunman stood up behind him and took aim at Miller and fired. The bullet clipped Miller in the shoulder, and knocked her backward where she landed hard on the floor. The soldier standing behind her squeezed the trigger on his M-16 and fired a short burst of three rounds into the chest of the gunman. It threw him into the rear bulkhead, and he was dead before he hit the floor.

Two more armed soldiers ran up the steps to assist; and upon reaching the top, the second one called down to Josh, "Medic, man, uh, woman down." Major Johnson unclipped the radio on his belt and quickly called the airport medical team. They arrived within minutes and hurried up the steps. While Miller's injury was being attended to, Josh came up the stairs and greeted Connie and Tara.

"Are you two okay? We have been worried sick," Josh asked.

"Where is Davin?" Connie asked concerned.

"Davin is in the hospital in Mexico City; he is doing fine. I have been talking to Stephanie every few hours; he is awake and breathing well. He still has a long way to go before he will be released. We will get you there as soon as possible. Now, please, let's get off this plane and to a safe location on base."

"Where are we?"

"GITMO," Josh responded.

"Cuba! How?"

"Long story, will tell you all the gory details as soon as we are able to sit down to a cold beer," Josh promised.

"I need a massage, a hot shower and a change of clothes," Connie commented as she grabbed Josh and hugged him as they exited the jet.

"I agree with that," Tara agreed and then added, "And a six pack of beer. And thank you Mr. Randal and Miss Miller."

"Let's first get you to a safe location, call the hospital and let Davin and Stephanie know you are safe. I also need to notify the President that you are safe, Ms. Tara," Josh said as he led the two ladies to the waiting black SUVs. "Wait here while I check on Agent Miller." Ten minutes later, Josh returned and hopped into the SUV.

"How is she?" Tara asked.

"Bullet went right through, lost some blood but with a few days rest she will be fine; the medic is patching her and they will take her to the base hospital for a quick check and then she will meet up with us later today."

Chapter 40 Recovery

"President Mitchell, we just got a call from Agent Randal; he informed me that they have caught Hans Bormann and Ms. Tara is safe at GITMO. They are planning on flying to Washington tomorrow. Is Air Force One available to pick them up, or should they hop a military transport?" Tony Sanford said as he entered the temporary Oval office.

"Is Tara okay, is she hurt?" Mitchell asked.

"No, she is fine. They are getting cleaned up and a good night's sleep will do them good," Tony replied.

"Good, send AF One to GITMO to pick them up," Mitchell ordered.

"Oh, yeah, Agent Miller was wounded in an exchange of gun fire; she will be fine, took a bullet in her left shoulder. The medics have her patched up and she will travel with Tara and Mr. Randal. I will send six agents along with AF One for added protection."

"Good, make it so," Mitchell said and then continued, "What is the status of the bomb?"

"Captain Gibson called down a few minutes ago, and told me that the bomb is stable and they are in the process of moving it to a safe location; the mall should be clear of any more explosives within the hour."

"Well, two bits of good news in the past few minutes makes my day," Mitchell commented.

"Now, Tony, is it possible that somewhere down in this drain hole there is a refrigerator with some cold beer in it. I really would love to sit back and enjoy a cold beer right now."

"Sir, the kitchen is fully stocked, what is your preference?" Tony asked.

"Dark beer, ice cold."

"Your wish is my command, sir," Tony said and then picked up the house phone. He ordered the beer and a few snacks to go along with them. "I hope you don't mind if I ordered a beer for me too, sir?"

"I hate drinking alone, Tony; did you also ask for some snacks?"

"Yes. Should be right in," Tony responded just as there was a knock on the door.

"Enter." The door opened and a steward walked in rolling a cart with a bucket full of beer and several trays of snacks. Mitchell reached over, retrieved a bottle, and twisted off the top. He took a long pull on it and said, "Ahhh. That is good."

****

"Mrs. Randal, there is a phone call for you," the nurse said as she entered the room, pointing to the phone on the side table with the flashing light.

"Thank you," she said and picked up the handset, "Hello this is Stephanie Randal."

"Stephanie, we have Connie and the President's daughter, Tara. We also have the disc. Mission accomplished. Well, almost, I have to fly to Washington tomorrow for a debriefing. How is Davin doing?"

"Touch and go, he has amnesia; can't remember who he is or how he got there."

"Damn, what does the doctor think? Is he going to get his memory back?" Josh asked, but knew full well that the doctor would not have that answer.

"He will know when we know. His body is recovering, slowly, but recovering. His mind is a different thing; with time, he should fully recover, but, well, only time will tell."

"I should be with you in a few days. Just take care of Davin. He will be better soon; I know it," Josh said.

"I know he will. Hurry back babe, I miss you and Connie," Stephanie said and hung up the phone.

****

Major Johnson, U.S. Marshal Davis and four armed soldiers escorted Hans Bormann and his surviving assistant to a holding cell and locked them in. After processing, they would be moved to a more permanent cell. The pilot and co-pilot were innocent charter pilots who had been hired two days prior to the flight; they knew nothing about Hans Bormann and the kidnapping of the two ladies. The steward on the flight was also an innocent, and she was released to return to Mexico with the plane and pilots. Their company would be reimbursed for the cleaning of the blood stains in the back of the plane. They would fly back to Mexico City early in the morning; until then, they were confined to quarters and under guard, mostly for their own safety because being on an active military prison that would ensure their safety as well as prevent them from going anyplace off limits.

At five thirty that evening, the pilots and steward were escorted to the dining hall and fed dinner. There they were able to relax and enjoy a full meal. They saw Connie and Tara. With their escort close behind, they walked over to the table where the ladies were sitting and the chief pilot said, "Mrs. Pierce and Ms. Mitchell, if we had known who you were and what was going on, we would have never agreed to the charter. We didn't know and we are very sorry. But also very happy that you are safe and back on home soil; well, at least, you know what we mean. Again, we are very sorry," and then held out his hand.

"Thank you, for your concern and have a safe flight back to Mexico," Connie said taking the pilot's hand when offered. The pilots and steward then returned back to their table.

Chapter 41 Cyber Warriors Strike Back

McDill Air Force Base had sustained a devastating blow, many had been killed or wounded and the Cyber Command building was eighty percent destroyed. It was completely unsafe to enter. Several techs were dead and their lead analyst was injured.

"Doctor, when can I get back to work?" Lieutenant Jessica 'Dusty' Moore asked as the doctor walked in her hospital room.

"El Tee, you are not going anywhere for a while; you have a shattered left arm and two broken ribs, which almost punctured your lung. Not counting the number of cuts, bruising and lacerations you have, we need to make sure they do not get infected and your bones need to heal."

"Okay, I can't leave; can I get a computer and Internet access? I have a mission to complete and can't do it without a computer," Dusty responded.

"I don't see any harm in you having a computer; however, you need to rest. But first, your commander is here to see you; and you can ask for the computer yourself," her doctor commented and then opened the door for Major Sorenson to enter. "She is all yours, Major."

"How are you doing, Dusty?" Major Sorenson asked as she walked in, standing at the foot of the bed with her own arm in a sling and a bandage over her right eye.

"Well, according to the doctor, I am pretty busted up, but look at you. Major, you look like crap. Is anyone else in here? Did we lose anyone? Oh, sorry for that remark."

"It's okay, I feel like crap too. Three of the team are down the hall, a bit busted up; and two, Murphy and Banks, didn't make it."

"Damn, they were good! We need to find some techs as good as them; otherwise, we will never defeat those geeks in Korea. Can I get a computer and access in here; and maybe, if whoever is down the hall, can also get computers and we can network and continue to work. We were very close to cracking in."

"Dusty, this place is not a secure facility and, damn I guess we could secure it with guards at all the doors and restrict access. I can set up in the waiting room or maybe they have a spare room for me and Wiggins."

"How is Wiggs?" Dusty asked.

"Couple broken bones and lots of cuts and bruises, but he will survive; he is tough as nails. He is still down in the emergency room getting patched up, should be up, soon. He ordered the medics to handle everyone else that needed help first. He was the last to get patched up," Sorenson said and stopped when Wiggins walked in and then continued, "I will be right back; I need to get the hospital director to allow us to set up a secure network in his hospital. Wiggins stay with her, she is trying to escape."

"Understood, Major, she will not escape, not on my watch," he joked and then to Dusty, "Okay El Tee, we survived the attack of the mutant Korean assassins. The one that lived is singing like a canary, finally. According to the intel group, we should be able to round up the rest of them in a few days and prevent anymore attacks."

"That's great, but we still have a problem with the infrastructure and need to get that back online as soon as possible."

"Yes, I know," Wiggins said sadly.

Twenty minutes later, Sorenson came back to Dusty's room and said, "Okay we have the go ahead on setting up a network in here. We can have it up and running by morning. In the mean time, I called base technical support to start the installation and also told them to bring over a laptop so you can start to work. They should be here in a few minutes."

"That's great, a good night's sleep; and then I will hit it hard in the morning."

"They are letting me use the room next door as an office for Wiggs and me. What else do we need?"

"Well, I could use my notebook, but I guess it is buried under the building."

"Yes it is; no chance of getting that anytime soon. You are going to have to wing it. They have started the clean up, classified information does not need to blow around in the wind. Now I think we need to get out of here and let you get some sleep. Tomorrow is going to be real busy," Wiggins said and started for the door. "You coming, Major?"

"Right behind you, Wiggs," Major Sorenson said, and they walked out into the hall.

"Have you talked to the President today?" Wiggins asked.

"Yes, and he told me that they recovered his daughter; she is in GITMO. He also knows that Cyber Command is down, at least temporarily. When we are back online, I will call him and let him know our status," **Spooky** replied.

"Anything going on up in D.C.?" **Wiggins asked.**

"Yeah, this is not public knowledge; so keep it to yourself; they had a nuclear bomb attack, but the bomb was a dud, lucky because it landed in the Mall just down the street from the White House. Mitchell is in the alternate White House, safe from harm."

Chapter 42 Discovery

"Wow, your dad sent Air Force One to get you home," Josh said as he, Connie and Tara walked out onto the tarmac at eight thirty the next morning.

"Yeah, since mom was killed in Boston, he has been overly protective of me. It is a little intimidating, but I understand completely," Tara commented as she looked at the big Boeing 747 sitting on the tarmac surrounded by armed guards.

"He is a good man, Tara. I met him a few months ago when Josh and Davin assisted in his rescue," Connie said. She pulled out her credentials and showed them to the guard at the foot of the stairs.

"Mr. Randal and this Davin fellow were part of the rescue team?" Tara asked Connie as they started up the steps.

"Yes."

"Mr. Randal," Tara yelled to Josh coming up behind them.

"Yes. What can I do for you Ms. Mitchell?" Josh responded.

"You saved my dad?" Tara asked Josh.

"Yes, guilty. Davin and I were part of the team that penetrated a hostile country and were very lucky to get him and the team out. We lost some very good men in the process, but the mission was deemed successful, with acceptable losses," Josh said almost too softly to be heard.

"How many died?"

"Miss, this is not the time and place to discuss this; I will fill you in once we are airborne and we are able to discuss it in the security of the flying oval office. Okay?"

"Sure, did not know it was classified. One other question, sir?" getting a nod from Josh she asked. "How did you find him and how did you find me?"

"Once we are settled in, I will answer your questions," Josh said as he continued up the stairs. Minutes later, the door was closed and sealed. The stewardess came around and asked everyone to buckle up for an immediate departure. She would serve drinks and a light breakfast once they reached cruising altitude. It would be a three hour flight to Andrews Air Force Base outside of Washington D.C. There were four F-35 Air Force fighters sitting at the end of the runway ready to take off when given the word from the pilot of departure.

"Eagle Flight, Gremlin One is ready for departure; you boys, oops, and ladies ready?" Colonel Keith Bell asked from the flight deck of Air Force One, correcting himself because he realized that two of the F-35 pilots were female Majors assigned for this mission by the base commander as a reward for getting promoted to Major on the same day.

"Gremlin, Eagle flight of four is hot and ready; let's rock and roll," Major Pamela Cunningham replied.

"Gremlin One taxiing to active runway, let's roll," Colonel Bell responded, as he and his copilot pushed the throttles forward. Minutes later, Air Force One lifted off the runway at GITMO and turned north for its flight to Andrews. The four F-35 fighters lifted off the parallel runway and formed up in a V formation, with one on each wing and two behind, one of which was flying high cover and the other low and further back to stay out of the wing tip vortices from the big Boeing. It was a short one thousand three hundred seven mile flight and each fighter carried enough fuel to make the flight without sacrificing the weapons they were able to carry to protect the Boeing.

After reaching their cruising altitude, Major Cunningham called on the secure frequency, "Gremlin One, Eagle One, got a good copy on secure three?"

"Go ahead Eagle One. On secure three, loud and clear," Colonel Bell answered.

"We have six boogies heading our way, climbing through Angels twelve. Turn right fifteen degrees to ensure we are out of their space. Weapons hot."

"Thanks for the heads up," Bell replied as he turned fifteen degrees right and switched on his air defense radar.

Minutes later, Eagle One heard a call on her guard frequency. "Unscheduled flight of five at flight level thirty-eight, please respond."

"This is Eagle One, Major Cunningham, to whom am I speaking?" she replied to the call.

"Flight commander Jose Martinez, Royal Cuban Air Force; we are no threat; we have been asked by our commander to escort you through Cuban air space. All our weapons are cold, and will only go hot if you are threatened by anyone during your short stay in our airspace."

"Thank you, flight commander; we appreciate your assistance," Cunningham answered.

"We will maintain flight level thirty-six west and ahead of your flight approximately three kilometers west of your flight path."

"Thank you, flight commander," Cunningham responded, and then turned her radio back to secure frequency channel three and told Gremlin of the situation. All eleven aircraft proceeded north over Cuba until reaching the invisible line that only shows on charts of the International line dividing Cuban airspace and international airspace. Once reached, Flight Commander Martinez called again. "Major Cunningham, it has been a pleasure escorting you and your team across Cuba; next time, you have to stay a while and enjoy our hospitality and, of course, our famous margaritas," Martinez offered.

"Flight commander, next time I come this way I will not be in an F-35, but on a commercial flight, so I can take you up on that offer. Thank you for a safe passage. May all your flights be as friendly."

"I can be located at Havana International airport, military side. Look us up," Martinez replied, "Good Flight."

"Good Flight Jose," Cunningham responded, switched back to secure, called Gremlin, and informed them that their escorts were departing. The rest of the flight went as planned; they landed at Andrews Air Force Base on time.

During the flight Josh sat with Tara and explained that she and her father had micro-bio chips implanted within their bodies which were used to track and monitor the health of the individual it was implanted in. In both cases, the ones in the President and Tara had helped teams track and recover each of them. She seemed to protest at first, but then decided that if it had not been for the chip she might be dead now, or worse.

Chapter 43 Bait and Switch

Late in the afternoon, the sun was unseen because of the heavy overcast. Sitting in his office overlooking the city of Munich, Gregory Dietrich, the grandson of SS Colonel General Josef 'Sepp' Dietrich of Hitler's closet friend was concerned; he had not heard from Hans Bormann in days. He was supposed to be back in Munich yesterday; yet, he had not gotten a call or text. It was time to make the switch. It seemed that he had lost his ace in the hole, Ms. Tara Mitchell and that computer drive. He needed to turn up the heat on the United States.

After picking up his cell phone, he punched speed dial and waited, "Hello General, Dietrich here. We need to turn up the heat some more."

"What do you want me to do? Our attack on Washington failed; the bomb did not explode," the General replied.

"Launch the attack on the west coast," Dietrich ordered.

"Consider it done," the General replied.

****

Dusty was sitting up in her bed with the keyboard on her lap working on relocating the cyber attacker she had found before the attack. With a head phone and mike hanging from her left ear, she could communicate with the other four techs, yet she wondered where Ensign Savage was. He wasn't reported killed or missing.

"How are you doing, Dusty?" Major Sorenson asked as she entered the hospital room smiling.

"Doing fine, almost back to where we left off before the attack," Dusty responded and then stopped and looked up at her commander and asked, "Where is Ensign Savage?"

"I knew you were going to ask; well, he is down in intensive care. He was hurt pretty bad and they are watching him very close. I just checked on him; he is doing fine, and the doctor says he will fully recover, but it will take some time," Dusty's commander replied.

"Didn't he get out of the building?" asked Dusty.

"No, he was still inside when it exploded; they pulled him out and rushed him to the hospital. He spent six hours in surgery, but they are confident he will be as good as new in a few months," Major Sorenson explained.

"When can I see him?" Dusty asked.

"In time, right now, we have a mission to complete and the entire country is counting on you and your team."

"But Savage is an important part of that team; without him I am not sure we can recover," Dusty stated.

"Yes you can! You are one of the best computer geeks I have ever had the pleasure to work with, you will succeed; and failure is not an option here, Lieutenant," Sorenson said sternly. "The country is severely wounded and you are one of the doctors with the cure."

"Yes, Major, you know I will do my best, but please keep me posted on Savage, please," Dusty responded.

"You know I will; now is there anything else you need here to stop these maniacs?" asked Sorenson.

"No I have everything I need for now. The computer and access is working great; those guys from the computer shop did a great job," Dusty replied.

"Okay, I will leave you alone; Wiggs will check in with you shortly. I have to run up to Washington to see the President. He wants a personal update; I leave in a couple of hours, so tell me what you have and your estimate of completion," commanded Sorenson.

"I just got his IP address and am about to spike him. We should be able to slam him sometime later tomorrow. It has to be..," she said stopping because Sorenson held up her hand to stop her.

"Don't need all the gory details, just make it happen and soon. The northwest is expecting more snow and the temperatures are dropping rapidly; they need their electricity as soon as possible," Sorenson reminded Dusty.

"Tell the President we should have the entire west back online by midnight tomorrow, unless of course, they have other sneaky things in there that we did not anticipate. I believe we have covered all the bases," Dusty indicated.

****

"Sir, we have an indication that North Korea is fueling their ICBMs" the chief technician at Cheyenne Mountain reported.

"How many?" the shift supervisor asked from across the room.

"Looks like eight. Yeah, eight, the ones on the coast, the ones that could reach our west coast," he replied as he flipped a couple of switches to bring the geosynchronous satellite over Korea and intensify the sensors to get a better picture of the activity at the Korean silos.

"They can launch in two hours with a flight time of four hours to Los Angeles," the tech confirmed.

The tech raced over to the secure phone located in the corner of the room, picked it up and punched in a three digit code; he waited for a tone, punched in the code for the White House, and waited until the White House answered. "This is NORAD at Cheyenne Mountain, we have a situation," he said immediately into the hand set.

"President's eyes only?" the operator asked.

"Yes, or the NSA," the NORAD technician stated.

"Hold one," the operator replied and then after a couple of clicks, Tony Sanford came on the line.

"National Security Advisor, Tony Sanford, what have you got?"

"Eight Korean ICBMs are in the process of being fueled. Launch expected in one hour and forty-eight minutes. Unsure of the target package, but assume the destination is the west coast; they can't reach anything east of the Rockies."

"Understood, I will inform the President, keep me posted," Sanford replied and then hung up the hand set. Within minutes, he had informed the President and they sat quietly for a few minutes.

"We can't evac all of the west coast; where would they go, and it would be a total mess. What do you propose, sir?" Sanford asked.

"What time is it in North Korea right now?" Mitchell asked, After Sanford told him it was around three in the afternoon, Mitchell ordered, "Get the Prime Minister of Korea on the line."

Tony Sanford walked over to the phone, spoke for a couple of seconds and then waited. The communications officer came back on the line and said she had the North Korean Prime Minister's assistant on the line and he said the Prime Minister was not available; she was eating an early dinner with her family.

"Comms, let me speak to the assistant," Sanford ordered and waited until he heard the assistant come online.

"Good afternoon Mr. President, this is Wun Sun Wo the Prime Minister's personal assistant, as I told your officer, the Prime Minister is busy and cannot be disturbed."

"Mr. Wo, I am Tony Sanford, National Security Advisor to the President, and he has an urgent matter to discuss with your Prime Minister, one that will save millions of lives in both our countries."

"How so, Mr. Sanford," Mr. Wo asked.

"I need to let President Mitchell discuss that with your Prime Minister."

"I will see if she is available, Mr. Sanford; I will be right back." The line went quiet and Sanford waited almost five minutes before he heard the hand set being picked up again. "Mr. Sanford, please put your President on the line, my Prime Minister is here," Mr. Wo said quietly.

"This is President Mitchell! Prime Minister; we have a serious problem, and I believe we can fix it right here and now."

"What seems to be the problem, President Mitchell?" she asked. President Mitchell wondered if she did not know her country was about to launch eight ICBMs.

"Are you aware that eight of your ICBMs are being fueled and readied for launch?" Mitchell asked straight out.

"No, I am not aware of that; I have given no order to prepare missiles for launch. We are at war with each other, but I have not given that order yet," the Prime Minister said nervously. "How do you know we are doing this? No, you won't tell me how you know, but you do know and I don't know. I need to find out who is doing this, and why; I do not want a nuclear war with your country and even though we are technically at war, I want a civilized war, no nuclear weapons. We may not agree on a lot of things, but nuclear war is not something we are ready for or want," she said being very contradictive of what was going on. She had admitted that they were at war with each other, but she had not really admitted that they wanted war. It was confusing to the President and Mr. Sanford.

"Ms. Prime Minister, I agree we don't want war; but you understand that I have to put my country on high alert and your country has attacked us, killing many of my citizens. Are we at war or not? With that in mind, we have, from what we can tell, about an hour and forty minutes before your missiles are ready for launch. You need to stop those launches; we will, if you can't."

"I will get back to you shortly, Mr. President," the Prime Minister said and then hung up the phone.

"Go to DEFCON One Tony; we just went to *'Cocked Pistol'*," Mitchell said quietly, using the official name for DEFCON One, meaning nuclear war was imminent. He stopped and let his mind drift as if thinking, and then commanded, "Contact Southern Command Korea and get, whoever is the commander there now, get him on the line. I need an assault team ready to go in twenty minutes to take out those silos before they launch, if the PM doesn't get it done. I still want them taken out no matter what she does; I am through with the Koreans."

DEFCON is short for Defense Readiness condition and starts at DEFCON 5 (Fade Out) for the lowest state of readiness or normal operations, DEFCON 4 (Double Take) is an increased intelligence watch and strengthened security measures, DEFCON 3 (Round House) is an increase in force readiness above that required for normal readiness, DEFCON 2 (Fast page) is the next step to nuclear war and finally DEFCON 1 (Cocked Pistol) means Nuclear war is imminent, maximum readiness. The readiness conditions were established in January 1960 and had been in use ever since.

"What if the government isn't behind this; what if she has a rat in the mist," Tony said, playing the devil's advocate.

"We have to stop those missiles! We don't have a choice, Tony. If they launch what do we have to stop them?" Mitchell asked.

"We have Star Wars," Tony acknowledged quietly, reminding Mitchell of the classified program designed to protect the United States from ICBM attacks. The system had been tested in simulation and in the lab but never on a real ICBM.

"But that isn't ready, is it?"

"It was launched, while you were kidnapped; yes, it is still untested, but it is up there and we can activate it. It is our last line of defense in this situation. That is the project the Vice President has been working on for several years; he has been in Florida at Cape Kennedy preparing the second phase of the program which will launch in two days. The first system is on station and active."

"Do you think it will work and stop all eight ICBMs?" Mitchell asked.

"I hope so," Sanford commented.

Chapter 44 Betrayal

Gregory Dietrich sat alone in his office looking intently out the large picture window overlooking his home city of Munich, Germany. He was in deep thought, the bait had been set; his North Korean General was about to start World War III with the United States and his government had no idea what he was doing. But the money he was receiving for his part in this scenario would let him live in a life style that he always wanted but not be in Korea. The villa he bought in the south of France had taking only a small part of the advance he received.

While America concentrated its efforts on the threat from the west, he now was about to turn on his master plan of destroying Washington D.C. and bring the United States of America to its knees. Ever since his grandfather was disgraced at the end of World War II and young Gregory learned about it, he was determined to bring down America. And now he was about to complete his lifelong mission.

"Hello Michelle, what brings you to my office on this beautiful day?" Gregory asked as his young beautiful wife entered his office.

"I don't mean to interrupt you, but I need to go to Frankfurt for a couple of days and do a show with Michelle. She has contracted with a designer and we are to model his new line. Sorry for the short notice, but Michelle just got the call, seems that two of his models came down sick and we are to replace them."

"Fine, I will send Josef with you; take the train. I would feel safer knowing Josef is with you. The roads should be clear enough to get to the train station; if we get more snow, then they may close, but he is a good driver. I have some work for him in Frankfurt anyway; the timing is perfect," Gregory said and picked up his phone to call Josef.

"Tell him we will be ready in an hour. I can get him a room at the same hotel we will be in," Michelle said.

"No, he will be going outside the city to meet with a company we have been working with. He will be staying with them for a few days. Now I also have work to do; have a safe trip," Gregory said and then spoke into the phone asking Josef to come to his office.

Michelle left his office as Josef entered, "Mr. Dietrich, you wished to see me?" Josef asked as he walked over to Gregory's desk.

"Please sit; I have a mission for you," Gregory said and pointed to an overstuffed chair at the corner of his desk. "Josef you are going with my wife and her friend to Frankfurt. But while you are there I need you to ..." He continued to explain his plan to Josef. It was known only to a select few individuals. Gregory Dietrich had been financing a project that was ready to deploy. Josef was the key to the deployment, and he was just learning he was and how he was about to change the course of the world as he knew it.

"Josef, there is an old military airport located ten kilometers west of Frankfurt. My grandfather used it during the war. There are bunkers and hangers located there, none of which can be seen from the air and the runway looks like a small lake. With the throwing of a few switches, the lake drains and exposes a paved twelve thousand foot runway. It was designed to launch fighters and bombers to attack London by day and night. The airfield has been a secret of only a few; you are to go there and meet with Dr. Heimlich. He will show you the project which you will help prepare for launch; and when I give you the command, you will launch. The pilots know the mission and will follow it until completed. Your job is to ensure the plane gets off the ground and report back to me. Understand?"

"Yes, sir. As the Americans say, I got it covered," Josef said and then stood to leave.

"Wait," Gregory said and then reached in the top drawer of his desk and pulled out a box about the size of a cigar box but painted black with a small padlock on it. "I want you to take this," he said and opened the box and showed Josef. In the box was a Lugar 9mm pistol in a brown holster with a gold SS emblem on the flap. "This pistol belonged to my grandfather's aide. I have my grandfather's pistol here also, but you are my aide and you may need this. Here is a box of ammo also. His aide was a Major and very dedicated to their cause and to my grandfather. I expect no less from you Josef."

"I will not let you down, sir," Josef said as he examined the pistol; it was in near perfect condition, and he noticed it was fully loaded.

Chapter 45 If Penguins Could Fly

At silo six on the coast of North Korea, a Korean General stood overseeing the fueling of the ICBM, and he was smiling. His plan was to launch all eight missiles at the United States and then hop on his private jet and fly to Hong Kong and then on to France and his new villa on the coast. He did not want to be around when the Americans came and destroyed his country. And they would destroy it; already South Korea was massing their forces for an all out assault. The Korean military forces outnumbered the American and South Korean military in numbers, but not in technology and firepower. The war would not last long and millions could die on both sides. He didn't care; he was rich, thanks to Gregory Dietrich. If the ICBMs didn't make it to their targets, he didn't care; his job was to launch them, nothing more. And that job was just about to be completed.

A young technician walked up to the General and came to an abrupt halt and stiff attention, saluted and handed the General an envelope.

"Thank you," the General said taking the envelope from the technician, who turned and left immediately. The General opened the envelope and smiled at what he saw. The coordinates for the eight targets in America were now in his possession. "Dr. Jang these are the coordinates, plug them into your computer, prepare to launch in forty-five minutes."

"Thank you my General; we are almost ready and we have a plane to catch," Dr. Jang said as he reached for the envelope and then flagged a technician to come over, conversed with him, and handed him the envelope. "Transmit those to the other sites, immediately."

"Yes, we do, is your lovely wife at the airfield?"

"She is there and ready. I thank you for letting me join you."

"It is my pleasure, my good doctor," the General said smiling. "The clock is ticking, Doctor, and your wife is waiting."

Twenty minutes later, Doctor Jang walked back over to the General and announced they were fueled and ready to launch. Both men walked over to the computer console. Doctor Jang sat and started to type on the computer. "I am bringing all the sites online; they are coming online now. Coordinates are in place, once we align the gyros, then we can launch. Just a couple of minutes."

"Good work doctor," the General said and then inserted his launch key into the key lock.

"Doctor please insert your key; we will launch in the following order, one then eight, two, seven, three, six, four and then number five."

"Start the count down," Doctor Jang ordered a technician sitting across from him.

"One minute and counting, sir," the technician stated, not understanding that they were about to launch nuclear ICBMs at the United States. He was under the impression that this was an exercise and they were only simulating the launch.

"All is ready, General. Please turn your key on my mark," Doctor Jang requested. "Three, two, one." Each turned their keys and then the General flipped open the covered launch button and held his finger over the button for a moment.

"Once I push this, we leave and do not look back, Doctor. Are you ready?"

"Yes, General, I am ready," Doctor Jang responded, and then the General pushed the button, starting the launch of ICBM number one which automatically launched the other seven in the programmed sequence. The General and Doctor Jang left the facility and climbed into the waiting car. They left the launch facility and headed to the airport.

****

"Mr. President, they have started a one minute count down," Tony Sanford stated as he entered the temporary oval office.

"Is Star Wars primed and ready? This has been one hell of a week. What could happen next?" Mitchell asked.

"Well, a hell of a lot," Sanford stated, "Your daughter landed a few minutes ago and they are bringing her and her saviors here. They should be here in about an hour."

"Great, I am so glad she is safe and will be here in this fortress underground," Mitchell commented slowly as if thinking about his next move. "What else have you got? Anything more serious than the eight nuclear ICBMs being launched at our west coast?"

"They should be launching right about now, sir. I will check with NORAD on Star Wars."

"You didn't tell me the other news."

"Bad news from Afghanistan, a shooter wearing an Afgan military uniform was able to get into a classroom where they had a guest speaker, Major General Robert Banks. The imposter opened fire wounding fifteen military students, and killed two including the General."

"Did they capture or kill the shooter?" Mitchell questioned.

"Yes, the shooter is dead and the base is on full lock down."

"Damn what else can go wrong?" Mitchell commented. As he paced around the office, the phone rang on his desk.

"President's office, Tony Sanford speaking," Tony said into the handset. "Go ahead with the call, comms." And he waited until the line was connected. "This is National Security Advisor Tony Sanford, to whom am I speaking."

"This is Andrew DeMarco, CIA Chief here in Munich. We have some intelligence that needs to reach the President immediately."

"He is standing right here, I will put you on speaker and you can tell him directly," Sanford said and pushed the speaker button on the phone.

"Go ahead Mr. DeMarco, President Mitchell. What have you got for me?" Mitchell asked.

"Sir, is this a secure line?"

"Yes it is; didn't you call in on a secure line; now tell us what you know," Sanford said quickly getting a little ticked off at DeMarco for asking that stupid question.

"Okay, we have been watching a suspected criminal element over here and have discovered he is about to launch an attack on Washington. We are still working on the how and when but all indications are that it will happen within the next twelve hours. I will have more information within the next few hours and will call again as soon as I get it."

"Do you have any idea of the delivery system? What kind of attack, air, ground, sea anything?"

"No sir, we just got this in and are verifying the facts, but this is from a credible source on the inside of his circle. I can't say anymore at the moment. Sir, I will have more shortly," DeMarco said and then finished by saying, "My contact is deep in the organization, but still has trouble getting information out. Our next contact is in two hours. I will call you as soon as I hear from my contact."

"Understood, we will talk again in two hours; thank you DeMarco, stay safe," Mitchell said, pressed the disconnect button, and looked at Sanford seriously. "Now we know, America has always been a target and now we are seriously hurt and they want to bring us down completely. Martial Law has been in effect for two days; riots have broken out in several cities, looting in others, and the civilian population has armed themselves for personal protection because the government can't protect everyone. I don't blame them and I know ninety percent of the population is armed and will do the right thing for themselves and the country; it is the other ten percent that I worry about."

"Me too," Sanford agreed.

Chapter 46 Berlin Germany

"What have you got for me today" asked Sepp.

"It looks like the American President has evacuated the White House; we are unsure where he has gone, but believe he is underground," his Lieutenant said.

"Have you heard anything from Hans?"

"No sir, we have not heard a word"

Gregory Dietrich needed a new plan. Hans had disappeared, his captives had disappeared, and the chartered Gulfstream had disappeared. Did they crash in the ocean, get shot down, what happened to them?

"Have you heard anything from the North Koreans?"

"Sir, the last we heard from the Korean General was that he was about to launch eight ICBMs at the United States. That was over two hours ago."

"Did he launch?"

"Yes sir, he launched," he replied after checking his tablet for confirmation. They also attempted to fly a Boeing 757 aircraft with a nuclear device onboard into the Washington metro area with plans to detonate over the White House. That plan failed miserably; the Americans shot down the Boeing 757 and it seems the nuclear device did not detonate as scheduled. We are unsure of the outcome of the device at this time."

"What the hell were the North Koreans thinking flying a jumbo jet into a restricted area; they knew they were going to get shot down. After those terrorists crashed jumbo jets into the World Trade Center in 2001, they have been very touchy about their restricted areas and are flying heavily armed fighter jets 24/7 in those areas. How stupid can they get?"

"We have a man stationed outside of Washington; I will contact him to see if he can find out any information about the detonation and what is going on in Washington. What else would you like me to do, sir?"

"Right now, just go find out from your contact in Washington what is going on. I will contact the Koreans," Dietrich said and then sat back in his chair with his hands flat on his desk in front, thinking. "Wait, wait, wait; don't you have a contact on the inside of the CIA?"

"I do, sir; but I am not sure if I can get a hold of him."

"I want you to try to contact him, and see if he knows what the hell is going on. Our plan cannot work while the President is still alive."

"Yes sir," his Lieutenant said and then abruptly turned and left the office.

Michelle Dietrich burst into the office and stormed over to Gregory's desk and stopped with her hands placed firmly on his desk and looked directly at him. "Gregory, what the hell have you done? Where is Hans?"

"My dear, what do you mean? I thought you were going to Frankfurt? I don't know what you are so upset about. I have done nothing to require you to come storming in here yelling. Hans is in California on business for me. Why do you ask?"

"So, you don't know what is going on in Washington?"

"What are you talking about, my dear, what is going on that I need to know about?"

"There has been an attack on the President, and an airplane crashed just outside the White House. And I know you are behind it. What are you trying to do, start another war!" she yelled.

"No, no war, not yet anyway and I had nothing to do with the plane crashing outside the White House. What makes you think I had something to do with it? And I guess since you believe I have something to do with it then it must be true. I don't want to kill the President; he is my friend and is actually helping me in my quest. And now that you believe you know what I am supposed to be doing, I guess I need to tell you the whole truth."

"The President is working with you?" she asked unsure as to what he was up to.

"NO, he does not work with me; he has no idea that when he was our captor in the desert that he was reprogrammed, as it were, and he is making decisions that he normally would not make. He doesn't even know he is working for me. He will soon make a decision to launch a full scale attack on North Korea. China and Japan will get involved, and, yes, we will have another war, but this one will be controlled by me, not President Mitchell. Some information will be leaked that will convince him that war is the only option he has."

"You can't do that Gregory, a war, Germany can't afford another war. We lost the first two wars and cannot afford another."

"Oh, it will be a short war, for sure. The North Koreans have already launched eight ICBMs at the United States and within a few hours China will launch a major attack with ICBMs from their submarine fleet and several of their surface ships. The west coast of the United States is already dark from the attacks on their infrastructure. They are unprepared for the massive attacks that are in the works. We will overrun the United States within a matter of days. And once we have taken control, I will step over and take charge as the new dictator of the United States of Germany."

"No..." she started to say then thought again only opening her mouth to speak yet nothing came out at first; then she said. "Actually that would be rather exciting; I have always wanted to be queen."

"Not a queen, my sweet little sister; just a sister of a Dictator of the soon to be greatest country on the planet."

"Okay, what do we do next?" she asked, and thinking to herself, *'I have to stay alive long enough to get another message out.'*

"Are you okay with what I am doing, my love? I truly hope so, your acting career is just getting started and I would hate for something to happen to you."

"No Gregory, it is okay. I understand completely," she lied, but being a good actress, she was able to convince herself that she was deceiving him completely. "Working together is something I have always dreamed about."

"Good. Now run along, go to Frankfurt and do some shopping. Everything will be fine in a few days," Gregory said smiling.

"Okay, see you in a few days," Michelle said and left the room.

Josef entered the office a few seconds later. Having overheard part of the conversation, he did not say a word.

"Josef, we have another problem that I need you to take care of. My sister has gotten a bit nosey about my business and I don't trust her. Make sure she and her friend have an accident before getting to Frankfurt," Gregory said.

"Consider it done, sir," Josef said and then turned and left the office. He headed down the stairs to the basement garage, where he met with his two passengers. "Ready to go, ladies?" he asked with a smile.

"Yes, please put our bags in the trunk, Josef," Michelle asked and then walked over to the front passenger seat and opened the door of the Range Rover, glancing casually at her friend and winked.

Chapter 47 Mount Weather

"Mr. President, we have recovered the missing computer drive, and I see your daughter has been safely returned to you," Ms. Ashley Peterson commented as she entered the temporary Oval Office.

"Yes, yes that is great. But we have bigger problems now. As you know, the Koreans have launched eight ICBMs at us, of which we were able to destroy six of them and the other two detonated in space causing no damage," Mitchell commented as he quickly paced around the office.

"Sir, that is the least of our problems; we have intercepted a communication that leads us to believe the Chinese are about to launch their own attack. We need to alert the military. This is an imminent threat, sir."

Reaching over, Mitchell pressed the button on his phone to call Tony Sanford, his National Security Advisor. "Sanford, come in here now," he ordered and then returned to his desk and sat, shaking his head.

"Right away sir," Sanford replied. Seconds later Sanford entered the office. "What is it sir?"

"Alert the military of an attack by the Chinese on the west coast," Mitchell commented to Ashley Peterson and Tony Sanford just as there was a knock on the door, Mitchell looked at the door and said, "Enter."

Tara Mitchell slowly opened the door and entered, "Daddy, am I interrupting?"

"No, come on in, we were just finishing, but you need to know what is going on. Please sit and listen," Mitchell said without looking up. He then stopped, turned to Tara, reached over and hugged her, and then continued, "Honey, I am going to need you to stay in this bunker until further notice. The country is under attack and I do not want to lose you."

"Dad, what is going on up there?" she asked sounding very scared.

"The Korean's have launched ICBMs at us, and the Chinese are about to join in. We are using our new unproven Star Wars system to stop them, but I am sure some will get through no matter what we do. The west coast and possibly as far inland as Saint Louis will be hit."

Stopping again he looked at Peterson and asked. "Has there been any indication of Korean or Chinese Naval activity in the Atlantic?"

"That is a good question, sir. Let me contact Admiral Hamner, Commander of the Atlantic Fleet and get his latest report. I will be right back," Peterson said and then stood and headed for the door.

"No, call from here; use that phone, it is secure. It is early enough, he should be in his office at the Pentagon. He has a secure line."

"Yes, sir," she agreed. She walked over and reached for the secure phone. She dialed Admiral Hamner's secure line, punched in the access code, and waited for the line to click through its security checks.

"Sir, we need to launch in retaliation," Sanford suggested understanding that doing so would ensure a nuclear war of epic proportion, destroying most of the population of the world in the process. Once launched, there would be no turning back.

"No, not yet," Mitchell replied firmly, "I am not ready to destroy the world."

"Admiral Hamner's office," a pleasant female voice answered.

"This is Ashley Peterson, Director CIA; may I speak with the Admiral?"

"One moment please," she said and the line became quiet.

"Admiral Hamner, how are you doing Ashley?" Admiral Scott Hamner said after a brief pause.

"I'm doing as well as can be expected. As you know, we are under attack from the Chinese and North Koreans. Have you got any Korean or Chinese ships in the Atlantic?"

Mitchell and Sanford continued to talk about retaliation. "Sir, they have launched; we need to shoot back!" Sanford insisted, almost to the point of yelling.

"As a matter of fact we do. There are three Korean attack boats and two frigates and at least four Chinese cruisers and two nuclear missile boats. We are tracking all of them, if there are any more, we don't have them. But it will be next to impossible to get past SOSUS and our other detection systems."

"Tony, we are not one hundred percent sure those countries are behind this. Intel is telling me that there may be rogue agents in the mist; and if we launch, we just committed to the end of life as we know it. Nuclear war is not the answer. We can stop those ICBMs, but if we launch, they cannot stop ours. And then they launch more, and we launch more. It will only end when life is gone or when everyone is out of missiles. So just get the football close, but I will not launch yet," Mitchell insisted. He then looked over at Ashley on the phone with Admiral Hamner and heard the start of the conversation.

"Damn, hold one, I am putting you on speaker so the President can hear this; and he may have some updated orders for you." Admiral Hamner repeated the report and then went quiet.

"Admiral, if any of those ships launch anything toward the states, your orders are to destroy the missile and sink them. Do not let them destroy our country. Destroy those ships at all costs," Mitchell ordered and then went quiet and stared before continuing. "You will be getting written orders within the hour. But consider this an Executive Order which you can act on immediately."

"Yes sir. Is there anything else? I have to contact my commanders with the new orders," Admiral Hamner stated.

"No, go to work, Scott. And good luck."

"This is the United States of America, sir; we don't need luck when we have the best military on the planet. We will prevail." Then the line went dead. Mitchell pressed the disconnect button and looked around the room. His daughter, Ashley Peterson, Director of the CIA and Tony Sanford, National Security Advisor all looked worried but had confidence in President Mitchell.

"We have work to do. Tara, would you please go down to my room and get the black binder that is laying on my head board. Don't open it until you get here; I will explain what it is when you get back. Tony, order us some food and make your calls. Get the staff in the Situation room in forty-five minutes; I don't care where they are, get them here."

"Yes sir," Tony said and then left the office right behind Tara.

Forty minutes later, they walked into the Situation room located sixty feet from the temporary oval office. Mitchell was carrying the black binder. Tara followed close behind; Sanford and Peterson brought up the rear. They entered and sat, but not before they looked at the trays of food and drink that had been placed in the room just prior to their arrival. Mitchell did not say anything for several minutes after he sat at the head of the table.

"Get yourself something to eat; this is going to take a while," Mitchell offered, finally speaking after a few minutes of silence.

"What is in that black binder, sir?" Sanford asked as he picked up a sandwich and soda.

"Everyone will know shortly, just wait."

Chapter 48 Cyber Meltdown and Nuclear Waste

"Dusty, how are the cyber warriors doing?" Master Sergeant Todd Wiggins asked as he walked into the hospital room of Jessica Moore, aka 'Dusty'.

"Master Sergeant, if only we could get out of this damn hospital. Maybe if we had a little more privacy and a little less hospital, we would actually get something done. We were able to get most of the west coast up and secure, but the Midwest is being a little more difficult. As soon as we get close, the system hiccups; and we have to start over. The power in this hospital is not stable enough to handle all the equipment we have. Can we move to the old SAC building; it has enough power; it is secure, and we will be able to get this fixed permanently."

"I will see what I can do. Be right back," Wiggins said and then headed out the door. As he passed a doctor coming in, he greeted him with a "Hi, Doc."

"How do you feel today, Ms. Moore?" the doctor asked as he picked up her chart hanging on the end of her bed.

"Feeling great, the drugs you are pumping in me must be doing a good job," Dusty replied as she reached over and closed the lid on her laptop computer.

"Good, I noticed Sergeant Wiggins going out in a hurry. Is there a problem?"

"No, just that we, meaning me and my team, need to get out of here; we have a lot to do and just can't get it done in here. Can you release us today? Sergeant Wiggins is on his way to see the hospital admin to see if we can go, but I guess it is really up to you."

"Well, let's see. All your numbers are good; but you were burned pretty bad. Two of your team are being released as we speak; one more can be, but I will need to assign a nurse to check on him and you three times a day for the next few weeks. If I release you and him, that is the rule; I can have a nurse check in with you three times a day until we are satisfied you are out of harm's way."

"Works for me, Doc. I can have Wiggins bring some clothes for us and be out of your hair as soon as you say."

"Okay, I will be right back," the doctor said and left her room. Dusty picked up her phone, called Wiggin's cell phone, and told him they were being released. She asked him to get her a uniform and one for Ensign Savage also. He said to hang on and would be back in about an hour.

****

Up on the Washington Mall, the nuclear disposal teams were standing around the remains of the Boeing 757 jumbo jet; and more importantly, they were looking at the large coffin shaped box that housed a Korean made nuclear bomb. There was a bomb that had counted down to zero, and did not explode. The men and women of Washington D.C. were considered some of the luckiest people on earth at the moment, but there still was a problem.

"Boss, what are your thoughts?" the young bomb disposal technician asked his boss as they stood looking at the unexploded device.

"Son, what I am thinking is, we should just pack up our stuff and run like hell as far away from here as we can as fast as we can. But we can't do that with a live nuclear device sitting six hundred yards from the White House. We need to make sure that thing is safe, and get it moved to a secure location as soon as possible," his boss replied, as he stood five feet from the bomb.

"Okay, I guess my job is to secure the device, right?" the technician said with a small chuckle, stepping closer to the bomb and kneeling down to examine it. "Looks like this Plexiglas cover doesn't have any trip wires; would you hand me the Phillips screwdriver, sir," he said. He reached back to retrieve the screwdriver from his boss who was standing behind him sweating, even though it was only thirty-three degrees today. The snow started to fall again and with the wind blowing at ten miles per hour, it felt like twenty-five degrees.

Twenty-four minutes later, all the screws were removed from the Plexiglas cover; he was ready to lift it off to expose the wiring and the bomb components.

"Sir, would you grab the other end of the glass," the technician asked as he stood, stretched and moved to the right side of the box.

"Let's do this slowly; you know how much I hate this right now?"

"Yes Sir, I hate this too. If I screwed up and missed a trip wire, we will be vaporized before, well you get the picture."

"Yes I do, I have been doing this for too damn long and have my required amount of time to collect a nice retirement check. I plan on punching out right after we save the city again."

"Sir, you can retire if we don't blow up the city in the next couple of seconds. I am not ready to retire Sir, I actually enjoy this, the excitement, the thrill, gets the blood running, and actually I get high on this stuff."

"Okay, lift slowly sir..." the technician said; "Holy shit!" he yelled.

"What did you do?" his boss asked.

"The timer has started again!" the technician yelled as they pitched the Plexiglas top to the side, he kneeled down and examined the timer and wiring. "Okay, no problem. The clock is ticking, but it is counting up from zero. That doesn't make any sense."

"Move over and let me look," his boss calmly said and then kneeled down to examine the bomb. "No, that doesn't make any sense; why would it be counting up?" He paused for a moment to think and then looked closely at the wiring. "We need to pull this thing out of that box and see the entire thing; grab the other end and lift on three."

"Damn, this is heavy... Hey you two come over here and help. Lift!" Gibson yelled to two of his assistants.

Two men reluctantly came over and started to lift.

Chapter 49 Who's in Charge Here

Standing in front of a room full of the most powerful men and women in the world, President Darrell Mitchell looked at each member one at a time, making eye contact with each one before he said a word. The concerned look on his face was unmistakable, he was scared; more scared than he had been since he was a pilot flying Hueys in Viet Nam. Going in and out of hot Landing Zones (LZ) with small arms fire all around, he sweated a lot; but he had a job to do, and he did it without concern for his own life. The men on the ground needed him to bring in ammunition and take out the wounded. He received several medals for his unselfish acts; although being wounded, he had continued to fly. As scared as he was then, today made that look like a walk in the park on a Sunday afternoon.

"I called you here, because, as you well know, our country is under attack by North Korea and possibly the Chinese. Attacks have already killed thousands of our citizens and they are planning to continue the attacks until we are all dead or dying. I also need to mention that the ISIS Groups are really ticked off at us for killing one of their teams and will probably start attacking us again soon," Mitchell stated and then sat and pulled his black notebook closer to him. "We need to stop this and stop it right now. To bring you up-to-date, I will have our National Security Advisor Mr. Tony Sanford brief you on what we know right now. Tony."

"As President Mitchell said, the attacks are hitting key points around the country; they have sleeper cells coming awake and they are well trained and have the equipment to complete the mission. So far, we have had an attempted destruction of the Hoover Dam, an explosion at the Supreme Court Building killing many, a Boeing 757 crash landed on the Washington Mall, killing nobody but had a nuclear bomb on board which did not explode, luckily. There was an attack at the Washington Navy Yard which left several dead, attacks at Fort Bragg, a Coast Guard Cutter off the coast of Key West and more attacks in San Francisco, Los Angeles, Dallas, Denver, and Chicago which left several hundred dead. The worst was North Korea launching eight ICBMs at the west coast, which is dark right now because our infrastructure has been compromised because of our lack of proper protection on the Internet. The ICBMs were all destroyed by our newly launched Star Wars program. It worked as designed, saving millions of lives. And our Cyber Command at McDill Air Force Base was attacked and destroyed along with killing a lot of our soldiers. We had a small terrorist group causing some of the attacks. The attack on the Navy Yard was committed by them. But with the cooperation with Great Britain and her Royal Commandos, backed up by Seal Team Six and others, the threat was eliminated with all traces removed. They are no longer a problem to us or any other nation. The only problem is they have friends, and we expect some retaliation from them. In a nut shell that is it, the complete rundown of everything is in the folder in front of you. We have activated the National Guard; and all reserve units have been activated and ordered to report to their centers and prepare for deployment in support of the National Guard. The country is under Martial Law and will remain in that condition until we have ended this. We will answer questions after President Mitchell completes briefing you about his plan to end this. President Mitchell, sir."

"Ladies and Gentlemen, the situation is grim, but this is America and Americans are the most resilient people on the planet. And we will survive. Right now, we need to decide, in this room, our next move. I have in this folder my ideas of what we need to do, but I am not the deciding factor here. We, you and me, need to decide to, well, let me outline what I believe we should do, and I will open the floor for discussion. Of course, we could do this one of several ways. As a unanimous vote from all of you and I sign the Executive Order putting the plan into effect, or the time consuming way of taking it to Congress, both the House of Representatives and the Senate, which will take a while to get it approved; or the final way is for me to act as a dictator and just sign the Executive Order. "

"Sir, what is your plan?" Admiral Hamner asked from across the room as he fixed himself a cup of coffee.

"First, Martial Law needs to stay in effect nationwide; second, we need boots on the ground in Korea. They have declared war with us and we need to retaliate immediately with more than just words. The Enterprise Carrier Group has been ordered to move to the Sea of China and prepare for battle. I have already ordered the other Carrier Groups in the Pacific to maintain coastal protection and to sink anything that fires on our country. I have the Executive Order prepared and ready to sign and put into motion. I do not want to launch nuclear missiles with hopes to prevent a nuclear war. Even though they shot first, escalating to that will only end in a nuclear storm of epic proportion."

"Mr. President, I understand the need for acting quickly; we are technically at war, but..." Homeland Director John Ramsey started to say but was interrupted by Admiral Hamner.

"Mr. Ramsey, sorry to interrupt your question, but if you are going to say something about not escalating this to the next level, well, we are already past the next level; they attacked us; the Korean Prime Minister is not talking. Hell, they cannot even locate him or be sure who is in charge over there; we have been talking to his female assistant, and she is not making any sense," Admiral Hamner said. "She told us they killed the PM and she was in charge, not true. They did shoot at us, but I agree with the President to not escalate to nuclear war."

"That is true, Admiral and Mr. Ramsey. The North Korean Leader has been missing for weeks, nobody seems to know where he is and his country has attacked us. We don't even know if it is a rogue group of insurgents. But the bottom line is, we have been attacked; and we need to protect our country; and we need to show North Korea that they cannot get away with this. We are at WAR!" President Mitchell shouted and then became very quiet, letting his mind drift for a few minutes. He was wishing he was someplace else, any place except here and as the President of the United States.

"The American people do not like the Martial Law, curfew and all that goes along with it. As far as the rest of the plan, I have no problem with it," CIA Director Ashley Peterson commented.

"It is temporary, Ms. Peterson, only until we have stopped the attacks. We need to control crime and possible trouble from our own people," Tony Sanford commented. "Most states have already bought into martial law and all the states have called up the National Guard."

"Yeah, I know temporary; the last time we went to Korea it lasted years and what about that temporary little war game in Viet Nam. I know temporary real well and so does the American public. I would hold off on rounding up Korean nationals like we did in World War II with the Japanese; it is not going to work," Eric Fredericks, Director of NSA stated. "I was in Nam, and if I am correct, so were you, Mr. President. That temporary action lasted, well, I was there for two tours and you, sir did three; three years in a war zone that was supposed to be temporary. Not too temporary, not saying that your plan is not temporary, sir but let's be careful with that word."

"Understood, Mr. Fredericks, let's look at the rest of it for now," President Mitchell responded.

"Mr. President, I have moved most of the available Atlantic fleet in for coastal patrol; and since I recently took over command of the Pacific Fleet also, I apologize for not having a good handle on the location of all the Carrier groups in the Pacific, but will by the end of the day," Admiral Hamner commented. "The Enterprise carrier group is already moving into the Sea of China, and will be on station within the hour."

"That is good news, Admiral. I want an update by four this afternoon on the rest of the fleets," President Mitchell ordered. "As for the rest, are we in agreement that we are at war and need to act now? Please with a show of hands, all those for the plan of action."

Five minutes passed and of the eighteen voting members discussed the issue. When the vote was called agreed with the President's plan. Four members did not agree.

Chapter 50 South of the Border

In the early morning hours the weather was crisp and cold, snow in the forecast. But in the country of Korea, things were very much different. The American military was about to cross into North Korea, something that had not been done since the early 1950s.

The weather on the border was cold, wet and rainy as usual. The temperature was dipping down to twenty-eight degrees, with a light fog covering the ground. It was like the majority of days on the 38th parallel.

"Open fire!" the order came down from command to the line of artillery located two hundred yards south of the 38th parallel, the border that divided North and South Korea.

The day broke with a quick succession of heavy artillery fire, reaching miles into North Korea. The North Korean Army had years to prepare defenses from attacks from the south; but even with all the preparation, they still were unprepared for the intense amount of firepower the United States and South Korean military could put deep into their country.

"Cease fire!" the order came down from command. After pausing for a moment, the General in charge of the operation sent the following message to the air operations command. "Commence air assault."

Seconds after the first barrage was fired, a flight of forty fighter aircraft flew over and started to bomb specific targets with smart bombs, which limited collateral damage, and only destroyed the military targets which had been identified over the past fifty years. These targets included truck parks, motor pools, missile emplacements, barracks, fuel storage and government facilities that were not classified as medical or emergency facilities. Over the next three hours, every military facility within one hundred miles of the 38th parallel was targeted and destroyed by American and South Korean aircraft.

"Ground troops move out!" the General ordered at nine fifty-five in the morning.

A short pause in the fighting took place at ten o'clock in the morning, and then the troops started across the border, meeting limited to no resistance from their enemy. The ground troops were supported by three hundred Apache and Cobra attack helicopters. This was one of the largest number of helicopters in attack mode ever to be assembled.

The war with North Korea started with the firing of eight ICBMs at the United States and ended with the American and South Korean mechanized infantry crossing the 38th Parallel in force. It was one of the shortest wars in history; actual fighting time lasted only ten hours.

At the same time our forces were crossing the border; multiple units of the North Korean military were overrunning the capital in search for their country's leader with the intent of overthrowing the government. The overthrow was also short; the political leaders surrendered to their own army; and in turn, when the American and South Korean armies arrived in the capital, they surrendered to them without firing a shot.

A North Korean soldier walked out of the city to meet with the attacking armies waving a white flag. He stopped at the edge of town and waited. The commander of the U.S. Army had his driver take him to the man with the white flag.

"Commander, I am General Wong of the North Korean Army; I am here to surrender to you and your forces. My men will come out of the city unarmed. We are tired of being suppressed, and want to become part of the new world." Upon stating this, the General handed his sword to the U.S. commander.

"Sir, we accept your surrender; please order your men to lay down their weapons and come out of the city."

"All troops lay down your weapons and exit the city," General Wong ordered over his radio.

"Where is your Prime Minister?"

"He is in the hospital, dying in a private room on the fifth floor, room 535. His body guards may not let you in without me, shall we go."

"Yes, in just a minute, I need to order my men to stand down so they will not accidentally fire on your troops." With that he called on his radio to order the U.S. troops to stand down and assist all the Korean soldiers to a containment area which needed to be set up outside the city.

Within days, their leader had been found, dying in a hospital room. After appointing an interim leader that wanted to reunite the north with the south, it now rested in the hands of the politicians. North Korea was ready to join the world as a free country, free from communism and dictators running the country and keeping the country in the dark.

****

"Dusty, you and your team have done a fantastic job with getting everything back online and setting up a system to protect our infrastructure with a better security system," Spooky commented as she stood in the new operations center.

California was the worst, having the weakest security and the most complicated computer programming on the planet. After removing the Trojan Horse and virus, they patched the holes in the programming and added an updated security system to each server and sub-station.

"I understand the hackers have been captured and disappeared again," Dusty commented.

"Yes, the Chinese authorities picked them up, six men and two women, and the last we heard was that they were placed in a Chinese prison, never to be seen again. Just so you know, Martial Law is still in effect in California; the gangs are trying to take over the state but are losing ground. The rest of the states that experienced infrastructure problems were able to control crime with local police and the National Guard as back up," Spooking stated between sips of her Coke.

"What happened in Washington?" Savage asked from across the room.

"The nuclear bomb disposal team that was tasked to remove the nuclear device that had crash landed on the Washington Mall had failed in their task. The bomb had reset to a countdown of fifteen minutes and started counting down and upon reaching zero it detonated," Spooky commented, pausing for a moment to let it sink in before continuing. "The detonation was not nuclear, but more of a large fire cracker; damage was minimal, but put both Gibson and his three technicians in the hospital. They were released within a week after being treated from burns, several broken bones, cuts and bruises."

****

Hector and his sniper did not locate the German or any other terrorists, but were successful in locating Roberto Guzman and four of his top men. After watching for a week noting his routine, they set up for a quick elimination operation. Four hours and twenty minutes after setting up, Jose took his first shot; he dropped Roberto Guzman with a clean hit in the head. After three more shots and three more confirmed kills, they attempted to hide; but the wall they hid behind was only six inches thick, too thin for proper cover from a BMG 50 caliber rifle. The fourth lieutenant was not present for the operation and would live another day or two.

****

"America has been seriously hurt and it will take time to mend. But she has been injured before and most likely will be injured again. September 11 was a devastating blow; the destruction of Boston, killing of millions of American citizens, and destruction rained down on this country will never be forgotten. Sure the names and faces of some of the heroes that played a vital part in saving the country might be forgotten, but America still stands tall and let any enemy whether foreign or domestic beware. These colors do not run, and we will fight for what is right and just." President Darrell Mitchell stated in his State of the Union Address, pausing for a moment before continuing. "I have and will continue to work toward making our country safe for all Americans..."

Twenty minutes later, he finished and asked, "May we have a moment of silence for our fallen families. Now it is time to heal."

After a minute of silence, the President lifted his head and started to speak, but he was unable to do so for a moment. The cameras were just about to turn off when he raised his right hand and said quietly, "Don't turn them off just yet, I have one more thing to say to the people of America." He paused for about fifteen seconds and then continued, "I wanted you to know that we, that is the FBI, CIA and DHS are working together to bring those that caused this to justice. Several of the leaders have already been taken care of and the rest are in our sights and will be apprehended soon. We will not rest until our nation has been rebuilt and those responsible brought to justice. Thank you."

Chapter 51 Healing

"Davin, how do you feel?" Connie asked as she walked out on the patio to check on her husband; he had been released from the hospital in Mexico City five months earlier and spent three more months at Walter Reed in recovery. Finally, after being released, he was able to return home under the care of his wife, Connie, and a visiting nurse four times a week. He was mending, but with the extent of his injuries it was taking time. His casts had been removed, and the bones had healed.

"I was fine this morning; I am fine now. I just need to get out of the house. Sitting around all day is driving me crazy," Davin commented. He was a little annoyed with being asked how he was all the time. His memory had returned about a week after the operation and slowly continued to improve.

"Well, we have visitors."

"Who?" Davin asked and looked up to see his partner Josh Randal walking out the door. "Josh, what brings you down to Palm Beach? I thought you were permanently glued to a desk in Washington."

"Just taking a little vacation. Stephanie will be right out, but I asked her to wait until I met with you first," Josh replied.

Davin stood and gave his old buddy and partner a big hug.

"Vacation, what is the newest Director of Covert Operations doing taking a vacation so soon after taking the job? What are you really doing down here?" Davin questioned, smiling at seeing his partner.

"Okay, I could never pull one over on you," Josh responded and then sat down across from Davin in the chaise lounge. "Well, it seems that we have a problem; and I may need some advice and possibly some help from you. But, first, I have a little gift for you," Josh continued and then handed Davin a cardboard box.

"Wait a minute, Josh. Look at me, my head is still not completely healed. My memory is still not complete; I forget things; short term memory is sporadic; and hell, I can't even remember where my shoes are most of the time. How can I help?" Davin said feeling like he had let Josh and the CIA down.

"Open it," Josh ordered and watched as Davin opened the box.

"Wow, how did you get it?" he said looking at his favorite Colt Commander Model 1911. "I thought this was long gone."

"You can thank Hector; he was able to recover it and Connie's also. I gave it to her when we came in. Now we need to talk." He paused for a second and then continued. "Davin, sitting in that chair feeling sorry for yourself is not going to get you well any quicker. I talked with Connie and the doctor; your recovery needs some assistance from me and the company. We have a problem and need your assistance."

"I'm retired and have a baby due in a few days. What can I do to help; how long will it take?" Davin asked getting interested. "Okay, tell me more."

"Let's wait till the girls are out here; they are being reinstated also, but they don't know it yet."

Connie and Stephanie came out with a tray filled with lemonade and sandwiches.

"I hope you are kidding, lemonade! Where is the beer?" Josh asked looking at the tray.

"Right here, dear. Davin can't have any yet, still on meds," Connie answered, handing Josh a cold beer.

"Now the ladies are here; I can get down to the meat of what is needed. Thank you, sweetie!"

"Quit beating around the bush, what is the mission?" Davin questioned, picking up a plate with his sandwich and a glass of lemonade

"First, this concerns all four of us, well, soon to be five. Davin you finally got your wish," Josh stated.

"What wish is that?"

"You are no longer the lead on any assignment unless I am not with you. As you know, I was promoted to Director of Covert Operations and I need an Assistant Director. The position is open and you are the only applicant. Do you accept, yes or no?"

"Assistant Director of Covert Operations, well, hell yeah. I think I can still drive a desk. But I have to report to you, not sure if I can do that; let me think on it a second or two." Davin paused for a couple of seconds and then responded, "I guess it could be worse, I accept. When do I start?"

"About twenty minutes ago, Connie had already accepted for you. She said you are driving her crazy and needed to go back to work."

"Connie, come over here," Davin ordered. She walked over and leaned down as best she could being eight and a half months pregnant, at which point he kissed her and said, "Thank you."

"Okay, do I get a big office?"

"Yes, but not right away; they have to clean up the mop closet and move in your desk," Josh joked. "But let's get down to business. Remember Bormann, captured him in Cuba. Well, we have discovered he worked for a German by the name of Gregory Dietrich, aka as 'Sepp'. Well, somehow Bormann escaped during a transfer to the states to stand trial. And we have intel that leads us to believe his old boss Sepp had a lot to do with it," Josh replied.

"Damn, that man almost killed me and Connie; any idea where they have gotten off to?" Davin asked, pausing for a moment to think, "This time if, no, when we catch them, I am going to put a bullet in both their heads."

"I will drink to that," Josh agreed.

But that is another story.

Brief History of American Military Deployments

War, what are we fighting for?

War, as described in Wikipedia, is an organized and often prolonged conflict that is carried out by states or non-state actors. It is generally characterized by extreme violence, social disruption and an attempt at economic destruction. War should be understood as an actual, intentional and widespread armed conflict between political communities, and therefore is defined as a form of political violence or intervention. The set of techniques used by a group to carry out war is known as warfare. An absence of war is usually called peace.

The history of war goes back before recorded history, warring tribes, countries and people fighting and killing for reasons from that in today's society seem trivial and the death toll for the wars unforgivable.

The Congressional Research Service (CRS), Congressional Budget Office (CBO), Department of Defense, Veterans Museum and Memorial Center, and Smithsonian Institution have cataloged 330 "notable deployments of United States military forces overseas" since 1798. Listing all of those notable deployments would take a whole book in itself, so below are several that most Americans may remember. At the end of this short list I have posted several more that you may not have heard of or remember.

History has shown us that the World War I, also known as the First World War or Great War, was a global war centered in Europe that began on July 28, 1914 and ended on November 11, 1918. More than nine million combatants and seven million civilians died during the war. It was one of the deadliest conflicts in history, paving the way for major political changes. The assassination of Archduke Franz Ferdinand of Austria on June 28th, 1914 triggered the war. He was the heir to the throne of Austria-Hungary. The assassination was carried out by Yugoslav nationalist Gavrilo Princip in Sarajevo. It was followed by a diplomatic crisis with the ultimatum delivered to the Kingdom of Serbia, which invoked the international alliances which had been formed over the previous decades. Within weeks, they were at war.

The Second World War (World War II) was a global war beginning in 1939 and ending in 1945. It involved a vast number of the world's nations, including all the great powers, forming two opposing military alliances, the Allies and the Axis. History shows it was the most widespread war in history, directly involving more than one hundred million people from over thirty countries in total war. During WW II, there were mass civilian deaths including the Holocaust where approximately eleven million people died. The war also consisted of strategic bombing of industrial and population centers where about one million people died, and the use of two nuclear weapons resulting in another estimated fifty to eighty-five million dead. World War II was the deadliest conflict in recorded history.

Japan wanted to dominate Asia and the Pacific and was already fighting with China since 1937. On December 7, 1941 Japan attacked the United States at Pearl Harbor, Hawaii, thus bringing the United States into the war in the Pacific.

Adolf Hitler was considered a monster, but he also created many monsters under him that followed his orders and also took things into their own hands. Millions of innocent people were killed; genocide of the Jewish population was one of their goals. There was little respect for life especially if you did not agree with their ideologies. Fortunately, Hitler did not win his quest to rule the world and to eliminate a group of people that had no ill will against him until he started to kill them.

The war in Europe ended when the Western Allies and the Soviet Union invaded Germany and captured Berlin. Germany surrendered on May 8th, 1945. The United States subsequently dropped an atomic bomb on Hiroshima on August 6 and Nagasaki on August 9th; and on August 15, the Soviet Union declared war on Japan and invaded Manchuria which ended the war in the Pacific and the end of the Axis bloc.

North Korea became an independent communist country in August 1945 when the Soviet Union declared war on Japan; and by agreement with the United States, they occupied Korea north of the 38th parallel. Russia controlled the north and the United States controlled the south. In June 1950, North Korea wanted South Korea back and invaded with permission from their sponsors, Russia. In June of 1950, the South Korean President Syngman Rhee executed one hundred thousand people starting the Summer of Terror in fear that the South Korean people would join the communists. On June 27th, 1950, the U.S. sent troops to Osan for what was thought to be a short war, but quickly discovered the North Korean Army was strong and could not be easily beaten. On July 4th, 1950, the U.S was defeated at Osan. On September 15th, 1950, General MacArthur led an invasion into Inchon and took it back from North Korea. China joined in the war in October 1950. They supported North Korea, and pushed the U.S. and South Korean troops back across the 38th parallel. In November 1950, U.S. troops were attacked by one hundred eighty thousand Chinese soldiers and forced a retreat. The war went back and forth until July 1953 when a truce was signed. In April 1954, Geneva failed to reunite Korea.

It all started again in Viet Nam; first in 1950, American military advisors started to arrive. United States involvement escalated during the early 1960s; troop levels tripled in 1961 and 1962. In 1964, the Gulf of Tonkin incident occurred when a U.S. destroyer had a clash with a North Vietnamese fast attack craft. This gave the U.S. President authority to increase U.S. military presence with regular combat units deployed in 1965.

U.S. military involvement ended on August 15, 1973. Saigon was captured by the North Vietnamese in April 1975 marking the end of the war. North and South Vietnam were reunified in 1976. The loss of human life was great; estimates of Vietnamese service members and civilians killed varied from eight hundred thousand to three million, one hundred thousand. Between two to three hundred thousand Cambodians, twenty to two hundred thousand Laotians and fifty-eight thousand two hundred twenty U.S. service members died in the conflict.

Islamic State (ISIS), Osama Bin Laden, and Al Qaida groups also have the ideology that all that do not follow the Islamic way are infidels and either need to convert or die. They have been fighting infidels for thousands of years and have now moved the fight to a larger front.

Desert Shield and Desert Storm in the sands of Saudi Arabia, Kuwait and Iraq was just a continuation of a war that had been fought for thousands of years between Middle Eastern countries. The war is still going on and has dragged the United States and many United Nation countries into a war that can never be won unless you kill everyone of the enemy.

The continuation of war in the Middle East brought the United States into another conflict. The Gulf War started on August 2, 1990 and ended February 28th, 1991, but was known as Operation Desert Shield (August 2nd, 1990 to January 17th 1991) to build up troops and defenses of Saudi Arabia. Beginning January 17th, 1991 and ending on the 28th of February

1991, Operation Desert Storm was the war of coalition forces from thirty-four nations which was led by the United States against Iraq. This was in response to Iraq invading Kuwait.

The initial conflict against Iraq troops in Kuwait started with aerial and naval bombardment on January 17th, 1991 and continued for five weeks. This was followed by a ground assault on February 24th which was able to liberate Kuwait and move into Iraqi territory. A cease fire was declared one hundred hours after the ground campaign started. Operation Iraqi Freedom continued well into 2003. This war was started with Saddam Hussein wanting to control the oil within Kuwait. In 1990, Saddam accused Kuwait of stealing Iraqi petroleum through slant drilling.

Wars throughout history have been started for many reasons; it only takes one person to start a war. When one person starts a war it takes many to end it; never in the history of the world has one person been able to stop a war. Hollywood shows us movies where one person becomes the hero and saves the world or ends the war. Life is not like that, it takes a team of people, sometimes millions, to end the conflicts.

History has shown us that no matter the reason for starting the war, the only thing that remains constant with war is that people die. Someone always loses, some lose more than others.

Other United States military deployments you may not remember:

Barbary Wars, 1801-1805 and 1915

War of 1812, 1812-1815

Indian Wars, 1813-1838 and 1866-1890

Mexican War, 1846-1848

Spanish-American War, 1898

Philippines, 1899-1901

Mexico, 1914-1919

Cold War, 1947-1991

Berlin Airlift, 1948-1949

Lebanon, 1982-1984

Grenada, 1983

Persian Gulf, 1987-1988

Vietnam War, 1965-1975

Panama, 1989-1990

Gulf War, 1990-1991

Iraqi Kurdistan, 1991

Somalia, 1992-1994

Haiti, 1994-1996

Bosnia, 1995-2004

Global war on terrorism/Operation Enduring Freedom/Operation Freedom's Sentinel/Operation Resolute Support, 2001-Present

Kosovo, 1999-present

Afghanistan, 2001-present

Iraq/Operation Iraqi Freedom/Operation New Dawn, 2003-2011

Operation Inherent Resolve, 2014-present

More information can be found at the following websites:
http://www.infoplease.com/ipa/A0931831.html
http://en.wikipedia.org/wiki/List_of_wars_involving_the_United_States
http://en.wikipedia.org/wiki/Military_history_of_the_United_States
http://www.loc.gov/crsinfo/ Congressional Research Service
http://www.defense.gov/ Department of Defense
http://www.si.edu/ Smithsonian Institution

Excerpt from Schutzstaffel Rising, Chain of Deceit, Book 6

Chapter 1: New Life

The waiting is always the hardest part for both parents; Connie wanted the pain to end and Davin was just worried. Davin lived his life on his terms and did not having anyone to worry about other than Connie for the past couple of years. Connie was a trained FBI agent and very capable in her own right. But this was different. Nature was taking over; childbirth was different for each woman and man. Some women had an easy birth, others not so. The men in their lives were a different story; some worried for no reason, and others felt that nature and good doctors would handle all of it. And to top it off, Davin had never really been good around children and now he was about to be a father. They had been at the hospital for three hours and still no baby.

"Josh, Stephanie, I do appreciate you two being here, but I know you both have work to do and this is just taking too long," Davin said trying to break the ice in the room.

"Yes, we both have work that we should be doing, but this is as important to us as it is to you. We will stick around until..." Stephanie stated but was interrupted when the nurse walked in and announced.

"Excuse me, Mr. Pierce and friends, would you please come with me to meet your new family," she said interrupting Stephanie, "Oh, sorry, but I believe you have been waiting for me. Now please follow me."

Minutes later, they entered Connie's room only to stop and stare at Connie and the two small bundles she was holding.

"Holy cow, two, it can't be!" Davin exclaimed; surprised at what he saw as he walked over to her bed. "Wow, Connie are you okay?"

"I am doing fine honey. I would like to introduce you to our new family; we have to name them soon so the doctor can fill out the birth certificates properly," she replied with a smile and chuckle, thinking about how Davin got his name. His mother wanted David and his dad wanted to call him Kevin and the doctor started writing David and ended up writing an 'n' at the end of David giving him the name Davin. It never got changed and he had been Davin since birth because of a mistake that was not caught until the certificate had been filed.

"What do you think of Joshua David for your parents and your best friend? And Amber Marie for mine." Connie asked.

"I think those will work just fine," David replied.

"Well Davin, ole buddy, I guess your nights are going to be full of dirty diapers and lack of sleep. Do you want a cot set up in your office so you can get some sleep?" Josh joked.

"Not yet, say hi to Joshua and Amber."Davin said as he picked up one of the babies. "Who do I have here?"

"That is your son; can't you tell the difference?" Connie asked. "And this is Amber with the wavy hair."

"Hello," Josh said into his cell after letting it ring only once. "Sorry, I have to take this," he said as he walked out of the room. Minutes later, he returned looking very unhappy.

"What is it, Josh?" Davin asked.

"Stephanie, stay here with Connie, I need to take Davin back to the office; we have a situation," Josh commented.

"Sorry honey, duty calls and when he calls I have to run. I will be back as soon as I can," Davin said and handed Joshua to Stephanie.

CIA Headquarters, Langley, Virginia

"Who do we have?" Josh asked his secretary as he and Davin walked into his outer office.

"You have visitors in your office and they are not very happy," she replied, and then glanced over at the side of wall to view three Secret Service Agents sitting comfortably in the brown overstuffed chairs provided to waiting guests. One was reading a current copy of Newsweek and the other two just looked bored.

"Who?" Josh asked as he looked at the two men and one women sitting in the chairs, and then realized who was in the office and said to himself. *'Oh hell!'*

"President Mitchell," she answered seeing that he figured it out himself, "Should I bring coffee or anything?"

"No, that's okay. Davin, what do you think he wants? Yes, get some coffee and water," he said and then changed his mind as he opened the door and entered Josh's office. "Mr. President and Mr. Sanford what brings you down to our humble office?"

"We have something to discuss with the CIA, Ms Peterson will be here in a minute," Tony Sanford, National Security Advisor stated and then took a seat beside the President. Just then Ashley Peterson, CIA Director stepped into the office.

"Good morning gentlemen, sorry I am late, traffic," she commented and shook the hand of each member present.

"Please take a seat, Ms Peterson. We have a problem," President Darrell Mitchell said as she walked in.

"Comes with the territory, sir. What have you got?" Josh commented as he walked around behind his desk and sat. "Georgia is bringing in some refreshments, so if you want to wait, she…"

"She has clearance, right?" Sanford asked.

"Yes, equal to mine and Davin's," Josh reported.

"Then please take a seat; this is not going to set well with any of you. Do you want to tell them, sir?" Sanford asked as he looked at Mitchell.

"No, go on, you tell them," Mitchell ordered.

"Okay, sir. We received this early this morning. It was in the morning mail," Sanford started, handing a copy of the letter to Ashley, Josh and Davin. "Please read and give back, please."

"Why now?" Davin asked.

"Now, because we are still in the process of recovery and still very vulnerable," Mitchell commented. "What do you think; do you believe he can pull it off?"

"Well, we do know that Bormann has some very high placed people with a lot of money backing him; so if anyone can, then he can," Josh stated looking very concerned.

"But seriously sir, this letter means nothing; anyone can send you a letter stating that we lost and he will return and this time he will succeed. How many death threats do you get?" asked Josh.

"Every president gets death threats and only a few have actually been assassinated and a couple others had close calls," Mitchell stated.

"But this Bormann had your daughter and Mrs. Pierce kidnapped; also almost killed Mr. Pierce and we have yet to prove if he was responsible in the deaths of several low lives like the 'Weasel' in San Francisco and a couple of people from the Guzman drug cartel," Sanford commented, looking a little disturbed.

"What's your point? We know the guy is bad, so does that mean he is or isn't going to attempt to kill me and who knows how many of our civilians," Mitchell argued. "Randal, read that letter and you tell me what you think."

"I have read it, sir; and it looks very much like Mr. Bormann has revived the Nazi party and is set on destroying you and this country. He does mention in this line and I quote, 'We will not lose, we have the manpower, the weapons, and resolve to bring your country to its knees.' According to Adolf Hitler they were on a quest, a religious quest to eliminate all those that opposed them. And his spiritual leader, Reichsfuhrer-SS Heinrich Himmler established the elite police force known as the Schutzstaffel commonly known as the SS and advised Hitler on everything in the scriptures. A recent show on the Discovery channel talked about the Nazi Gospel and how they were destined to rule the world." Josh summarized.

"They what?" Mitchell asked.

"It really gets deeper than that; history as taught in our schools about the Nazis is a little behind the curve. They were very nasty people, brain washed from a young age, thinking that the Aryan race was the super race and denied all non-Aryans many rights and privileges that the super race had. That was the start of the first race-based laws," Davin added. "I studied and researched the Third Reich in college and it has been a pet project of mine over the years."

"No, sir, it means we need to take this seriously. We know that Mr. Randal and Pierce have good reason to go after this guy. Let me ask, Randal, Pierce, do you have any idea as to the location of Bormann or the money he is being financed with?" Sanford asked looking at the two Covert Operations men in charge.

"Sir, yes, we have been using all our resources to locate this scumbag; but every time we think we are close, we run into a brick wall. Our last known location is GITMO and then he was being transported to DC for trial when he escaped. It was well planned and executed. Two officers were injured, but are back on duty. From there, we were able to track him to Columbia where we last lost him. We know he has connections with several drug cartels and political higher ups so he was able to disappear. Exactly who, we are working on, but we have hit more road blocks than we can count."

"With Ms Peterson's blessing and resources we want you to turn up the heat." Mitchell stated. "This country has endured enough from those people, Nazis or not. I am about to give you an order that technically I can't but in this room, right now, I will. Turn up the heat, locate Bormann and whoever is financing him and kill them. Take no prisoners. And if we need to send the military, I will. Understand."

"We will handle it personally, sir." Josh said in agreement and then looked over at Davin and Ashley, getting a nod from each of them. "And as far as the military, put them on standby. We may need them to take care of his army. We may still have World War III on the horizon."

The saga continues with <u>Chain of Deceit</u>, Book 6.

www.ingramcontent.com/pod-product-compliance
Lightning Source LLC
Chambersburg PA
CBHW061636040426
42446CB00010B/1436